Mafias on the Move

Mafias on the Move ———————

HOW ORGANIZED CRIME CONQUERS
NEW TERRITORIES

Federico Varese

PRINCETON UNIVERSITY PRESS

PRINCETON & OXFORD

Copyright © 2011 by Princeton University Press

Requests for permission to reproduce material from this work should be sent to Permissions, Princeton University Press

Published by Princeton University Press, 41 William Street, Princeton, New Jersey 08540

In the United Kingdom: Princeton University Press, 6 Oxford Street, Woodstock, Oxfordshire OX20 1TW

press.princeton.edu

Jacket art: *Four-headed Man with Nail.* 1980. Oil on canvas. 195 × 235 cm by Oleg Tselkov.

All Rights Reserved

Library of Congress Cataloging-in-Publication Data

Varese, Federico.
    Mafias on the move : how organized crime conquers new territories / Federico Varese.
        p. cm.
    Includes bibliographical references and index.
    ISBN 978-0-691-12855-9 (hardcover : alk. paper)   1. Mafia—History.   2. Organized crime—History.   3. Transnational crime—History.   I. Title.
    HV6441.V37 2011
    364.106—dc22   2010040304

British Library Cataloging-in-Publication Data is available

This book has been composed in Adobe Garamond

Printed on acid-free paper. ∞

Printed in the United States of America

10 9 8 7 6 5 4 3 2 1

Contents

Acknowledgments vii

ONE Introduction 1

TWO Mafia Transplantation 13

THREE The 'Ndrangheta in Piedmont and Veneto 31

FOUR The Russian Mafia in Rome and Budapest 65

FIVE Lessons from the Past: Sicilian Mafiosi in New York City and Rosario, circa 1880–1940 101

SIX The Future of the Mafias? Foreign Triads in China 146

SEVEN Mafia Origins, Transplantation, and the Paradoxes of Democracy 188

Notes 203

References 237

Index 263

This book stands on the shoulders of four hard working and dedicated assistants. I was extremely fortunate to employ Paolo Campana on a grant to code and analyze the data on the Russians in Rome. Paolo has worked well beyond the call of duty and the expiry of the grant, helping me to collect data on Bardonecchia as well, and accompanying me on research trips to Piedmont and Rome. He has also read the entire manuscript and made innumerable suggestions. I hope that readers will appreciate the range of Chinese-language sources I have been able to use. This is the work of a researcher based in China who was employed full time for a year on this project. I have at times bombarded him with requests for further data and information, and he complied fully and with the best possible attitude. For reasons that should be obvious, he prefers not to have his name revealed in print. Professor Carina Frid guided me through the history of the city of Rosario. She pointed me in the right direction many times, answered numerous questions, and read a version of chapter 5, offering most helpful suggestions, and showing a deep knowledge of the economic and social history of the city. Carina also collected data on construction permits on my behalf. We plan to collaborate further. Finally, Borbála Garai translated some press reports on the Russian mafia in Budapest and helped compile the data set on migration to Hungary in the 1990s. Although none of the valiant individuals mentioned above are responsible for the remaining omissions and errors, they have made this work more credible and offered me much intellectual pleasure.

The Leverhulme Fund proved to be a model funding institution. It generously supported some data collection in Italy and imposed the minimum amount of bureaucracy at all stages. Carlo Morselli acted as my referee and offered useful comments on the project. I have also been the recipient of a grant from the European Union Seventh Framework Programme (Theme 10, "Security") as part of A New Agenda for European Security Economics consortium. Professor Tilman Brück at the German Institute of Economic Research acted as the intellectual leader of the project, and navigated the rather complex application and auditing process. John Holmes, also at the German Institute of Economic Research, showed great patience and competence in dealing with my part of the work. The Oxford University John Fell Fund and the Law Faculty Research Support Fund funded aspects of my research as well. Sarah Parkin at the Centre for Criminology managed these grants on my behalf. She was most effective, and displayed great stamina in dealing with several jurisdictions, banking systems, and funding bodies' regulations. Ray Morris at the Law Faculty Office and Matthew Smart in the Division Office gave advice that facilitated my work in many ways.

Gaining access to data is notoriously difficult in my field of study. I was lucky to find officials who made my research possible. The mayor and the staff at the Comune of Bardonecchia opened the town archive to us, making it possible to collect the data presented in chapter 3. Prosecutors, judges, and archivists at the Turin, Rome, and Bologna courts cooperated to secure my access to criminal cases. I would like to thank in particular Luigi De Ficchy, Paolo Giovagnoli, Aurelio Galasso, Guido Papalia, Morena Plazzi, and the late Maurizio Laudi for sharing their views with me on cases in which they were involved.

Several people read the entire manuscript at some point of its evolution. Timothy Frye and Susan Rose-Ackerman acted on behalf of Princeton University Press. Their encouragement and critical comments greatly helped my work. It is a pleasure to finally thank them in public. Liz David-Barrett served two roles, as editor of the text and sharp critic of the arguments I try to make. Her comments went well beyond the call of duty. Cindy Milstein copyedited the text for the publisher superbly. Edoardo Gallo also read the entire text. I am particularly grateful for his suggestions regarding the summary tables that run through the book. As always generous and incisive, Diego Gambetta showed an interest in the project from the start and commented in depth on several chapters, especially chapters 5 and 6. At the 11th hour, Iris Geens spotted innumerable typos and errors in the proofs. Her suggestions extended to several aspects of my argument and presentation.

A number of scholars have taken time away from their busy working lives to read sections of the book. Jane Duckett read an early version of chapter 6. Ko-lin Chin, Tiantian Zheng, and Yiu Kong Chu read a much-reworked version of that same chapter. They steered me away from errors, and the text improved as a result. David Nelken commented extensively on the whole project while I was his guest in Macerata. David Critchley, the author of a groundbreaking volume on the early history of the Italian American mafia, answered numerous questions of fact and engaged in a long series of email exchanges on a subject he knows so much about. Vittorio Bufacchi, an old friend, read the introduction more than once, and it magically got better every time. Anna Zimdars also gave me much valued comments. Gavin Slade, a doctoral student at Oxford, pointed me in the direction of relevant material on Georgia, while at an early stage of this research Valeria Pizzini-Gambetta alerted me to the story of the Rosario mafia. Luca Ricolfi and Ray Yep helped me in practical ways in Turin and Hong Kong, respectively. The author Mimmo Gangemi was a most gracious host and guide in Rosarno, Calabria. Osvaldo Aguirre kindly supplied me with photos of two of the people he wrote about in his study of the mafia in Argentina, while Norma Lanciotti shared some information on the construction industry in Rosario. A conversation with Jon Fahlander made me change my mind on the title of this book. I am grateful to my Oxford colleagues Julian Roberts and Laurence Whitehead for their support and suggestions. The untimely death of my friend and colleague Richard V. Ericson affected me and many others deeply.

Misha Glenny and Roberto Saviano have encouraged me at crucial moments as well as shared their expertise with me. A fortunate coincidence put me back in touch with David and Jane Cornwell as I was working on this book. While discussing David's latest work, I benefited from his and Jane's advice and hospitality in London and Cornwall. I could not have been more fortunate with my editor at Princeton University Press, Ian Malcolm. He was patient and supportive, and steered the production process brilliantly. Leslie Grundfest, also at Princeton, did a superb job in getting the text ready for publication. In Italy, my agents Marco Vigevani and Alberto Saibene believed in this work from the beginning.

As with my previous book, I benefited from my association with Nuffield College. The college not only provided me with a place to work but also with a most stimulating intellectual environment. I am grateful to the warden and the bursar for their hospitality. The Centre for Criminology and the University of Oxford granted me a sabbatical term to finish the manuscript. I am particularly indebted to Ian Loader, the director of the Centre for Criminology, for fostering a friendly and productive working environment.

I presented chapters from this book at several universities, where the audiences were most receptive. These venues include Nuffield College, All Souls College, Columbia University, the Centre of Criminology at the University of Toronto, the University of Macerata, the University of Hannover, and the City University of Hong Kong.

Last but not least, I am most grateful to all the people who agreed to be interviewed. Some of the names of individuals and locations have been changed. This is indicated by italicization of the name the first time it is mentioned.

Once again, my parents have been a constant source of support and inspiration. My wife read the entire manuscript and assisted me in several ways. Although he had no input in this book and will never read it, our special son deserves credit for enriching my life in ways that I never thought were possible.

I published a shorter version of chapter 3 as "How Mafias Migrate" in *Law and Society Review* 40, no. 2 (2006): 411–44. I am grateful to the editor and the publisher for allowing me to reproduce some parts here.

Sections of this work are based on judicial evidence. Such evidence is used simply for analytical reasons, and there is no intention to imply any criminal responsibility of the individuals mentioned in this work.

ONE

Introduction

On September 11, 1996, *Boris Sergeev*, the director of an import-export company based in Rome and father of two, a stocky man in his late forties, arrived in Moscow to finalize a valuable contract for the importation of frozen meat. The Russian partners were Agroprom, a giant Soviet agricultural concern that was now in private hands, and two prominent banks, the Nuovo Banco Ambrosiano and Promstroybank. The former had a somewhat bumpy history—its CEO Roberto Calvi was found hanging from beneath Blackfriars Bridge in London in 1982—but was now under new management and aggressively trying to enter the Russian market. Promstroybank of Saint Petersburg was a safe bet—formerly the largest state bank in the Soviet Union and now a joint-stock company. Even Vladimir Putin once sat on its board. Some twenty million U.S. dollars were at stake. Sergeev had several meetings with top officials at both banks and the Ministry of Agriculture. His most valued contact in the political world was a Soviet-era politician who had taken part in the coup that tried to oust Mikhail Gorbachev in August 1991 and was now a lobbyist for agro-industrial interests.

By the end of the week, Boris had secured the funding and felt confident. Despite fears voiced by his family before the trip, nothing bad had happened. He could relax and spend the last few nights in his native city in style. He took a suite at an upscale hotel located on the central Tverskaya Ulitsa, the street a few yards from Red Square that runs northwest from the Manege toward Saint Petersburg. On the night of September 23, he was sipping predinner drinks at the bar on the fourth floor when two men entered the hotel looking for him. Even with the closed-circuit television system and heavily armed guards that patrolled the hotel's granite lobby, entry was not difficult. The pair showed a bogus hotel pass and boarded the elevator to the fourth floor. Sex for sale was on display at the bar. Yet they moved on, past the gaggle of women flaunting their heavy makeup and cheap jewelry. They stopped in front of Boris's table and extracted two TT pistols with a silencer. Their victim was hit in the head by four bullets (some reports say five). The killers, who were seen on the closed-circuit television camera, calmly took the elevator back to the lobby, walked on to the busy Tverskaya, and climbed into an old Zhiguli that was waiting for them. They were in the hotel for no more than six minutes, between 6:55 and 7:01 p.m.

In the meantime, some fifteen hundred miles away, a special unit of the Italian police was picking up a lot of chatter on the several telephone lines that it was tapping. More details on the murder emerged. Boris's brother, *Sasha*, who lived in Vienna, had joined him and was sitting on the same sofa when Boris was shot. At 7:51 p.m. Moscow time, Sasha, still in shock, called Boris's wife, *Nadia*, in Rome from the police station where he was being interrogated. At first she thought he was joking, but then she asked if it was a "Georgian" who had shot Boris. Sasha replied: "It happened very fast, but the man was dark skinned." The next day they spoke again. Boris's distraught wife could not comprehend how the murder could have happened in one of the best hotels of the city, in front of so many people, with no reaction whatsoever from the hotel "security." "The police say," replied Sasha, "that the murder had the hallmarks of a professionally planned operation, with the intention of sending a clear message to others as well. Nadia, believe me, there is no chance the culprits will ever be found."

The victim in question was no ordinary businessman. Born in Russia in 1948, he had used at least four aliases in the previous ten years. He moved to Rome in 1993 to set up an import-export company. By then, he had already been prosecuted in Italy, Austria, and France on several charges related to the possession of weapons, forgery, polygamy, and fraud. He was rumored to own a large villa in Vienna and hold bank accounts worth at least thirty million U.S. dollars. Official papers state that his company, *Global Trading*, dealt in the import and export of frozen meat and other food products along with oil, alcohol, timber, and coal. The company also conducted, so the papers claim, "market research." Intent on covering his tracks, Boris had taken a rather roundabout way to reach Moscow:

he flew from Rome to Milan, then crossed the Swiss border in a rented car, and finally took a plane from Zurich to the Russian capital. While in Moscow, he carried a gun at all times. The Italian authorities were certain that Global Trading was a front for the Solntsevskaya, the most important crime group to emerge from the collapse of the Soviet Union. The Russian mafia had created an outpost in a faraway territory and was expanding fast. It was high time that someone took notice. When I was shown the files for this investigation, almost ten years ago, I decided to devote my research to the study of mafias' ability to transplant in new and distant territories. This book is the result.

One reading of the Tverskaya hotel murder would support the conventional wisdom on globalization and "transnational organized crime" that has emerged in recent years, especially thanks to authors such as Claire Sterling (*Crime without Frontiers*), Manuel Castells (*The Rise of the Network Society*), Moises Naim (*Illicit*), Louise Shelley (*Global Crime Inc.*), and Phil Williams, and is influential among policymakers: organized crime migrates easily, due to the spread of globalization and population migration, and criminal multinational corporations are increasingly unattached to a specific territory. "International organized crime," writes Shelley, the director of the Transnational Crime Institute in Washington, DC, "has globalized its activities for the same reasons as legitimate multinational corporations." She maintains that "just as multinational corporations establish branches around the world to take advantage of attractive labour or raw material markets, so do illicit businesses."[1] For Williams, organized crime now "can migrate easily."[2] Castells, who also describes this phenomenon, lists a number of localities where (he thinks) well known mafias have opened outposts, such as Germany for the Sicilian mafia, Galicia for Colombian cartels, and the Netherlands for the "Chinese triads."[3] These and other authors go further by arguing that the notions of territorial entrenchment and control are becoming obsolete for a "Global Crime Inc." that "transcends the sovereignty that organizes the modern state system."[4] Factors often cited to explain the globalization of criminal activities and the geographical expansion of criminal firms include technological innovation in communications and transportation along with disappearing language barriers.[5] This position reflects the broader debate on the nature and consequences of globalization, and is consistent with the view advanced by authors who emphasize the de-territorialization of economic power.[6]

The "transnational organized crime consensus" is influential among policymakers. Mafias have now become "liquid," as argued in a recent report by the Italian Anti-Mafia Parliamentary Commission (CPA). Liquidity in this context does not refer to the availability of cash but instead to a version of modernity where control of a territory has been superseded by a rather unspecified fluidity. Politicians from both ends of the political spectrum find ammunition in the assertions promoted by the consensus: sections of the Right peddle unqualified fears of migrants, while some on the Left are only too happy to blame globalization and "neoliberal policies" for local state failures.

The world of international crime is more complicated than these authors wish to admit. Chapter 4 and chapter 7 will expand on the context of the Tverskaya hotel murder and unpack its mechanics. Here I wish to direct the reader's attention to the fact that most authors interpret globalization as a process that facilitates movement and eventually transplantation. In order to evaluate the effect of globalization on organized crime generally and mafias more specifically, one needs to spell out the motivations for a group to open a branch abroad and the effects that different motivations have on how those outposts are created as well as explore whether globalization might have the opposite effect—namely, that of enabling a mafia to acquire resources produced in other countries simply by buying them on the open market rather than by setting up foreign branches. Furthermore, not all attempts at transplantation are successful. To outsiders, a mafia group might seem like a giant and unbeatable octopus about to take over the world from its headquarters in an unreachable Eastern European city. Looked at from the ground up, transplantation is fraught with difficulties.

Does it follow that mafias can never be found in faraway territories? Both Peter Reuter and Diego Gambetta, arguably the foremost scholars in the field of mafia studies, have emphasized that these organizations are hard to export and tend to be local in scope. An illegal organization opening a branch abroad would find it difficult to monitor its agents in distant localities. Outside their home region, mafiosi would struggle to corrupt the police and collect reliable information. Finally, it might be taxing to make victims believe that the person standing in front of them belongs to a menacing, foreign mafia. A reputation for violence depends on long-term relations, cemented within independent networks of kinship, friendship, and ethnicity. It is next to impossible to reproduce them in a new land.[7]

And yet under particular conditions, mafia groups have been able to open branches in distant territories. In the 1950s, members of the Calabrese 'Ndrangheta migrated to the northern Italian region of Piedmont, managed to penetrate the construction sector of some towns outside Turin, and soon became entrenched. In 1995, the president of Italy disbanded the city council of Bardonecchia, which hosted the 2006 Winter Olympics, as a result of the 'Ndrangheta's enduring influence. This was an unprecedented decision for a town in the north of Italy. An attempt by the 'Ndrangheta to set up a branch in the Veneto region at around the same time, however, failed.

Similar dyads, although neglected in the literature on organized crime, are not that rare. Most strikingly, the migration to the United States of Italians, some with mafia skills, at the turn of the nineteenth century gave rise to a set of powerful mafia groups known as the "five families" in New York City. Italian migration to another seaport, the city of Rosario in Argentina, failed to generate long-lasting criminal groups of Italian descent. After a relatively brief spell, the "Rosario Mafia" disappeared and is now a forgotten episode of local history. Why? The central question of this book is why in some cases mafia transplantation succeeded while in others it failed. In order to answer this question, I have used a wide range of data and traveled to several parts of the world during the past ten years.

Below I consider cases of both successful and unsuccessful attempts by mafias to open branches outside their territory of origin. Chapter 3 is a matched comparison between Bardonecchia and Verona, while chapter 4 is a study of efforts by the Solntsevskaya to create subsidiaries in Rome and Budapest. Chapter 5 takes us back to the turn of the twentieth century with a matched comparison between New York City and Rosario. The final chapter of this book explores the movement of Hong Kong and Taiwanese triads to mainland China. In chapter 7, I outline a general perspective of mafia emergence and transplantation, and offer some considerations on the relation between democracy and mafias.

Before I proceed further and anticipate the conclusions I reach, I should say a few words on the unit of analysis (mafia), the phenomenon (transplantation), and the structure of the argument. I focus below on a specific type of criminal organization, defined as a group that supplies protection in the territory of origin. The 'Ndrangheta, the Sicilian Cosa Nostra, the

Italian American mafia, the Hong Kong and Taiwanese triads, the Solntsevskaya and other Russian *gruppirovki*, and the Japanese yakuza are essen-
tially providers of extralegal governance, and can be collectively referred
to as mafias.[8] These groups engage in extortion—the forced extraction of
resources in exchange for services that are *not* provided.[9] But such behavior
is not their defining feature.[10] Rather, they are groups that aspire to govern
others by providing criminal protection to both the underworld and the
"upper world."[11] They can supply genuine services like protection against
extortion; protection against theft and police harassment; protection for
thieves; protection in relation to informally obtained credit and the retrieval
of loans; the elimination of competitors; the intimidation of customers,
workers, and trade unionists for the benefit of employers; the intimidation
of lawful right holders; and the settlement of a variety of disputes. For example, in his classic study of Chicago organized crime published in 1929,
the U.S. ethnographer John Landesco highlighted the enforcement of cartel
agreements as a service provided by mafia groups. Producers have an incentive to enter into cartel agreements but also to undercut fellow conspirators,
placing themselves in a classic Prisoner's Dilemma. The mafia offers to enforce the cartel agreement among producers, thereby deterring conspirators
from cheating on the deal.[12]

I take the word "transplantation" to mean the ability of a mafia group
to operate an outpost over a sustained period outside its region of origin
and routine operation.[13] Although in principle the new territory could be
contiguous or faraway, I will focus mostly on territories that are not contiguous (a better word for transplantation in contiguous territories might
be expansion). The actors involved are "made" members of the organization of origin; in other words, they are bona fide mafiosi who have gone
through an initiation ritual in the territory of origin. If transplantation
succeeds, such rituals may come to be performed in the new environment
and recognized by the group of origin. Mafiosi might find themselves in
the new territory by an accident of history, such as migration, or because
they have been forced to reside there by a court order. In such cases, their
presence is due to exogenous factors rather than an explicit *ex ante* plan
to set up shop in a new region. Alternatively, or in addition, the mafia of
origin might consciously decide to open a branch in a new land. In both
scenarios the "foreign" mafiosi actively work at creating a new group, relying on the skills acquired beforehand. The new entity or "family" is either

affiliated to or a branch of an established existing mafia family. The outpost might become financially autonomous and able to generate its own profit, or continue to rely on transfers from the center. A rather crude indicator of the phenomenon is whether the mafiosi in question reside in the new territory, although they might be seen occasionally to travel back "home." Over time, the branch organization might drift away from the original "firm" and become fully autonomous as well as financially independent, or retain a degree of dependency with the homeland.

The above definition helps distinguish transplantation proper from several phenomena that are often lumped together in the category of transnational organized crime. Criminals crossing a border (physically or virtually, as in the case of Internet frauds) with an illicit good or a person do not automatically qualify as either mafia or transplantation but rather as a form of illegal *trade*, and need to be placed in a conceptual box that differs from attempts to control markets or territories abroad. Similarly, members of mafia groups traveling abroad do not constitute transplantation of the group, nor do conspiracies between mafiosi and foreign criminals to smuggle workers, drugs, weapons, and other illegal commodities either into or out of their country.

In this work, I try to identify distinctive factors in the narratives that I present. One is the generalized migration of the population from territories where mafias are well established, such as western Sicily and Calabria. It seems plausible that when large groups of individuals migrate from territories where mafias are pervasive, some with criminal skills would also relocate and be more likely to engage in mafia activities in the new territory (I am referring here to resettlement prompted by non-mafia-related reasons). A second possible boost to mafia transplantation might be the migration of people specifically trained in violence and with mafia skills. In the case of Italy, we can evaluate this dynamic thanks to *soggiorno obbligato*, a policy that punished convicted mafiosi by forcing them to relocate outside their area of origin. Third, I consider the extent to which members of mafia groups are pushed to migrate in order to escape mafia wars or prosecution in their areas of origin, or whether they are in search of particular resources or investment opportunities.

In each chapter, I then discuss the conditions under which mafia groups are likely to become entrenched. A key dimension is the presence of a

demand for criminal protection in the new place. The presence of large illegal markets, booms in construction, an export-oriented economy, incentives to create cartel agreements, or the inability of the state to settle legal
disputes quickly and effectively usually generate such a demand. I also
examine whether lack of trust and low levels of civic engagement would
predict a higher likelihood of mafia entrenchment.

Let me anticipate the main conclusions of this study. In all the cases narrated in this book, mafiosi find themselves in the new locale not of their
own volition; they have been forced to move there by court orders, to escape justice or mafia infighting and wars. They are not seeking new markets
or new products but are instead just making the most of bad luck. I had
not anticipated this result, and certainly did not choose the cases in order
to conform to this finding. What might appear the product of globalization is in fact the consequence of state repression exporting the problem
to other countries (even mafia infighting can to an extent be the product
of pressure put on the group by the state). This finding does vindicate an
aspect of the perspective suggested by Reuter and Gambetta—namely, that
mafias would not normally move out of their territory. An additional issue
I explore is that even if they do not move willingly, they can still to an extent choose *where* to move. I find that they move to places where they had
a previous contact, a trusted friend or a relative.

Is the presence of mafiosi in a new territory enough for a mafia to
emerge? No. A special combination of factors must be present. First, no
other mafia group (or state *apparati* offering illegal protection) must be
present. It is too much of an uphill struggle for an incoming mafia to set
up shop in the presence of a powerful local competitor. Second, a mafia
group is most likely to succeed in transplanting when its presence coin-
cides with the sudden emergence of new markets. To the degree that the
state is not able to govern new markets, the possibility of mafia emergence
or entrenchment from abroad is strong. States might be unable to clearly
define and protect property rights, and market operators hence would develop a demand for alternative sources of protection. In addition, states by
definition cannot protect dealers of illegal commodities. In both instances,
significant opportunities exist for mafias to govern access to valuable markets, offer genuine services of dispute settlement and protection, enforce

cartel agreements, reduce competition, and thus serve the interests of a sector of society. These opportunities can be easily taken up when a supply of people trained in violence, either local or from abroad, is at hand.

The presence of a supply of mafiosi and the inability of the state to govern markets are the key factors that link cases of successful transplantation, such as the 'Ndrangheta in Bardonecchia (chapter 3) and the Russian mafia in Hungary (chapter 4). In Bardonecchia, disenfranchised migrant workers from outside the region accepted illegal employment over unemployment, thereby forgoing membership in trade unions and more generally state-sponsored protection. Entrepreneurs not only hired illegal workers but also schemed to restrict competition. The structure of the local labor market and the booming construction industry (in which firms compete locally and there is a strong incentive to form cartels) led to the emergence of a demand for illegal protection. Members of the 'Ndrangheta Mazzaferro clan resided in this territory. They offered certain firms privileged access to this market, and were able to settle disputes between workers and employers.

Although Piedmont does not have a new market economy like those of Eastern Europe, a striking parallel exists in the successful transplantation of the Russian mafia's Solnstevo criminal group in Budapest (chapter 4). In that instance the state failed to create a system to adjudicate disputes quickly and effectively, thereby leaving significant sectors of the emerging market economy unprotected by the law, as was the case for immigrant workers in Bardonecchia. When vast numbers of economic agents operate in an unprotected market, they develop a demand for nonstate forms of protection. In both Bardonecchia and Budapest, skilled criminals were available to organize a mafia group and offer a variety of services, such as the settlement of disputes and elimination of competitors in local markets.

A powerful set of mafia groups emerged in the United States around 1910 because of the unintended consequences of police reform and it was able to expand later thanks to Prohibition (chapter 5). Until then, illegal markets were protected by a combination of local politicians and corrupt police officers. When the mayor of New York enacted far-reaching reforms that curbed grand graft, illegal markets such as gambling and prostitution were in search of new protectors. In legal markets, like garment production, poultry, garbage collection, and construction, existing operators were only too happy to turn to an agency able to ensure the continuation of cartelization. Unemployed immigrant workers, mostly from southern Italy and equipped with some mafia skills, stepped in.

The case of China allows us to spell out in greater depth some crucial mechanisms. The state has been unable to offer swift and efficient avenues of dispute settlement for the new players in the rapidly emerging market economy, and a significant sector of the workforce operates in the informal economy, where state protection is absent. In addition, large illegal markets, such as in prostitution, gambling, and drug trafficking, have developed since the opening of the Chinese economy in the 1980s. On the "supply-side" of the story, "brothers" (triads members) from Hong Kong and Taiwan have moved to the Middle Kingdom. They have failed (so far) to become entrenched and offer generalized protection, however. Why? Chapter 6 shows that in China, a powerful actor is already in place to offer such services—that is, corrupt fragments of the state apparatus, which work as the "protective umbrella" for both legal and illegal businesses. In the cases of successful transplantation, no other mafia (or bent state apparatus) was already on the ground to compete with the outsiders.

Globalization hinders mafia transplantation in a way that has escaped most contributors. In the case of two of the failed attempts to transplant mafias, the local economies relied on exports—Verona on exported furniture, and Rosario on exported agriculture. There is no demand for cartels in the export-oriented sector of the economy since producers export to different parts of the world. In order to stop competition for producer A in, say, northern Europe, the mafia would need to scare away producers in a variety of different countries who all export to northern Europe. Thus, as economies become more export oriented due to globalization, the likelihood that mafias will transplant themselves may diminish.

Migration as such is clearly not a cause of mafia transplantation. Despite roughly similar patterns of migration from the south to the north of Italy, a southern mafia did not transplant itself in either Rome or other towns of Piedmont. Only when migration is coupled with illegal employment and the absence of state protection does a demand for criminal protection emerge that can be met by a mafia. In other words, migration—even from regions with a high mafia density—does not necessarily carry the seed of a new mafia. Rather, it is the state's failure to offer effective legal protection and the lack of avenues for legitimate employment that set in motion a chain of events that might give rise to a new mafia.

The Italian policy of soggiorno obbligato, flawed as it might have been, cannot be blamed for successful transplantation. In the case of Bardonecchia, the supply of foreign mafiosi went hand in hand with a genuine demand for criminal protection. When it did not, transplantation failed. Moreover, other parts of Piedmont and northern Italy also experienced an influx of skilled mobsters forced to migrate due to the soggiorno policy, but mafias did not develop. Similarly, the Russians in Rome failed to establish a successful group because there was no demand for their services. Even a supply of specialized criminals (as distinct from generalized migration) is not enough to produce successful transplantation.

Contrary to what is suggested by the seminal work of Robert D. Putnam, a high level of generalized trust and "social capital" among the law-abiding population is not enough to prevent transplantation. The study of Bardonecchia suggests that high levels of trust among the general population are not sufficient to prevent transplantation and social capital might remain high while a mafia flourishes. The mafia was able to offer to a large enough section of the local population protection against competition, a workforce cheap enough to reap the opportunities generated by the construction boom, and more generally capital and employment. Those who rejected this state of affairs, recognizing that it was built on violence and disrespect for the law, were soon ostracized and marginalized.

Not only do I show that a mafia can transplant itself in highly civic northern Italy and that some local groups can rally to its defense. I also establish that in Verona the dense network of social trust allowed the drug trade to operate without recourse to third-party enforcers. This network reduced the demand for third-party enforcement by the mafia and thereby inhibited mafia migration. The more general point is that social capital can be used for good or ill depending on the goals of the actors involved.

In all the cases narrated in this book, mafiosi were forced to move, but once in the new territory, started investing in the local economy, as the Russian mafia did in Rome and the triads did in China. Yet investments alone are not sufficient to lead to long-term transplantation. When investments combine with a supply of mafiosi and a specific demand for protection services, a group can become entrenched.

Finally, the incentives to open outposts abroad in order to obtain resources such as labor, intelligence, and specialized equipment are few, and decrease as the mobility of goods and people increases. Globalization will increase the ability of mafia groups to obtain some of the resources that they need without having to move. To put it more generally, globalization will affect the way crime is committed in a given locale. For instance, labor mobility *toward* traditional mafia territory can well increase, allowing mafias to import labor from trusted suppliers. A feature of globalization that we observe in legitimate firms—the ability to outsource work, such as opening call centers in India—will not be an option for mafia groups; workers cannot be located in India to run protection rackets in New York City. To the extent that mafias seek specialized technical equipment, like arms, globalization could increase the number of international locations from which a mafia group obtains its resources, but will reduce the motivation to open outposts abroad.

Can the conclusions on transplantation form the basis of a general perspective of mafia emergence and transplantation? A relatively recent body of research has shown that mafias emerge in societies that are undergoing a sudden and late transition to the market economy, lack a legal structure that reliably protects property rights or settles business disputes, and have a supply of people trained in violence who became unemployed at this specific juncture. This perspective—I call it the "property-right theory of mafia emergence"—has been applied to cases such as Sicily, Japan and post–Soviet Russia, to explain how mafias might emerge in times of rapid but flawed transitions to the market economy. I suggest that this perspective is a special case of a broader phenomenon. Mafias emerge and transplant when certain key structural conditions are present in the economy. The critical factor is proximity to a sudden market expansion that is not properly regulated by the state and the presence of people who can step in to regulate such markets. In a nutshell, opportunities in the market economy bring about mafias. Effective states can ensure the orderly development of markets, and hence neutralize a mafia's transplantation or emergence. In chapter 7, I address the unintended consequences of some state policies along with the complex relationship between democracy and mafias. I also return to Boris's murder at the Tverskaya hotel and offer a clue to identify the culprit.

TWO

Mafia Transplantation

Does transplantation ever take place? It is often difficult to gauge what the police, judicial authorities, or press reports mean when they claim, for example, that the Russian mafia is active in at least twenty-six foreign countries, or that the Calabrese 'Ndrangheta is present in more than twenty countries.[1] From the few academic studies that mention the phenomenon, we know that mafias are rather stationary. Peter Reuter, while discussing U.S. "illegal enterprises" (of which mafias are a subset), notes that they tend to be "local in scope."[2] In *The Sicilian Mafia*, Diego Gambetta writes that "not only did the [Sicilian] mafia grow mainly in Western Sicily, but, with the exception of Catania, it has remained there to this very day." More generally, the mafia, he adds, "is a difficult industry to export. Not unlike mining, it is heavily dependent on the local environment."[3] Similarly, Yiu Kong Chu argues that "Hong Kong Triads are localized and they are not international illegal entrepreneurs whose wealth and connections may enable them to emigrate to Western countries." Although Hong Kong triads might be involved in international crime, observes Chu, they "are not likely to be the key organisers."[4] Peter Hill, the author of *The Japanese Mafia*, dates the beginning of the foreign activities of yakuza from the 1970s, when the Ishii Susumu branch of the Tokyo-based Inagawa-kai started to organize gambling trips for wealthy Japanese. A few years later, corporate racketeers began to target Japanese companies abroad. Yet "more usually foreign travel has been recreational or to invest either in real estate (usually very unsuccessfully) or weaponry. At no time however, have the yakuza managed to extend their core protective role beyond a native

Japanese market."[5] Moreover, the opposite claim—that a Chinese mafia is invading traditional yakuza turf—is, according to Hill, for the moment incorrect and politically motivated.[6]

Reuter and Gambetta offer several theoretical insights into why mafias find it difficult to become entrenched in foreign countries.

Ability to monitor agents. Distance makes it harder to monitor an employee, and ensure that the agent works efficiently and honestly. The agent can misappropriate capital (both tangible and organizational) from the enterprise by embezzling it and engage in activities that are not sanctioned by the principal, thereby attracting police attention and endangering the entire organization. In order to get off, the agent might even inform on the bosses back home.[7]

Information collection and communication. The collection of reliable facts on what people do is a vital part of a mafioso's job, but they are likely to find it hard to come by this information in an unfamiliar region, where they cannot rely on an extensive network of friends and accomplices. Furthermore, agents and bosses need to be in touch frequently, thus increasing the need for communication traffic between the two territories. Since face-to-face meetings would be the exception rather than the rule, the likelihood that the police might intercept such communication increases with distance.

Reputation. Reputation is a crucial asset for mafiosi to carry out their jobs. The greater one's reputation for the ability to wield violence, the lesser one's need to resort to violence, since victims comply more readily. Reuter writes that investments in violence, which yield a reputation for being able to deliver threats, have a higher return when the criminal has contacts, through a continuous chain of other persons, with at least one witness to the violent act. It is more likely that such a chain is broken with distance. Along similar lines, Gambetta maintains that a reputation for effective violence depends on long-term relations, cemented within independent networks of kinship, friendship, and ethnicity. It is next to impossible to reproduce such networks in a new setting.[8]

Still, transplantation does take place. In his memoirs, Catania mafia boss Antonio Calderone reminisces that during his time, there were two recognized branches of Sicilian mafia families in central and northern Italy. Another family operated for a while in Tunis, its existence having been recorded since at least the 1930s. "At the time," writes Calderone, "Tunis was a haven for many mafiosi fleeing Fascism. . . . [There] they had formed a regular family with a representative."[9] In his study of southern Italian mafias' expansion and entrenchment in nontraditional territories within Italy, Rocco Sciarrone shows how a concatenation of mechanisms accounts for the expansion of the Neapolitan Camorra in the neighboring region of Apulia in the late 1970s and early 1980s. First, a number of Camorristi had been incarcerated or forced to resettle in Apulia. By the 1980s a new smuggling route from Yugoslavia had opened, and Apulia had become a crucial node. As the former Yugoslavia descended into war in the early 1990s, Apulia offered even greater criminal opportunities for smuggling drugs and people from the ruins of the former Communist bloc. Finally, the leader of the Neapolitan Camorra, Raffaele Cutolo, decided to expand into Apulia, putting into action a long-term plan that included establishing relations with corrupt officials. Yet the final outcome was not as Cutolo had planned: soon the local criminals tried to free themselves from their masters and founded the Sacra Corona Unita, a new mafia invoking the regional Pugliese identity against the intrusion of the foreign Neapolitans.[10]

Moving beyond Europe, we encounter other instances. The charismatic leader of Taiwan Bamboo United, a major triad group, has been living in Cambodia for several years, where he appears to broker deals between visiting businesspeople and the local elite. At least thirty other Taiwanese gangsters live and operate in Phnom Penh.[11] According to reports, the reign of Evgenii Petrovich Vasin, a Russian mafia boss of the Far East, has been succeeded by that of a triad boss, Lao Da, now "the main organized crime figure in Vladivostok."[12] Xiangu Du, a Chinese national, led a gang in the Russian city of Khabarovsk for four years (1997–2001).[13] But at the same time Russian groups moved westward. Two subsidiaries of the Moscow-based crime group Solntsevskaya operated in both Rome and Budapest, as I will show in chapter 4. As for the Japanese case, although Hill downplays the presence of the yakuza abroad, he suggests that "the presence of non-Japanese criminals in Japan is likely to become more significant in the future."[14] Thus, transplantation seems to be a real phenomenon in need of an explanation.

Factors Conducive to Transplantation

Why do mafias succeed in setting up branches in a new territory? I have organized the factors into two broad categories: supply, and local conditions relevant to demand.

SUPPLY

Migration is the explanation for mafia transplantation most often cited by the press, academics, and prosecutors.[15] Although never properly unpacked, a straightforward quantitative logic lies at the root of this theory: assuming that a given proportion of a population consists of criminals, the greater the migration of individuals from that population, the larger the number of criminals that will reach a new territory. Moreover, migration from territories of origin where there is a high proportion of mafiosi appears to carry the greatest threat of mafia transplantation.[16] Thus, the large migration from southern Italy to the United States at the end of the nineteenth century included many individuals with "the necessary skills for organizing a protection market."[17] The view that links migration to mafia transplantation can take simplistic and crude forms. Within Italy itself, the Northern League labels all southerners as a potential crime threat and has called for controls over south-north migration in order to prevent the spread of organized crime. The notion that Italian migration alone is responsible for the creation of the Italian American mafia in the United States is part and parcel of the now-discredited "alien conspiracy theory" of organized crime.[18] The presence of migrants from mafia territories, although clearly a contributing factor, is not sufficient for the establishment of new mafias, otherwise we would find mafias in every country to which southern Italians have migrated in the past.

A specific push factor for mafia transplantation in the case of Italy was the perverse policy of forcing convicted mafiosi to reside outside their area of origin as a form of punishment.[19] Based on a naive view of the mafia as a product of backward societies, forced resettlement (soggiorno obbligato) started in 1956, and was predicated on the assumption that away from their home base and immersed in the civic, law-abiding culture of the North, mafiosi from the South would abandon their old ways. Since the mid-1950s this policy has brought hard-nosed lawbreakers to the northern regions of Italy, including Lombardy, Piedmont, and Emilia-Romagna.

The mafioso-turned-state-witness Gaspare Mutolo commented that the policy of forced resettlement "has been a good thing, since it allowed us to contact other people, to discover new places, new cities."[20] The soggiorno obbligato selected for forced migration individuals with specific mafia skills, and unintentionally allowed them to expand their networks and knowledge of the world (see chapter 3).

Criminals, including members of mafia groups, are also pushed to migrate in order to escape mafia wars or police repression in their areas of origin. Such cases abound in the history of mafias. For instance, Antonio Deodati escaped from Sicily to New York City in the 1860s to save himself from a "death" sentence passed on him by fellow mafiosi (he was nonetheless murdered in Brooklyn in 1865; see chapter 5).[21] *Ivan Yakovlev*, the Russian boss in Rome, was eager to move from Moscow to Italy because he was afraid of being killed by the Solntsevskaya ruling elite (see chapter 4). Vyacheslav Kirillovich Ivan'kov, often described as the Solntsevskaya envoy to the United States tasked with creating the Russian mafia in that country, in fact left Russia in 1992 because "it became too dangerous for him there."[22] Many yakuza active in the Philippines are actually ex-members who have been expelled from their groups.[23] Georgian *vory-v-zakone* (a type of mafia boss in the Soviet Union) "migrated" to Russia whenever there was a change at the top of the Georgian Soviet Republic's political elite, since every new first secretary would try to impress Moscow by conducting purges as well as cracking down on corruption and crime.[24] Following the Rose Revolution of 2003–5, the new Georgian president launched a harsh repression of what was left of the Georgian *vory*, referred to now by their Georgian-language equivalent of *kanonieri kurdebi*. A direct consequence of the repression was the escape of several leaders to Moscow (again), Spain, and other countries.[25] Similarly, Taiwan's campaigns against organized crime in 1984, 1990, and 1996 facilitated the relocation of triad bosses to China. As crime expert Ko-lin Chin aptly put it, "Even though initially they [Taiwanese triad members] had no intention of staying away from Taiwan for long, they ended up living abroad for months, or even years. . . . As many fugitives started new lives abroad, they not only became entangled in the affairs of the overseas Chinese community, but also established connections with local crime groups in the host societies" (see chapter 6).[26] Fascism's repression of the Sicilian mafia led to families emerging outside the island, such as Tunis, and some leaders arriving on the shores of the American continent, both in New York City and Rosario (see chapter 5). A systematic study of a Camorra clan shows that out of fifty-one members, only four individuals resided abroad, in Aberdeen and Holland. All four were escaping from the Italian police.[27] Thus, a neglected aspect of globalization is at work here: repression in one corner of the world has an unintended effect on another.

The factors that I have reviewed so far are unintentional (migration, forced resettlement, and fear of punishment). Yet mafia bosses are also capable of deliberate and strategic thinking. Below I explore whether mafias sometimes act like legitimate firms and rationally decide to expand to new territories in order to exploit special business opportunities, unprompted by police repression or mafia infighting. At least in theory, mafias might be after specific resources or investment opportunities, or wish to invade a new market.[28]

Resources. For a legitimate firm, the decision to open a branch abroad may be motivated by the desire to acquire a specific resource, such as a mineral or labor, at a lower cost. Resources also include intangible goods like knowledge, innovation capabilities, and management or organizational skills.[29] The motivation to open a branch abroad is predicated on the fact that the resources desired by the firm cannot be simply bought on the open market or accessed remotely.

For a mafia, resource-seeking motivations might include looking for labor, a key input factor. Is it plausible that a mafia would open a branch abroad to recruit "workers" for its operations back home? Broadly speaking, mafias hire two kinds of workers: casual and permanent. Casual workers include specialists in explosives, chemists, translators, people familiar with certain premises, and government officials. It is possible that some occasional helpers are hired from faraway lands, but it is unlikely that a mafia would open an outpost in order to do so. Such hiring is unusual. Permanent employees normally undergo an initiation ritual and work under the direct orders of the head of a group.[30] One indispensable quality for full-time workers is dependability; another is the proven ability to use violence. It follows that recruitment normally occurs within the area in which the group operates. Only by having known the recruit for many years can a boss be confident that the newcomer is not an undercover agent.[31] The boss will also know the family relations of the aspiring member, making it easier to threaten him in the event that he decides to turn state witness. Still, at least one significant case of labor mobility exists in the history of the Italian American mafia. In the 1970s, a capo in the Bonanno New York mafia family recruited cold-blooded Sicilian killers in order to help him distribute drugs on the East Coast of the United States. At first this strategy proved highly successful and he was able to corner a significant segment of the market; but eventually the killers betrayed him and the capo was himself assassinated.[32] In this case the Bonanno family imported workers rather than employ them in a subsidiary abroad, and the source of recruitment was closely allied to the Bonanno family.

Other resources of interest to mafias include technical equipment (such as arms, hideaways, and spying technology), passports, and bank accounts. Mafias are more likely to access resources on the open market when their quality can be clearly defined, as with technical equipment, weapons, and surveillance tools. Mafia members might want to acquire foreign passports in case they need to escape quickly, open bank accounts to deposit their money, or hire the services of lawyers in a foreign country, but the group as such would not need to relocate abroad. Like ordinary firms, it is possible that mafias could hire a workforce from another territory, and then that workforce would relocate to the mafia's territory of origin. As the mobility of people and goods grows, there will be even fewer incentives for mafia groups to establish outposts in distant territories in order to acquire specific input resources.

Investments. A legitimate firm might wish to reinvest the proceeds of its core activity in other businesses. Such decisions might be motivated by tax and performance incentives provided by governments, or by the desire to operate in more efficient financial systems. This type of investment-seeking location decision will be affected by new technologies, as greater integration between different markets makes it easier to invest in other countries' assets without the need to physically open a branch in the new territory.

It is harder for a mafia group than for legitimate firms to monitor remote investments. Like other firms, mafias seek to reinvest their proceeds in profitable enterprises. Mafia investments, though, are informal and often involve cash, and no recourse to the legal system exists in the event of a dispute. Moreover, money laundering and investments in the legal economy can involve several hundred one-shot transactions between business associates of the criminal group and legitimate firms in foreign and inhospitable countries. Those tasked with undertaking these decisions enjoy a significant amount of discretion and are hard to monitor. Investments can go wrong, and the bosses back home cannot easily verify claims and reports. This situation generates specific incentives for bosses to go abroad to monitor transactions with legitimate entrepreneurs directly. For instance, the Sicilian mafia opened such an office in Rome at the beginning of the 1970s by sending Pippo Calò, the boss of the Porta Nuova family. Passing himself off as an antiques dealer, Calò invested large amounts of money, mainly in real estate, for several mafia families. In connection with his activities in Rome, he was accused of the murder of Roberto Calvi, the chair of Banco Ambrosiano. Calvi was killed in 1982 in London, allegedly because he lost funds entrusted to him by the mafia when his bank collapsed.[33] Similarly, after the Chicago outfit decided to invest some of its money into casinos in Las Vegas following the Second World War, it regularly sent an envoy to ensure that profits were "skimmed" and channeled back home to families in Chicago, Kansas City, Saint Louis, and Milwaukee. The partly fictionalized movie *Casino* (1995) recounts the exploits of one such enforcer, Anthony Spilotro.

Markets. A legitimate firm might open a subsidiary in a different country in order to carry out its main activity in a new market. For mafias, the core business of the firm is control of a territory or market. Would a mafia, unprompted by police repression or mafia infighting, rationally decide to colonize a virgin territory? It is unlikely that a mafia group would undertake to invade a foreign territory already dominated by another criminal group, or that if it decided to do so, it would be successful. Thus one local factor—namely, the presence or absence of an existing group—must be one consideration in calculating the pros and cons of any colonization strategy. It is still possible that a mafia rationally decides to expand when it perceives that there are no local competitors and the opportunities are great enough to offset the considerable start-up costs of such a venture. In the course of presenting the case studies in subsequent chapters, I will evaluate whether mafias ever think in this way, or whether mafia transplantation is more likely an outcome that is not fully intended, at least at first.

In conclusion, the incentives to open outposts abroad in order to obtain resources such as labor, intelligence, and specialized equipment are few, and are set to further decrease as globalization spreads. Globalization increases labor mobility generally, and therefore a mafia probably does not need to open an outpost abroad to attract workers to its traditional area of operation. Moreover, mafias hire people they trust locally, rather than open a branch abroad to recruit workers for their home turf. To the extent that mafias seek specialized technical equipment, such as arms, globalization could increase the number of international locations from which a mafia group obtains its resources, and thus there would be no need to open a branch abroad. They can simply buy the goods on the open market. Some mafia investments might require close scrutiny and give rise to incentives to open outposts abroad to monitor investments in distant territories. Such was the reason for the mob presence in Rome and Las Vegas. Market-seeking ventures of mafia groups are unlikely to involve the takeover of territories already occupied by existing local groups, unless the local groups are particularly weak and the incentives to move there are overwhelming. More generally, I do not expect a rational decision to open a branch in order to conquer a territory in a faraway land. Transplantation is more likely the outcome of unintended consequences.

CONDITIONS IN THE NEW TERRITORY AND THE "DEMAND" FOR MAFIAS

Once mafiosi find themselves in the new territory, under what conditions do they succeed in becoming entrenched?

The level of generalized trust (trust in others whom we do not know) in the new land is, for some authors, an important variable that could explain the entrenchment of mafias. James Coleman has pointed out that a low level of trust reduces actors' ability to cooperate and communicate, inhibiting collective action.[34] The less that trust exists among law abiders, the less likely it is that civil society will organize to oppose the entrenchment of a mafia group. One can further predict that the lower the trust among lawbreakers, the greater their demand for protection services will be; a mafia facilitates exchanges among criminals who distrust each other by offering the enforcement of deals and promises. This line of reasoning implies that mafias are more likely to transplant successfully to regions with little trust among law abiders and lawbreakers (each condition is independent of the other).

How is trust created? Robert Putnam's classic studies *Making Democracy Work* (1993) and *Bowling Alone: The Collapse and Revival of American Community* (2000) posit that local voluntary (nonpolitical) groups that bring people together provide private benefits to participants. In addition, he suggests that such groups can generate "social capital" that is *transferable* to society as a whole, thereby increasing the stock of generalized trust and promoting democratic values. Putnam shows that southern Italy is trapped in a long-term vicious circle of a lack of trust and civic virtue, whereas such virtue is robust in the North. Regions such as Sicily, Campania, Calabria, and Basilicata consistently score the lowest in terms of social capital, while Piedmont, Emilia, Veneto, and Lombardy score the highest. As Putnam explains, "In the most civic regions . . . citizens are actively involved in all sorts of local associations—literary guilds, local bands, hunting clubs, cooperatives and so on. They follow civic affairs avidly in the press, and they engage in politics out of programmatic conviction." By contrast, in the less civic regions such as Calabria, citizens take part in the political process because they are motivated by particularist short-term individual benefits rather than an interest in general issues. "An absence of civic associations and a paucity of local media in these latter regions mean that citizens there are rarely drawn into community affairs." Putnam traces levels of "civicness" in Italy back to medieval times and finds a remarkable stability over the centuries for which comparable data are available.[35]

Since levels of trust and civic culture are highly stable across the centuries, and organized crime is correlated with low levels of trust and social capital, Putnam's work implies that mafia transplantation to an area that traditionally experiences high levels of social capital is ceteris paribus harder to achieve. Thus, areas in northern Italy that historically have had high levels of trust and social capital along with no mafia should be more resistant to mafia attempts to immigrate and establish themselves. This view implies that high levels of trust and criminal protection are inversely related: when one is high, the other is low or absent.

Putnam's work has been criticized—most eloquently by Susan Rose-Ackerman—for failing to show a link between participation in civic associations, and the production of generalized trust and democratic values.[36] My critique is different. Moderately high levels of social capital and civic engagement can coexist with the presence of mafia protection. Such a "service" may be welcomed by sectors of the population because it provides an advantage in a given market. Alternatively, or in addition, a demand for mafia protection emerges among those dealing in illegal commodities. This perspective suggests that civic engagement and the demand for private protection are independent of each other. If we think of private protection in a broader sense to include the enforcement of cartel agreements, the reduction of competition, and the organization of illegal markets that supply goods in high demand among a population (such as prostitution or alcohol), it is evident that criminal organizations may supply a solution welcomed by significant sectors of a society. Indeed, protectionism, though an enemy of global competition, is promoted by legal as well as illegal means—as, for example, when local governments impose restrictions on nonnative business groups and workers in order to protect entrenched local interests. Therefore, a high level of civic engagement does not in itself prevent mafia transplantation; the private protection supplied by mafias is orthogonal to social capital and civicness as defined by Putnam. In order to substantiate these suggestions, I consider territories in nontraditional mafia areas where trust and social capital are reportedly high (see chapter 3).

A key argument of this book is that the presence of a genuine demand for criminal protection, the core activity of mafias, leads to long-term transplantation. A demand for criminal protection is a critical factor that prompts both the birth of homegrown mafias and the migration of established ones. Such a demand interacts with a number of local conditions. In legal markets, the more incapable a state is of protecting its citizens and settling disputes among actors in the economy, the greater the demand for alternative sources of protection. Such demand arises because of the state's lack of competence to act as a credible third-party enforcer of agreements.

A second type of demand for protection emerges when entrepreneurs seek to sell legal commodities illegally. This might take the form of trying to wipe out competition or organize cartel agreements with mafia support. A sector of the economy that typically generates high incentives to create cartels is construction: firms compete on a local market, and the barriers to entry are relatively low. Construction cartels often emerge without the need for mafia enforcement. A small number of firms simply corner the market. Yet a sudden explosion in the construction market would open up the market to new entrants. Incumbents might then develop a demand for protection against outsiders. Given this, construction sector booms might lead to a demand for criminal protection. Below I explore in depth two such cases, in Bardonecchia and Rosario.

On the other hand, economies that are export oriented will generate less demand for mafia protection: the mafia cannot help exporters to penetrate distant markets by harassing another entrepreneur who lives in the same place but exports to a different part of the world. For the mafia to be effective, producers must compete in the same market. On the other hand, several exporters of the same product to the same market would benefit from mafia protection. In the area north of Naples, for instance, the Nuvoletta family ensured that only certain food products, including Parmalat milk and Bauli Panettone, were carried in shops and supermarkets. The large producers from the North, such as Parmalat and Cirio, were willing to enter into direct contact with the Camorra in return for a near monopoly. Only after the police uncovered the scheme did these multinationals claim that they had been the victims of "racketeers."[37]

The demand for property rights protection in illegal markets is rife. Not only is state protection absent by definition, but state action is aimed at arresting actors in such markets and confiscating their "property" ("That's what the FBI can never understand," says Henry Hill in the book *Wiseguy*, "that what Paulie [mafia member Paul Vario] and the organization offer is protection for the kinds of guys who can't go to the cops").[38] As a consequence, illegal assets are highly vulnerable to lawful seizure and theft, and property rights are disputed to a much greater degree than in legal markets. Moreover, information about the quality of goods as well as the identities and whereabouts of the actors is particularly poor in illegal markets; entrepreneurs in these markets cannot freely advertise their good reputation, creditors disappear, informants consort with the police, and undercover agents try to pass themselves off as bona fide fellow criminals. As documented by several studies, mafias offer protection to criminals in the underworld and, in so doing, make illegal markets run more smoothly. It is thus plausible that the larger the illegal markets are, the greater the demand for protection will be. When there is a time lag between the emergence of a demand for protection and the provision of suitable local supply, the opportunity to supply mafia services may be seized by transplanted groups.

As such, the state's lack of competence in legal spheres and unwilling-ness to protect illegal activities leads actors to look for alternatives, and so increases the demand for mafia services. In the presence of a suitable sup-ply, foreign groups might become entrenched in a new territory.

Other features of the new territory are related to transplantation, such as size and the presence of local protectors. For instance, ceteris paribus, the smaller the new territory or the market, the easier it is to penetrate it. As mentioned above, the construction market is vulnerable to mafia pen-etration. It is easier to control a construction sector populated by thirty players than one populated by three hundred, however. If a mafia tries to penetrate politics through the control of votes, it is easier to control politics if the district is small. It takes more voters to influence the election of the mayor of a large city than of a smaller one. Where local protectors, such as a mafia or fragments of the state apparatus, are present and effec-tive, it might be next to impossible for incoming mafiosi to dislodge them. When Taiwanese triad bosses and foot soldiers were forced to flee their home country and landed in places like Thailand and Vietnam, they soon discovered that the locals controlled all the criminal markets and they had little chance of replacing them. One brother in Vietnam said that "there are also Vietnamese gangs here, but we will never get into any conflicts with them because, the bottom line is, it is their territory. It is impossible for us to be in command here."[39]

Large constituencies or markets and export-oriented economies are negatively related to a demand for mafia protection and thus transplan-tation, while construction booms and large illegal markets are positively related to such a demand.

REPUTATION, INFORMATION, AND MONITORING

Let's return to the challenges to transplantation raised by Reuter and Gam-betta—that is, advertising one's reputation, the collection of information, and the difficulties of monitoring agents in a distant territory. Clearly, the incoming mafiosi must be able to persuade the local population that they truly belong to a menacing established mafia (cases of individuals faking such membership have been recorded).[40] Although a difficult task, it is not impossible. Reuter himself, in a classic article on the decline of the Italian mafia in the United States, notes that Colombian drug dealers in the 1980s managed to develop their own reputation for ruthless violence—a reputation that has become more menacing than that of the U.S. Cosa Nostra.[41] "Advertisement" in this domain might well rely on indirect strategies: newspaper investigations, popular culture, and the media unintentionally promote the name of a mafia when depicting it in movies or reporting on its activities. Gangsters indeed welcome movies about them. One producer told Italian film critic Tullio Kezich that "organized crime does not mind movies about the mafia; on the contrary it considers them with a dose of pride, as something that can shed an appealing light [on them], especially if a boss is played by a popular actor."[42] In this specific domain, aspects of globalization might be coming to the aid of the incoming mafia. One would expect that the increase in communication and the spread of media news would make it easier for a new group to signal to a wider audience its arrival in town along with its connections to a menacing homeland. Yet the mafiosi abroad still requires their audience to link them as individuals with the worldwide reputation of their groups. They therefore should be working hard at reinforcing markers such as ethnicity that associate them with the mafias of their origin. Paradoxically, mafiosi might exploit prejudices against immigrants to their own advantage.

A key resource for a mafia group is the ability to collect reliable information. Both Reuter and Gambetta suggest that a mafia working in a new territory would find it impossible to carry out this task. A tangible and long-term presence in the new territory is fundamental. But how long is "long"? It is plausible that a number of years would suffice to create a network of informants. In addition, the information to be collected need not be about complex transactions or numerous locales. It might well be about a local market in the new territory, as in the case of the construction industry in Bardonecchia (see chapter 3). To the extent that a mafia can count on migration networks in the new locale, some information will be easier to come by. Significant economic investments in the new territory by associates of the incoming mafia can also be a conduit for data gathering for a criminal group. In sum, the collection of information in the new place is not an insurmountable obstacle to transplantation, only a challenge.

A final point of skepticism about the ability of mafias to transplant indicates that agents abroad are harder to monitor. They might take risks while away, thereby increasing their chances of being arrested and the danger for the boss back home. The case of Anthony Spilotro supports this viewpoint. While in Vegas, he started to run a burglary ring, endangering the mafia investment due to renewed police attention. The bosses back home ultimately punished him with a gruesome death. Yet the Chicago outfit did not plan to exercise territorial control in Las Vegas but simply wanted to ensure that its investments were safe. In the framework of this book, they were motivated to open a branch abroad to monitor investments. Any illegal investment raises the danger that the agent might cheat, since the principal cannot undertake it directly but instead needs to go through fronts, lawyers, bankers, and the like.

More generally, the "hard-to-monitor" argument hinges on the assumption that a mafia group, like a standard company, rationally decides to open a branch in a distant territory that is directly dependent on the homeland. A more plausible mechanism of mafia diffusion is through the unintended consequences of state action or mafia wars, as I will show below. A mafioso finds himself in the new territory because he escapes from his homeland. Once there, he will have the chance to explore local opportunities and negotiate arrangements that reduce the need for complex ways to monitor his actions by the homeland. It is unlikely that he will receive a salary from the boss back home. Rather, he will have to earn his own money by entering the local market. The group of origin may do no more than bestow a seal of approval on the existence of the outpost, which has a great deal of autonomy. The outpost abroad is not a branch of a corporation but rather a semiautonomous unit allied to the homeland. If seen in this light, the objections raised by these authors vanish.

THE KEY FACTORS IN SUMMARY

Table 2.1 presents a summary version of the factors discussed above. "Supply" refers to unintentional and intentional factors that account for the presence of the mafiosi in the new territory. They could also be thought of as "push" factors. The table includes a line for generalized population migration and another for mafiosi migration. Such latter migration can be willing or unwilling. "Willing" aims to describe whether the mafioso migration is due to intentionally seeking resources, investments, or markets. "Unwilling" refers to the soggiorno obbligato policy, mafia wars, and the attempt to escape prosecution. Among the "local conditions," I include the level of trust in the new locale (as measured by Putnam), the presence

TABLE 2.1

Factors Facilitating Mafia Transplantation

	Factors facilitating mafia transplantation
Supply of mafiosi	Generalized migration Mafiosi migration (willing/unwilling)
Local conditions	Level of trust/civic engagement Presence of local illegal protectors Size of locale New and/or booming markets*
Demand for mafia services	
Transplantation	

* The markets considered are construction (Bardonecchia and Rosario), drugs (Verona and China), property rights (Budapest and China), oil (Budapest), alcohol (New York City), gambling (New York City and China), and prostitution (China).

or absence of local protectors, such as an existing mafia or corrupt officials and police, and the size of the locale. By "new and booming markets," I refer to whether the economy has undergone some sudden change. For instance, a construction boom would qualify as one. Also a wholesale transition to the market economy or the sudden outlawing of alcohol consumption would create new and booming markets. I suggested above that some such factors are causally linked to others: a construction boom, the sudden outlawing of alcohol, or low levels of trust could give rise to a demand for criminal protection. Such a connection, however, is not mechanical; if actors in a given market are able to regulate the sudden changes in the market and cope, they would not develop such a demand. If the state is efficient at defining and protecting rights in a new market economy, a demand for criminal protection would not arise. If the operators in the drug market are able to settle disputes without recourse to a third-party criminal enforcer, such a demand again would not emerge.

In the remainder of the book, I evaluate empirically whether the factors listed in table 2.1 have generated such a demand, and whether a foreign mafia was able to intercept such a demand and become entrenched in a faraway territory (transplantation).

CASE SELECTION

A final word on how I selected the cases. Researching criminal organizations is a hazardous enterprise, and often chance encounters with data direct the scholar toward a particular case study. The main criterion that I have followed, however, is the "possibility principle." The said principle prescribes the inclusion of cases where the outcome of interest—in this instance, transplantation—is possible. In some of the cases included transplantation did not occur; nevertheless, it was tried. A related criterion for inclusion is variation in the "dependent" variable (transplantation). Only by presenting cases in which mafias failed to transplant as well as ones where they succeed can one hope to identify the factors that are most likely to cause transplantation. The negative cases of this study are the failed attempts of the Mazzaferro family to create an outpost in the city of Verona, in the Veneto region, in the 1980s; the Moscow-based Solntsevskaya to open a branch in Rome in the mid-1990s; and a mafia to emerge in Rosario, circa 1910–40. Foreign triads have also so far failed to establish themselves in China. In all instances these organizations tried to transplant. The two criteria combined—the possibility principle and variation in the dependent variable—led me to exclude "irrelevant" cases—namely, cases where there was no transplantation and also no indication that it was ever attempted.[43]

I have used three further criteria for selection. First, among the territories of destination, I discuss both advanced market economies and newly created ones. Variation on this dimension allows me to establish whether similar (or different) reasons account for transplantation to newly created and advanced market economies, and make it easier to generalize from my findings. Second, I include regions, among the territories of destination, where the level of interpersonal trust and civic engagement was high along with those where it was low before the arrival of the mafia. In particular, Piedmont and Veneto are high-trust regions in Italy, while Rome, Budapest, and China have low levels of interpersonal trust. Since the level of trust in the territory of destination is a factor that I suspect might affect the ability of mafias to entrench themselves, variation in this independent variable was crucial.

Ultimately, this is a study with many variables and few cases. In order to control as much as possible for intervening variables, I have tried to match cases. For instance, the movement to Bardonecchia (Piedmont) is matched by the failed attempt of the same mafia group to move within the same part of the same country (the city of Verona in northern Italy). Although not a perfect control, we can assume that many intervening variables, such as the level of corruption and policing, are similar. At any rate, the conclusions that I reach must be considered tentative, and this work calls for more instances to be studied and compared with the ones that I cover in this book. In this field of study there is no substitute for detailed narratives and in-depth discussions of specific cases.

THREE

The `Ndrangheta in Piedmont and Veneto

THE `NDRANGHETA

"The `Ndrangheta is as invisible as the other side of the moon" remarked a prosecutor in Florida in the 1980s.[1] Indeed, the organization managed for a long time to remain under the radar of many police forces around the world, in part thanks to the small number of turncoats. In the same period, Tommasso Buscetta, the highest-profile Sicilian mafioso turned state witness, even suggested impishly that it might not exist as an autonomous entity.[2] Notwithstanding Buscetta, historians have documented the existence of the `Ndrangheta since the late nineteenth century, although at that time it did not yet have a name of its own. Official sources refer to Calabrian criminals as *Camorristi* and occasionally also as mafiosi. Other terms used were *Picciotteria* and, oddly, *Famiglia Montalbano*, also the title of a novel. The very word `*Ndrangheta* was first recorded only in 1909. The etymological origin is the Greek *andragathos*, meaning a brave and daring man.[3]

Another word of Greek origin, `*ndrina* ("a man who does not bend"), refers to the basic unit of the organization, and is the equivalent of the Sicilian mafia's family or *cosca*. According to the Italian Anti-Mafia Parliamentary Commission (CPA), each `*ndrina* is "autonomous on its territory and no formal authority stands above the `ndrina boss."[4] The `ndrina is usually in control of a small town or neighborhood. If more than one `ndrina operate in the same town, they form a locale. In some cases, *sotto* `*ndrine* have been established. A rather elaborate internal structure is shared by most `ndrine, and includes the boss and six lower ranks. Each rank could be further differentiated into further internal ranks.[5]

The village of San Luca on the Aspromonte Mountains in the province of Reggio Calabria is the core `Ndrangheta territory. The Sanctuary of Our Lady of Polsi (located in the San Luca district) has long been the meeting place of affiliates, and the `ndrina based in this village is granted special authority. Every new group must obtain the authorization of the San Luca family in order to operate. Former members report that "every *locale* deposits a small percentage of their illicit proceeds to the principal of San Luca in recognition of the latter's ancient supremacy."[6]

From at least the 1950s the chiefs of the `Ndrangheta have held annual meetings, fittingly called *crimini*, at the Sanctuary of Polsi between September and October (the exact date is constantly changing). Cesare Polifroni, a former member, testified that at these meetings every boss "must give an account of all the activities carried out during the year and of all the most important events taking place in his territory such as kidnappings, homicides, etc."[7] The *capo crimine*, who is elected every year, is in charge of convening the meeting, but far from being "the boss of the bosses," actually he has little authority to interfere in family feuds or control the level of interfamily violence. The `Ndrangheta equivalent of the Apalachin meeting took place in October 1969, when the police raided the gathering and captured more than seventy `Ndranghetisti—although many more managed to escape. Allegedly, the purpose of the meeting was to suggest a unified command structure of the `Ndrangheta and support a right-wing conspiracy to take over the Italian state. Both plans failed.[8]

Bosses from outside Calabria, from as far away as Canada and Australia, regularly attend the fall meetings at the Sanctuary of Polsi—an indication that the `ndrine around the world perceive themselves as being part of the same collective entity.[9] Nonetheless, and as in the case of other mafias, separate units have often been at war with one another. For instance, in Siderno, a town on the Ionic coast, the theft of some guns belonging to one of the family chiefs led to 34 people being killed in a "war" that lasted from 1987 to 1991. One conflict between two `ndrine in Reggio Calabria claimed hundreds of lives. Mafia killings in Calabria took the lives of 680 people during 1986–91 alone—a figure that approximates the number of deaths in civil wars.[10] From 1991, attempts have been made to create a Sicilian mafia-style regional commission but they have not yet succeeded, although loose mechanisms of communication, coordination, and dispute settlement have existed since the end of the nineteenth century.[11]

The 'Ndrangheta is ultimately a loose confederation of mafia families, most of which (eighty-six) operate in the province of Reggio Calabria in southern Calabria.[12] This mafia has systematically forced local entrepreneurs to pay protection money, corrupted officials, and penetrated politics.[13] Politicians have been threatened, wounded, and killed, while bosses have successfully stood in local elections. In the 1990s, the Italian government disbanded eighteen city councils due to the 'Ndrangheta's ability to pervert local electoral processes.[14] In 2007 killers from San Luca, this mafia's stronghold, murdered six people outside an Italian restaurant in Duisburg, in northwestern Germany, bringing the ruthless nature and international reach of the organization home to the European public.[15]

The key difference between the 'Ndrangheta and mafias from Sicily, the United States, Russia, Hong Kong, and Taiwan is the role of kin. While other mafias try to minimize the number of blood relatives accepted into each family, within the 'Ndrangheta blood family and membership of the crime family overlap. By and large, the 'ndrine consist of men belonging to the same family lineage. An antimafia prosecutor in Reggio Calabria, Salvatore Boemi, maintains that "one becomes a member by the simple fact of being born into a mafia family," although other reasons might attract a young man to seek membership, and nonkin can also be admitted.[16] A former member, Pasquale Barreca, confirms that "in most cases one becomes 'ndranghetista through family links."[17] Marriages help to cement relations within each 'ndrina and expand membership. As a result, a few blood families constitute each group, and for this reason "a high number of people with the same last name often end up being prosecuted for membership of a given 'ndrina."[18] Indeed, since there is no limit to the membership of a single unit, bosses try to maximize the number of descendants.[19]

The kinship link has meant that the 'Ndrangheta has experienced significantly fewer defections (*pentiti*) than the Sicilian mafia, as shown in table 3.1, since turning oneself in to the police or informing on partners in crime amounts to informing on one's own extended family.[20] The same applies to the Neapolitan Camorra, which has an organizational structure akin to the 'Ndrangheta.[21]

The coincidence of blood and mafia family also seems to have helped the 'Ndrangheta expand beyond its traditional territory—a dynamic suggested

TABLE 3.1

Membership of Mafia Groups, Number of Pentiti (Mafiosi Who Have Turned State's Witness) per Group, and Pentiti as Percentage of Membership

	Membership*	Pentiti (1995 data)	Pentiti 1995 as percentage of membership
Cosa Nostra	5,487 (1995)	381	6.9
`Ndrangheta	5,000 (1994)	133	2.6
Camorra	6,700 (1993)	192	2.8
Total	17,187	706	4.1

* Date of estimate in parentheses.
Sources: For the membership of Cosa Nostra and `Ndrangheta, see the official data quoted in Paoli 2003, 26, 30; for Camorra, see CPA 1993b; for the number of pentiti, see CD 2000.

by the authors of one of Italy's parliamentary reports on this mafia: "The familial bond has not only worked as a shield to protect secrets and enhance security, but also helped to maintain identity in the territory of origin and reproduce it in territories where the family has migrated."[22] The `Ndrangheta has clearly demonstrated a remarkable ability to establish branches abroad. `Ndrine are reported to be operating in northern Italy, Germany, Belgium, Holland, France, Eastern Europe, the United States, Canada, and Australia.[23] According to the Anti-Mafia Parliamentary Commission, the dependency of the subsidiary groups is significant: a subsidiary "is an outpost of the original cosca and depends on it to function."[24] Still, the activities of these subsidiaries vary, and more research is necessary to detail the relations between groups. In 2000, prosecutors pointed out that Germany, Eastern Europe, and Australia were areas where the `Ndrangheta invested the proceeds of its illegal activities heavily rather than aspiring to establish control over territory.[25] Yet there have been no in-depth studies of the `Ndrangheta's transplantation into new territories. I now turn to such a case, in the town of Bardonecchia in northern Italy.

THE `NDRANGHETA IN THE VAL SUSA VALLEY, PIEDMONT

One has to travel more than fourteen hundred kilometers from Calabria to reach the valleys outside Turin at the center of the story of the `Ndrangheta taking root in Piedmont. The town of Bardonecchia (three

Figure 3.1 Map of Italy

thousand inhabitants) lies in the Val Susa Valley, the most western part
of Italy, bordering France. Bardonecchia has throughout its history been
a transit zone, with many armies, traders, and smugglers passing through
the tortuous mountain crossings of the Cottian Alps (Alpes Cottiennes).
In the mid-nineteenth century, the Piedmontese government gave the order
to start work on a railway line to connect Turin to the (now-French) city

of Modane, running under the Frejus tunnel and through Bardonecchia. The Frejus railway line, completed in 1871, gave a massive impetus at the end of the nineteenth century to the town's tourist industry, and members of the aristocracy and upper classes from Turin and Genoa began building pleasant summer villas in the art nouveau style. By the beginning of the twentieth century winter sports had developed, and in 1908 a skiing club was founded in Bardonecchia. Local histories also recall the exploits of the two Norwegian brothers, Harald and Trigwe Smith, who in 1911 broke the world record for trampoline jumping with a forty-four-meters-long jump. The trampoline had been constructed in an area that was to be named after the Smith brothers, Campo Smith. The land was given to the city by one of those wealthy families that had patronized Bardonecchia at the turn of the twentieth century, with the explicit provision that it should be made into a public park and remain so in perpetuity. Eighty-five years later, the same area had acquired immense real estate value, and was at the center of a major scandal involving local officials, construction companies, and the Mazzaferro clan of the `Ndrangheta. The scandal led to the mayor being arrested, and the city council was disbanded for "mafia penetration"—the first instance of this kind in a city outside the south of Italy (the mayor was eventually acquitted).[26] The data I present below suggest that the `Ndrangheta was best placed to exploit the lucrative opportunities in the construction business in the Val Susa Valley and in particular Bardonec-chia in the 1960s.

According to established theories of social capital, Piedmont—one of the most industrialized areas of the country and home to the Fiat car manufacturing company—is a most unlikely territory for a mafia to take root. In contrast to the vicious circle of low interpersonal trust and unre-sponsive local institutions that is typical of southern regions, Piedmont scores among the most "civic" regions in the country, with a high level of interpersonal trust and highly effective local institutions, as measured by Robert Putnam's Civic Community Index. Putnam's historical index of "civic traditions" for the period 1860–1920 has Piedmont scoring even more favorably—second only to Emilia Romagna—as the most civic re-gion of Italy.[27]

Let us now turn to immigration from high mafia regions of the country. Could this be the factor that explains mafia transplantation in the Val Susa Valley? To be sure, since the 1950s Piedmont has experienced significant flows of immigrants, which in turn have changed its ethnic composition dramatically. Between 1951 and 1961, 440,040 immigrants moved to Turin (the largest city in the region), increasing its population by 42 percent. The share of the population born outside the region more than doubled from 1951 to 1971. It should be noted, however, that other cities, such as Rome and Milan, also experienced dramatic increases in population, yet did not succumb to mafia entrenchment. The data in table 3.2 show that Rome had higher immigration from "mafia regions" than Turin in the 1950s and 1960s, and a similar level of immigrants in the 1970s and 1980s. And yet no mafia became entrenched in Rome.[28] (A potentially revealing parallel with Bardonecchia is the small town of Buccinasco, outside Milan, where the 'Ndrangheta appears to be entrenched and to control the construction sector).[29] Migration is not the whole story.

In chapter 2, I drew a distinction between generalized patterns of migration and the migration of specific individuals who belonged to a mafia group. The presence of even a small number of the latter can be highly significant because these are specialized criminals, well equipped to set up criminal groups.

Because of the policy of soggiorno obbligato, we know how many people had been forced by court orders to reside in the region. In the period 1961–72, fifty-four individuals were ordered by the courts to resettle in Turin Province. Compared with other regions, however, Piedmont experienced only an average number of such forced migrations of specialized criminals. For instance, 15 percent of the criminals who were sentenced under the soggiorno obbligato policy relocated to Lombardy, 10 percent to Emilia Romagna, 9 percent to Tuscany, and 11 percent to Piedmont. Furthermore, Piedmont's provinces of Cuneo, Asti, and Alessandria likewise experienced an influx of hardened criminals in the period 1961–72 (respectively, sixty-three, thirty-six, and fifty-four individuals), but mafias did not become entrenched there.[30] Thus, no direct link exists between soggiorno obbligato and mafia formation.

I now turn to a discussion of the local conditions that existed in this part of Piedmont, starting with a look at the construction sector. Between 1950 and 1959, this sector of the economy was virtually monopolized by three local companies that had roughly 50 percent of the market between them, as measured by the number of licenses that they obtained to build new homes in the town (table 3.3).

TABLE 3.2

Regions of Birth for Residents of Turin, Milan, Rome, and Verona Provinces, 1951, 1961, 1971, and 1981 (%)

1	2	3	4	5	6
Census Year	Province	Percentage of residents born within the region	Percentage of residents born outside the region	Percentage of residents born in Sicily, Campania, and Calabria	Percentage of residents born in Calabria
1951					
	Turin	80.3	17.1	2.4	0.5
	Milan	79.3	18.9	2.2	0.3
	Rome	67.0	30.6	7.4	1.7
	Verona	93.2	5.6	0.5	0.1
1961					
	Turin	68.7	28.8	6.2	1.9
	Milan	72.0	26.1	4.3	1.0
	Rome	64.4	33.3	8.9	2.4
	Verona	91.1	7.6	0.9	0.1
1971					
	Turin	60.8	36.7	12.2	3.7
	Milan	66.2	31.8	8.8	2.3
	Rome	64.1	33.0	9.8	2.6
	Verona	89.9	8.6	1.2	0.2
1981					
	Turin	63.6	34.1	12.8	4.0
	Milan	68.1	29.8	9.6	2.5
	Rome	69.4	27.9	7.1	2.3
	Verona	88.4	10.1	1.7	0.4

Notes: Columns 3 and 4 do not sum to one hundred because individuals born outside Italy have been excluded. The province (provincia) is an official administrative unit and includes territories beyond the city limits.
Sources: Data based on ISTAT 1951, 1961, 1971, 1981.

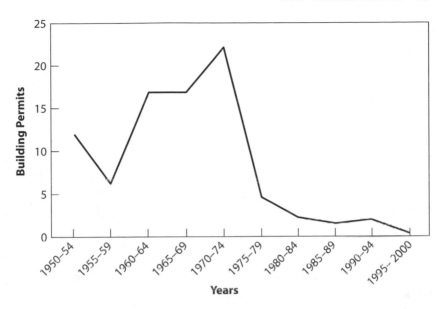

FIGURE 3.2 Number of licenses to build new dwellings, city of Bardonecchia, 1950–2000

As a consequence of the expansion of tourism in the early 1960s, a strong demand for housing developed. During a period of fifteen months in 1967 and 1968, some eighty thousand new dwellings were built in Bardonecchia alone.[31] Figure 3.2 gives a quantitative, albeit partial, picture of this trend. Like table 3.3, figure 3.2 is based on data about legally obtained licenses to build new residential dwellings issued in the period 1950–2000. These data were collected in the archives of the city of Bardonecchia and had never been examined previously. Typically, each license refers to a major construction project, since it was common for a single application to be made for the construction of one building (or sometimes two) containing a minimum of eight flats and a maximum of fifty.

The market peaked between 1960 and 1974. (In the same period, a new highway and the Frejus tunnel to France worth some 170 billion lira—the equivalent of approximately US$275,000,000 in 1971 dollars—were under construction.)[32] In the period 1985–94, a further 1,300 dwellings were built—a total of 282,000 cubic meters of construction worth 500 billion lira, or approximately US$310,000,000 in 1994 dollars.[33]

The arrival of new actors in the market is partially captured by the data on building licenses that I collected in Bardonecchia. Table 3.3 gives the

TABLE 3.3

Percentage Shares of Licenses Obtained by Four Firms to Build New Dwellings, Bardonecchia, 1950–79

Firm/five-year period	1950–54	55–59	60–64	65–69	70–74	75–79
Gibello	28.0	12.0	15.8	1.4	7.6	5.9
Carisio and Pesando	14.0	20.0	10.5	5.6	1.8	5.9
Patané and Raitieri	0	0	7.9	13.9	6.3	5.9
Zedda Aldo and Iginio	4.0	16.0	18.4	1.4	0	0
Total	46	48	52.6	22.3	15.7	17.7

Sources: Data collected in Ufficio Licenze Edilizie, city of Bardonecchia.

percentage of the market share for the four biggest companies operating in Bardonecchia between 1950 and 2000. In the 1960s a new firm, Patané and Raiteri, energetically entered the market and obtained 8 percent of all the licenses granted in the period 1960–64. Zedda Aldo and Iginio, one of the original firms that had been operating in Bardonecchia since at least the 1950s, saw its share of licenses fall in the period 1965–69; by 1970 it was out of the market. Overall, the market expanded, and the top four companies accounted for only 22.3 percent of the sector between 1965 and 1969, and even less in the next two periods. Rather mysterious *immobiliari* (literally "real estate companies") appeared and disappeared frequently from the 1960s onward, but when present, they were involved in major works such as Immobiliare Patrizia, which gained 5 percent of the market in 1970–74. Another new company gained almost 9 percent in the same period. Both disappeared in the next period.

The sudden expansion of the construction market had two key consequences: local construction companies did not have a large enough workforce to meet the new demand, and new firms entered the market. Some construction firms in the Val Susa and nearby Canavese valleys therefore turned to "fixers" who supplied immigrant workers, typically with little education and unable to find employment in large companies like Fiat. Many of the new immigrants lived in appalling conditions in Turin. These poorly qualified and nonunionized workers accepted short-term, temporary employment and low salaries, and worked without accident insurance coverage. Several firms welcomed the possibility of hiring cheap labor in order to save on mandatory health contributions and safety costs, and more generally to bypass trade union controls. Moreover, by hiring the workforce indirectly, the firms avoided having to pay transfer, catering, and accommodation costs.[34] New construction companies also entered the market at the suggestion of the Calabresi who had been residing in the valley under the soggiorno obbligato policy. These new firms, too, employed an illegal workforce and turned for protection to the Calabrese mafia. Many residents were able to sell their plots of lands at considerably high prices to the constructors.[35]

Mario Corino, the mayor of Bardonecchia in the 1970s and a fierce antimafia campaigner, summarizes the situation in the town as follows:

> I have been active in politics for 40 years as a member of the Christian Democracy Party. I was the elected mayor of Bardonecchia from December 1972 until 1978. Since 1990, I have been the Leader of the Opposition in the City Council. As early as the 1960s I realised that, for the good of the city, we first had to study the mafia phenomenon, and then to make it clear that we did not condone it. Once my position became known, I found myself the object of night-time displays of aggression and was in a constant state of fear for my life. . . . During my term as mayor of Bardonecchia, my position became even more delicate. The mafia were a long-term fixture (it was pointless trying to deny it) and I would have to choose one side or the other. I therefore made the decision that it was my duty to fight this phenomenon, which I considered to be unacceptable. In particular, those years saw the emergence of labor racketeering. When I became mayor, I discovered that more than 72 construction sites had been opened in Bardonecchia, in which a number of workers who had come from the south, and especially from the Gioiosa Ionica area [Calabria], lived, literally "camped out" in extremely unhygienic conditions. Many of them had criminal records and weren't legally allowed to work.
>
> The managers of these construction sites gave me no guarantees as to either public order or the working and living conditions of those who worked on them. Independently of any investigations I was making, the Work Inspector also decided to carry out checks on the sites to ascertain the position of these people. However, they

were usually forewarned of the Inspector's arrival, and nowhere to be found. It was all extremely and uncomfortably illegal. Faced with this problem, I tried to confront it by involving the Trade Unions Associations as well, and together we obtained an audience with the Anti-Mafia Commission. Following our audience, a delegation presided over by MP La Torre [later murdered by the Sicilian mafia in Palermo in April 1982] began various investigations into, and checks on, these sites to verify what we had said. This was, however, just one part of a wider situation which was endangering the safety of the city.[36]

The current mayor of Bardonecchia has a rather more positive outlook on the same events:

> My view is that these individuals [originating in Calabria] entered the construction sector using the carrot rather more than the stick. One must recall that there was a significant expansion in the market in the 1970s, especially an increase in second homes and homes for tourists. Local entrepreneurs often were short of labor, and these people delivered it. Thus, they performed a service for the local economy. They brought to Bardonecchia some unqualified, as well as qualified, workers, and found them employment.[37]

Some firms and workers that had not been hired through the racket were intimidated, and eventually forced to exit the market.[38] As the racket expanded, more local firms started to hire illegal workers. The final outcome was that a number of firms—some local, and some newly arrived from Calabria—came to rely on workers supplied by the Calabresi and employed them illegally. In all, the racket was beneficial to both nonunionized immigrant workers and construction companies (a phone intercept testifies to workers' support for the main fixer: "The Calabresi respect him because he finds them work").[39] Such an equilibrium, however, meant that workers could not turn to trade unions in the event of disputes with employers, and employers could not turn to legitimate sources of protection in the event of disputes with this vast contingent of workers. A demand thus emerged for an alternative, nonstate source of protection. Entry into this market was policed by the mafia, which also oversaw

Mario Corino (1929–2010), the primary school teacher who became the mayor of Bardonecchia in 1973 and took on the 'Ndrangheta at great personal costs. He is now a largely forgotten figure in the valleys that he loved so much and an unsung hero of the fight against organized crime in Italy. Photo credit: *La Luna Nuova.*

employer-employee relations and used violence to achieve control of the construction industry.

A spate of cases of intimidation led to an investigation by the Anti-Mafia Parliamentary Commission, which first visited the area in 1974, as recalled by Mayor Corino above. The investigation recorded "widespread intimidation, improper allocation of workloads, exploitation, improper salary reductions, and racketeering," and estimated that 70 to 80 percent of the labor force in Bardonecchia was hired through this racket.[40] In one instance, a group of mafia-backed Calabresi workers showed up fully armed at a construction site, and forced the bricklayers to quit their jobs then and there. The firm that had (legally) hired the bricklayers was forced out of

Bardonecchia.[41] It was not uncommon for construction sites to be set on fire.[42] In 1970, a worker at a building site was killed with a *lupara* (sawed-off shotgun), and his body was found in a nearby town.[43] In 1975, Mario Ceretto, a Cuorgnè developer, was kidnapped and murdered. A former 'ndranghetista testified that the man had been targeted because he was a competitor in the construction business.[44] When in 1976 two thieves were caught trying to steal from a construction site, they were tortured for several hours and one of them became paralyzed in both legs as a result.[45]

The main organizers of labor racketeering in Bardonecchia were two Calabresi who had moved there as a consequence of the soggiorno obbligato policy: Rocco Lo Presti and his cousin Francesco (Ciccio) Mazzaferro. Both came from the town of Gioiosa Ionica and were members of the Mazzaferro clan.[46] Lo Presti, a stocky young man with a sharp look and pitch-dark hair, had moved to Bardonecchia from Calabria in 1952. By the time of the construction boom in the 1960s, Lo Presti had become the main illicit supplier of cheap labor to the area and had called in construction companies from Calabria. He also established several firms of his own and obtained unlawful subcontracts, especially in the area of plastering and framing. A Turin-based construction entrepreneur testified to the following:

> Everybody knew that one could work in the construction business in Bardonecchia only after having obtained Lo Presti's approval. One could obtain such approval only if introduced by somebody from Calabria, and by paying up. I recall what happened to me in 1979: at the time, I wanted to obtain the contract to build sewerage in Bardonecchia, but I was told that I needed Lo Presti's approval. Thus I obtained an introductory note for Lo Presti. Eventually, I did not bid for the contract, because I was told that another company was supposed to win.[47]

By the early 1970s, Lo Presti had been convicted three times by the court of Turin for a variety of crimes, including "violation of the law on hiring workers and workers' protection." He was charged with—and acquitted of—murder (1982), fencing (1987), and extortion and mafia activities (1995 and 1999). It was not until 2002 that he was found guilty of engaging in mafia activities and sentenced to six and a half years in prison. Recently, he was serving his sentence in a private clinic. On January 22, 2009, he was confined to bed, hardly able to talk and fighting a degenerative form of diabetes, when he was ordered to move from the clinic to the convicts' wing of the Turin Molinette hospital. After the officers read the removal order to Lo Presti forcing him to serve his remaining sentence in prison, he shook their hands and whispered, "I follow you." He died the next day.[48]

Lo Presti's associate Mazzaferro was found guilty in Calabria in the early 1970s of heading a mafia organization that exercised a monopoly over transportation in the area of Gioiosa Ionica. As a consequence of this verdict, the court ordered him to reside outside his region of origin, and he moved to Bardonecchia in 1972. There he started a transport company servicing construction sites and obtained several contracts related to the construction of the Fréjus tunnel. The then mayor of Bardonecchia recalls the arrival of Mazzaferro in town in 1972:

> It was around this time that a number of people who were linked to mafia families such as the Mazzaferros were sent to the Bardonecchia area. When they arrived in Bardonecchia, the Mazzaferro family member would come into my office and say, "You have received instructions from the Locri Tribunal to find me a job and somewhere to live. But don't worry about it: I will find them on my own." And indeed, it was not long before an excavation company (with a never-ending supply of trucks) sprang up that effectively monopolized the market in that area.[49]

In fact, a Turin court found that Mazzaferro had acquired these contracts "through the use of force and intimidation."[50] Throughout the 1980s he was charged with a variety of offenses in three regions—Piedmont, Calabria, and Sicily. In 1987, he was found guilty of being the boss of a "mafia group" based in Piedmont that was involved in several crimes, including drug trafficking and illegal money lending.[51]

The pattern described above is virtually identical to that in the neighboring Canavese Valley, where two individuals of Calabrese origin, who had migrated to Cuorgnè in 1972 and 1963, undertook activities in the construction industry similar to those of Lo Presti and Mazzaferro. The Turin court accused them of having created a mafia group.[52] By the mid-

1970s, entry into the construction industry in the two valleys (Val Susa and Canavese) was thus completely controlled by the 'Ndrangheta.[53]

The mafia's control of labor and the overall construction industry soon evolved into a wider protection system. A city council employee is known to have handed over Lo Presti's business card to people applying for business licenses in the area. In one case he was heard saying, "You should get in touch with Lo Presti in order to avoid problems." Inspectors sent by the prefect of Turin noted that "in Bardonecchia, everybody assumes that it is necessary to obtain Lo Presti's endorsement in order to engage in any commercial activity."[54] Another telling instance is narrated by a member-to-be of the 'Ndrangheta (who then turned state witness). In 1987, this man had started a fight at a disco because the bouncer would not allow a friend of his to enter. Shortly after the incident, "Lo Presti got in touch with me, and asked for an explanation of what had happened, because the disco was *under his protection*. At that time, I was not yet a member of the Belfiore family. I explained myself and he agreed with my reasons and let me alone."[55]

Violence now extended beyond the construction industry. Lo Presti was charged by the police with ordering the assault of and inflicting grievous bodily harm on a local politician (and future mayor) in 1963.[56] The first "mafia murder" in Bardonecchia took place in 1969, when Lo Presti's brother-in-law killed a man.[57] In Cuorgnè, a Calabrese who had been forced to relocate to the town came into conflict with Lo Presti and Mazzaferro, and was murdered in 1972.[58] Between 1970 and 1983, twenty-four people originally from Calabria were killed in Turin Province (which includes Bardonecchia and Cuorgnè), while Turin's Procurator Office recorded forty-four mafia murders.[59] The most high-profile murder was that of Bruno Caccia, the chief public prosecutor of Turin, who was gunned down by members of the 'Ndrangheta, among them Mimmo Belfiore, the brother of a developer from Calabria operating in Bardonecchia and an associate of Lo Presti.[60] According to a police investigation, Lo Presti received a phone call on the day of Caccia's murder allegedly saying, "Here is your birthday present" (Caccia had investigated Lo Presti several times; no one suggested that Lo Presti was directly involved in this murder).[61] Violence continued steadily throughout the 1980s and 1990s.[62]

The judicial system and the police also felt the full weight of mafia pressure, and ominous mafia messages were sent to local officials. In 1990

Lo Presti threatened a police officer, proving that he was aware of the secret investigations directed at him. In 1991, another officer was suddenly
transferred to high-density mafia territory in Calabria after having written an investigative report on Lo Presti. In 2000, the carabinieri station
chief was charged with favoring criminal suspects but was later acquitted.
The ruling acknowledged that he was conducting "friendly and improper
relations" with Lo Presti. Several officers were also removed.[63] A woman
who had testified against Lo Presti in the pretrial phase in 1999 later refused to confirm her statement at the trial, explaining in tears that she
felt threatened and scared.[64] A solicitor who was a member of the town
committee that dealt with building applications suggested an increase in
the environmental fee (*onere di urbanizzazione*) to be paid by a construction company. When he returned home, he found a large knife stuck in
his video-recorder. He immediately resigned, citing "health reasons."[65] Another "unreasonable" solicitor hired by the city council had the door of his
house burned.[66]

To what extent did the high level of interpersonal trust and the potential for collective action function as a barrier to mafia entrenchment,
as hypothesized in chapter 2? At first local politicians and trade unions
resisted the mafia. Corino, the mayor of Bardonecchia between 1972 and
1978, and later an opposition politician, openly denounced the presence
of the mafia in the town and rejected its offer of electoral support (he had
been physically assaulted in 1963).[67]

The Turin section of the Construction Workers' Union alerted the authorities at its annual conference in Bardonecchia in 1972. In only one
of sixty building sites were workers able to elect delegates to the conference, and only twenty people attended an antimafia trade union rally in
Bardonecchia. Trade union officials were directly intimidated by phone in
advance of their tour of the building sites in Bardonecchia and, once there,
found that workers did not want to speak to them.[68]

The reaction of civil society was not sufficient to prevent the mafia from
becoming entrenched. The `Ndrangheta was able to forge a vast social
constituency among both migrant workers, who generally remained grateful for even illegal employment, and employers. The mafiosi extended their
protection to other spheres of the social life of immigrant workers, who
were often ostracized by the native population. Shrewdly, the mafiosi also
offered protection to Piedmontese residents by punishing those Calabresi

residents who misbehaved. For instance, they punished Calabresi who offended local women outside bars and nightclubs.[69] Their territorial control allowed the group to branch out and protect other criminal businesses, including arms trafficking, drug dealing, and money laundering. For example, a laboratory producing ecstasy tablets was found in Val Susa in 1994.[70] Ominous signs of the expansion of this mafia group were also highlighted by an investigation in the late 1990s into racketeering by construction companies in nearby towns.[71]

The step from a successful protection racket to the penetration of local politics was a short one. The mayor of Bardonecchia discovered that, by the time of the 1971 census, some three hundred people all originating from the area around Lo Presti's birthplace in Calabria had recently registered as residents in Bardonecchia. This number amounted to almost the entire increase in population since the previous census. As the voters numbered some fifteen to sixteen hundred adults, the newly registered residents could have accounted for up to 19 percent of the electorate (it is not known whether all the new residents were of voting age, although the mayor seemed to think so).[72] Lo Presti boasted in a phone call of controlling five hundred votes and influencing elections to the point where the majority of the city councillors were in his pocket.[73] He tells a candidate in another phone conversation: "We have never lost [an election]."[74] To a local paper he declares: "No administration [in Bardonecchia] is elected without the support of the southerners [*meridionali*]. I can tell you that I do not need to tell my friends how they should vote. They know my ideas and, if they love me, they know for whom they should vote."[75]

In 1975, the Turin court noted that a power struggle was under way between the incumbent mayor (Corino) and the Calabrese clan of Lo Presti. In 1979, a new administration was elected that was more favorable toward the Calabresi. Lo Presti himself declared, "Some days ago, [the new mayor] asked for help, and I helped."[76] In effect, the political coalition that won the elections in 1979 has been reelected ever since. A report produced for the prefect of Turin notes that in 1988, the mayor was voted for unanimously by both the winning coalition and the opposition councillors (mayors were at the time elected by the city council).

In 1994, Bardonecchia hit the national headlines. The mayor and other councillors were arrested for their involvement in the illicit allocation of construction permits (*speculazione edilizia*), unjustified variations to planning decisions, and undercharging for and underselling valuable land (it should be stressed that they were later acquitted at the appellate stage and had been compensated by the Italian state for the judicial error). The father of the mayor appears in the license records above. The land in question is Campo Smith, where the Smith brothers established the world record for trampoline jumping in 1911. In essence, the case involved underselling a valuable green area to a developer controlled by Lo Presti and then granting him permission to develop it. The land, estimated to be worth 1.6 billion liras in 1995, was sold for 17 million liras. The overall value of the development was later estimated to be 90 billion liras by the authorities investigating the case. The developers and contractors entrusted with the work included individuals sentenced for violent crimes and drug trafficking rather than bona fide professionals.[77]

This situation resulted in an unprecedented move for a town in northern or central Italy: in 1995 the president of Italy suspended the democratic process and disbanded the city council because of "mafia penetration."[78] Nonetheless, in the 1996 election the ticket that had supported the disgraced mayor campaigned for "continuity" and obtained almost 70 percent of the votes. Both the left-wing Partito Democratico della Sinistra and the right-wing parties supported this ticket, while the leader of the opposition reported pressure on one of their candidates during the electoral campaign. The 1996 administration included four individuals (among them the new mayor) who had served in the disbanded 1995 administration and had been under investigation. The 2001 administration was also a political heir of the disbanded 1995 local government; it included two individuals who had served in the 1995 administration and seven who had served in the 1996 administration. Despite presidential intervention, there was clear political continuity between these administrations.[79]

As in other mafia territories, Bardonecchia saw the emergence of a code of silence (omertà). Police officers and investigators "found among the population a very low propensity to help the authorities in their investigation."[80] In 1994, when the elected officer with the tourism portfolio was asked about his plans to keep the mafia out of local politics, he answered, "Our job is to manage local affairs; police officers (and there are plenty of them in town) should worry about the mafia."[81] Similarly the mayor, charged with being involved with the mafia, and son of the owner of the construction company, declared that "unlike my colleagues,

I don't play the policeman," and "we should be grateful to the soggiorno obbligato policy, which brought to our town people like Lo Presti and Mazzaferro."[82] After the 1996 elections the newly elected mayor stated, "We are cooperating with law enforcement to clarify what went on in the past, but, believe me, in town nothing ever went on, there were no connections between local politics and the mafia (assuming that the latter ever existed)."[83] As late as 2001, the mayor was still demanding a "public apology" from the state for disbanding the city council in 1995.[84] The mayor elected in 2001, in contrast, established links between his office and antimafia campaigners based in Turin and was supportive of the present study, although he belonged to the same political faction as the mayor who was under investigation, and considered the 1995 suspension of the city council futile and wrong.[85] The passing away of Mario Corino, the antimafia mayor of Bardonecchia, on February 2, 2010, went virtually unnoticed. Contrary to the extensive press received by Lo Presti for his death (including a full page in the national paper *La Stampa*), Corino's death elicited only two short articles in news bulletins with a local circulation in the Val Susa Valley. One such piece did not mention his efforts against crime and described him as a difficult man who, "for good or for bad," had an impact on his community. His courage went unsung.[86]

Collective action was now working in the opposite direction to virtuous social engagement, with people being mobilized in order to support mafia-tainted politicians. The parish priest of Bardonecchia organized a four-hundred-person march in support of the disgraced mayor, with the endorsement of the bishop, who himself went on record as saying, "I would deny the presence of the mafia in this area."[87] Both clergymen were later interviewed by the investigating magistrates about their roles in the march and claimed that they were simply supporting a group of parishioners who had "spontaneously" organized the rally themselves.[88] A march against mafia penetration into the North, organized by the Northern League in the town on May 27, 1995, failed to attract any support whatsoever, according to a police report from June ("indeed, the population even avoided being seen anywhere near the site of the march").[89] No other political party organized rallies of this kind. After the dismissal in 1995 of the local administration, *La Stampa* interviewed a number of casually selected residents and long-time vacationers; the former expressed their support for the mayor, while the latter favored the presidential measure, indicating some local support for the criminal state of affairs.[90]

Was social capital depleted as a consequence of the mafia penetration, as predicted by Putnam's work? If one measures social capital as voting in referenda and the European elections—where the constituency covers the whole of northern Italy and thus the link with a specific candidate is rather loose—the answer is negative. For instance, in 1979, 85.13 percent of the electorate voted in the European elections, virtually identical to the turn out in Turin Province (87.09 percent) and the northwest electoral constituency (88.75 percent). Similarly, in the last referendum (2009), although the turnout in Bardonecchia (25.52 percent) was lower than in Turin Province (36.87 percent), it was higher than in other Piedmontese provinces, such as Asti (17.78 percent), Cuneo (23.92 percent), and Verbano-Cusio-Ossola (15.46 percent).[91] Mafia presence does not seem to have led to a drop in civic engagement as measured by electoral turnout.

Connections exist between the homeland and the groups operating in Piedmont. In order to gain entry into the Bardonecchia `ndrina, a would-be member had to travel back to Calabria to undergo the initiation ritual.[92] This suggests that the mafia of Bardonecchia is a branch of the Mazzaferro family rather than an independent entity. Other evidence of connections exists. Piedmontese clans are expected to assist fugitives from Calabria, support other members imprisoned in the region, distribute drugs, and more generally invest capital from Calabria in the legal economy.[93] Construction companies in the two valleys—Val Susa and Canavese—have been found guilty of laundering drug money from Calabria, with the help of local professionals.[94] ("It is easier to launder money through a construction project," maintains a police investigator who has worked on Bardonecchia extensively, "than to invest it in immovable property, as there are many expenses, many of which can be settled informally, without issuing official invoices.")[95] Giuseppe Ursino, the cousin of the Ursini-Scali family boss based in Gioiosa Ionica and Lo Presti's nephew, was arrested in Bardonecchia in 1993, along with another fifteen Calabresi who had settled in the Turin area.[96]

Other mafias have also made an appearance in Bardonecchia. In the 1970s, some members of the Sicilian and U.S. mafias tried to enter the construction industry—in particular members of the Gambino and

Spatola families—but they were eventually dissuaded by the `Ndrangheta and left town, according to confidential police reports. A summit involving Calabrese, Italian American, and Sicilian mafiosi was to take place in the town in 1975, but it was canceled at the last minute, possibly because it was known that the police would have raided it. Still, contacts with the U.S. Gambino family and the local `Ndrangheta continued, and relationships remained friendly. In the 1990s, Sicilian fugitives passed through town and a boss, Salvatore Inzerillo, resided there for a few months. An as-yet-unpublished piece of evidence alleges that Totò Riina, the so-called boss of bosses of the Sicilian mafia, visited Bardonecchia as he was interested in investing money in construction. He disappeared before he could be arrested and remained a fugitive for several more years.[97]

To conclude, the story of the `Ndrangheta in the Val Susa Valley is closely linked to the expansion of construction in the 1960s, which brought significant profits to a vast part of the population. Local firms could not meet the demand for new homes and started to hire illegally, through Calabresi fixers, unemployed immigrants who had moved to Turin. New firms from Calabria also entered the market at the suggestion of Calabresi who had found themselves in Bardonecchia due to the soggiorno obbligato policy or had simply started to work in the construction sector. Neither this large workforce nor its employers could turn to the state to settle any disputes that might have emerged. Moreover, the Calabresi involved in the labor racket began to offer criminal protection to both workers and employers as well as enforce a cartel of market incumbents. Violence was used to force some firms out of the booming construction sector. Over time, individuals who were favorable toward the mafia penetrated politics. Initial high levels of trust did not prevent transplantation. It is hard to tell whether trust was depleted as a consequence of the arrival of the mafia, but surely civic engagement (as measured by voting in referenda and the European elections) remained high. Portions of civil society even mobilized in support of mafia activities.

To fully understand why the `Ndrangheta succeeded in becoming entrenched in Bardonecchia, one needs to compare this case to another instance where the `Ndrangheta tried but failed. To find a comparable city is a challenge. First, the city in question must be in a part of the country that is as similar as possible to Bardonecchia in as many ways as possible (so that we can discount them) while at the same time having been subject to such an attempt. An added complication is that, typically, information on failed cases is harder to come by.

THE 'NDRANGHETA IN VERONA

The journey from Reggio Calabria to Verona is almost as long as the one to Bardonecchia, and the Northern city could not be more different from the one in Calabria. Instead, Verona and the Veneto region share many features with Turin and Piedmont. Putnam's Civic Community Index puts Veneto—like Piedmont—among the most civic regions of Italy. Verona sports an array of positive indicators, such as the highest gross domestic product and highest disposable income in Veneto, virtually full employment, high levels of cultural consumption, and one of the lowest crime rates in Italy.[98] It is world famous for the opera season at L'Arena running every year from June to August, and for the setting of the doomed love story *Romeo and Juliet*. In a street just off the main square, Piazza delle Erbe, stands a house falsely claiming to be Juliet's home. A short passageway covered with slips of paper containing love pledges leads to a narrow and always-crowded courtyard. Above one's head towers Juliet's balcony, while a bronze statue of William Shakespeare's heroine occupies the center of the paved *cortile*, one breast shining indecently as a result of the thousands of hands that have touched it for luck.

And yet Verona is a city that does not live in the past. The economic structure of the district changed after the Second World War from being mostly agricultural and based on sharecropping to being export-led, competing successfully in international markets for goods that require a high level of craft and skill, such as wooden furniture, footwear, engineering, wine, confectionery, and graphic design.[99] Pino Arlacchi and Roger Lewis, the authors of a study on drug consumption in Verona, describe the city as a tight-knit community where informal social control is exercised by "the bar owner, the newsagent, the teacher, the priest, the doorman, parents, and women talking on their door steps."[100]

Verona's population grew dramatically in the period 1951–81 as a result of immigration. Between 1951 and 1961 the net population increased from

185,482 to 215,733, with immigrants making up 34 percent of the total population by 1961.[101] Overall, in the period 1951–71, the population of the city grew by 29.2 percent (slightly more than the figure for northeastern Italy, which was 27.2 percent in the same period). Despite the rise in population, however, the demographic makeup of Verona did not change as it did in Turin. As shown in table 3.2, more than 93 percent of the 1951 population was born in the city or the Veneto region, 13 percentage points more than the equivalent figure for Turin. Still, the divergence between Verona and the other cities discussed above is even more striking in the succeeding decades. In the 1961 census, Turin, Milan, and Rome had between 26 and 33 percent of people born outside the region, while Verona had just 7.6 percent. By the 1981 census, Verona had almost 90 percent of residents born in the same region, roughly 20 percentage points more than in Milan and Rome, and 30 percentage points more than in Turin. Throughout the period covered in table 3.2, the number of residents originating from Calabria, Sicily, and Campania was negligible.

Where did the new residents of Verona come from? In contrast to the pattern experienced in Turin, Milan, and Rome, the new residents of Verona came from the surrounding region and mainly consisted of agricultural workers seeking better employment in the local factories. These immigrants managed to find employment in local industries. At this time there was a net increase in the supply of jobs relative to demand, and the rate of unemployment remained low and also considerably lower than the Italian average.[102]

As in the case of Piedmont, several members of 'Ndrangheta families had been forced to resettle in Verona during the 1960s and 1970s through the same soggiorno obbligato policy described above.[103] In the period 1965–74, some one hundred people moved to the province for this reason. Not all of them had been found guilty of mafia crimes. For instance, in February 1974, out of sixteen such felons residing in Verona, only four had been found guilty of mafia-related crimes in the South.[104] Another source of people trained in the use of violence and specific to Verona was the vast contingent of neofascists, who over the years had been involved in, and charged with, several violent crimes. In particular, the neofascist Ordine Nuovo was founded in Verona, while most members of the Rosa dei Venti and the Nuclei Armati Rivoluzionari, two other extreme right-wing groups, lived in Verona. Veronese neofascists were questioned and investigated in connection with the bomb placed in Brescia in May 1974 that killed eight people and injured more than a hundred.[105]

The only significant illegal market in Verona in this period was that for drug consumption and trafficking. Some 10 percent of young people used drugs regularly. According to police estimates, roughly eight thousand people were habitual consumers in the late 1970s.[106] Consumption and trading were rather open, involving local youths influenced by the revolution in personal behavior of the late 1960s. In 1974, police raided an apartment where teenagers openly smoked and traded hashish (it was reoccupied shortly afterward). Most business occurred in Piazza dei Signori and Piazza delle Erbe, both central city squares not far from Juliet's balcony.[107] Arlacchi and Lewis estimate that up to 60 percent of those involved in heroin use and trafficking in Verona at that time were educated, self-employed proprietors, or managers of small businesses, and came from relatively well-off families. In other words, operators in the market belonged to the same social milieu that had given rise to a flourishing economy, and adopted the same norms of fair dealing and commercial practices that characterized the legal sectors of the economy. Transactions in the illicit drug market took place according to shared rules of fair bargaining, and punishment took the form of exclusion from future exchanges as well as refusal to offer credit and discounts. In addition, a significant level of barter and individualized exchange took place, and no third-party mechanism to punish defectors existed. Most of the arrests of both consumers and local traffickers were for direct violations of drug laws rather than violent crimes connected to the drug trade, and most of those arrested were sent to prison only once rather than being repeat offenders.[108]

Operators in the drug market seemed able to satisfy the growing demand. At first, supplies of morphine and heroin arrived in the city with users who had visited Bangladesh and Pakistan in the early 1970s. In a matter of a few years (1974–75), individual consumers, small-time local traffickers, and consumers' cooperatives started to buy heroin that came from southeast Asia via Amsterdam and Munich, and from the Middle East via Yugoslavia. Over the following years the quality of the product increased, as did the sources of supply (between fifty and eighty kilograms were sold monthly in the city, according to police estimates).[109] A Communist Party official at the time and antidrug activist, Dino Facchini, recalls an aspect of the heroin transportation routes into the city:

A significant element facilitating drug trafficking was the Interporto terminal. The terminal provides infrastructure for freight activity, making available multiple modes of transport. In essence, it means that goods may arrive by different means—say, by rail—and then be loaded onto trucks. The Interporto is located at intersection of the Brenner (north-south) and Serenissima (east-west) turnpikes, and is directly connected to the Verona airport. There is also a customs office. More than four hundred companies have offices there, and it employs some four thousand people. I know this well because I served for several years on the board of the Interporto [board members are political appointees]. Thus, the heroin was arriving from Eastern Europe by truck and by rail, was going through the terminal, and then entered the rest of the Italian market.[110]

Suddenly, Verona found itself at the center of an international drug route, and its heroin, the so-called La Veronese, acquired a national reputation as cheaper and purer than many other variants. Local consumers introduced trusted outsiders—especially consumers based in the surrounding towns—to sellers, and the market gradually spread to the rural areas.[111] As this illegal market was expanding, the number of people under eighteen years of age charged with drug-related offenses actually dropped in the period 1970–87.[112] Prior to the arrival of the Calabresi, violent conflict was virtually absent, as evidenced by the data on murders: the rate in Verona city was lower than the average of the Veneto region, and six times lower than the national average.[113]

A colorful character from this time is a young local lad, thin with pock-marked cheeks, best known by his nickname, "Gengiva" (Gum). He is credited with having introduced considerable quantities of heroin into the city over a twenty-year period. A carpenter by trade, he started his career—after a brief spell as a bank robber—with other like-minded locals, also known by their nicknames, such as "Camay," "Gancio" (Hook), "Bistecca" (Steak), "Gamba" (Leg), "Perry," "Elio il bello," and "Volante d'oro" (Golden Wheel). In his time, Verona came to be known as "the Bangkok of Italy," and the long line of cars visiting the city from all over northern Italy to buy heroin was dubbed "the Ho Chi Minh Trail."[114]

In the 1970s, the Calabresi in town decided to muscle into the legal and illegal markets. As early as 1973, they began trying to extract money from legal entrepreneurs. For instance, in early January 1974, in the city of Ronco, near Verona, several prominent entrepreneurs and politicians received threats and demands for money.[115] In the eastern and southern parts of the province of Verona, home to successful export-oriented furniture makers, police uncovered extensive extortion. Some one hundred thefts of trucks carrying furniture reportedly took place in 1973 alone. The Calabresi claimed that they could offer protection against such occurrences.[116] Violence and crime increased in this period, with businesspeople in particular experiencing a rise in intimidation, robberies, and homicides.[117] Answering a confidential survey administered to two hundred local entrepreneurs, 38.2 percent of the respondents stated that extortion was "common," 9.3 percent stated that it was "all-embracing," while 45 percent declared it was "limited." Only 4.6 percent answered that the phenomenon did not exist in Verona.[118]

The Calabresi also tried to gain control of the drug market by using violence against existing traders and establishing direct links with suppliers. Six murders connected to disputes in the drug market took place in rapid succession. One of the victims was murdered mafia style (*incapretare*). This involved tying his hands and feet behind his back with a rope that also went around his neck; death came as a result of self-inflicted strangulation.[119] The large drug suppliers whom the Calabresi contacted (Sicilian mafiosi and Turkish heroin suppliers) demanded payment in cash on consignment. Since the Calabresi faced a chronic shortage of funds, they decided to raise capital by kidnapping wealthy Veronesi for ransom, relying on their region of origin for hiding places. Ten Veronesi were kidnapped between 1974 and 1978.[120]

The key organizer of the transplantation attempt was Cosimo Ierinò, a prominent member of the Mazzaferro clan, born in Gioiosa Ionica, the Calabrian hometown of Lo Presti. Like Lo Presti, he was related to the Mazzaferro, having married the sister of Vincenzo and Giuseppe Mazzaferro. In a curious twist, Ierinò disappeared from Verona for a while and surfaced in Bardonecchia. Other prominent individuals involved were two sets of brothers—the Corsaro and Camera brothers.[121] The group recruited local petty criminals and neofascist activists in an attempt to create a protection racket and control the lucrative drug trade. They planned to establish a system of concessions whereby a set of local criminals (thieves, con artists, extortionists, pimps, and smugglers) would be identified and put in charge of a given territory, encouraged to extract protection payments from local businesspeople, and forced to hand over a portion of their earnings to the Calabresi. The Calabresi, in turn, would offer services such as dispute settlement, refuge and hiding places for people and illegal goods, and the intimidation of political and law officials. As part of this strategy, they started to hand out bribes to local law enforcement and party functionaries.[122]

A clear attempt to penetrate politics is also on record. Several drug dealers and other individuals from Calabria became card-carrying members of the tiny Partito Social Democratico Italiano. Shortly thereafter they were elected to positions of responsibility within the party. Reputedly, the local party leader, also from Calabria, was supporting them. Their acceptance into the party and rapid rise through the ranks generated internal opposition, resignations, emergency meetings, and alarm in the city.[123]

Violence spread beyond the drug market. The highest-profile murder at this time was that of Fabio Maritati, the son of a police officer, possibly a case of mistaken identity (the real target was his father), on December 21, 1979. The murder was related to Maritati's investigations into truck thefts (he was with the transport police). At the trial, it transpired that another police officer had helped the killers.[124]

As in the case of Bardonecchia, civil society was quick to mobilize against outside criminal elements. At the forefront of this grassroots movement were the Catholic church, the local chapter of the Italian Communist Party, and the newly created Association of Concerned Families against Drugs.[125] A large rally against drugs and organized crime took place in December 1980, and some ten thousand people signed a petition to the same effect in 1981.[126] At the instigation of the Communist Party, an even larger and televised march of protest, attended by the speaker of the House of Representatives, was organized for October 1982.[127] All local political leaders (with the exception of the neofascist Movimento Sociale Italiano) denounced drug dealing, and resolutions were passed in the city and provincial councils in support of the fight against organized crime.[128] The local paper, L'Arena di Verona, rallied behind the efforts to free the city from these criminals, and ran several features openly opposing the presence of the Calabresi in town, often using bigoted language.[129]

Local campaigners were targeted and violence was used against them. On December 8, 1980, the editor of L'Arena di Verona was the victim of an attempt on his life.[130] Members of the Association of Concerned Families, a priest, and Communist activists were all threatened, affronted, and physically attacked.[131] In contrast to the outcome in Bardonecchia, however, the concerted pressure of civil society on both the police and judiciary yielded tangible results—namely, the removal of officials and politicians who had accepted bribes from the mafia.[132] The attempted penetration of the Partito Social Democratico Italiano was short-lived. Unable to control a significant share of votes in a city much larger than Bardonecchia, the Calabresi were unable to influence the outcome of elections.

By the mid-1980s, the long-term plan of establishing a protection racket and controlling the drug market in Verona had failed. Ierinò, for instance, resumed his activities in Calabria and was eventually arrested in 1995. In the meantime, the drug market continued to flourish according to the rules of fair bargaining and reciprocity described above, and was being run by entrepreneurs beyond suspicion.[133] For example, in February 1988, the police intercepted eighty-five kilos of pure heroin, with a street value of 150 billion liras (or US$128,000,000). The masterminds of the traffic were a former postal worker, a wine producer, and the owner of a livery stable. An in-depth newspaper investigation concluded in 1988:

> Going over the occupations of those arrested for drug trafficking, one often comes across hairdressers, manicurists, small entrepreneurs, pasta makers, bar owners, door-to-door salesmen, individuals with regular jobs. And entire families, spanning from grandfathers to grandchildren. Reportedly, a couple of years ago local entrepreneurs even formed an investment company to collect funds to invest in the heroin traffic, with a 30 percent guaranteed return.[134]

For his part, Gengiva returned to drug trafficking in Verona. In 1988, the police found some eighty kilos of heroin in one of his villas. In 1994, he realized that his luck had run out—a police officer who had helped him throughout had just been arrested for favoring criminals—and flipped, revealing the ins and outs of the local drug market. Courtesy of a local veteran crime correspondent, I met Gengiva in 2005. Excessive drug and alcohol consumption had taken their toll on his health. He was spending most of his days sitting at a central café, just opposite the Arena, not far from Piazza delle Erbe. Gaunt, with darkened teeth and scant hair, he wore dark glasses and was dressed smartly. He willingly recounted some details of his previous life, but mainly evoked for me the many places that he had visited in the Far East and the many properties that he had acquired. Gengiva had also grown wiser. In heavy Veronese dialect, he said that it is not worthwhile misbehaving in life, as you will pay for it in the end. Frail and ailing, he died in 2008, at age fifty-three.[135]

A combination of factors accounts for the Calabresi failure at transplantation. First, the new immigrants found official employment in the local industries. In the legal markets, extortion was directed at export-oriented firms that were not in direct competition with each other. In contrast to the case of Bardonecchia, employers would not benefit from the creation of a cartel of a few locally based firms to exploit a local market, since they were mainly exporting their goods to diverse markets in northern Europe and the United States. The service offered by the Calabresi turned out to be purely extortionary. Collective action, fostered by an active civil society, thereby became more effective than in Bardonecchia.

One would expect that the expanding drug market in Verona shared key features with the expanding construction market in Bardonecchia, giving rise in both instances to a demand for mafia-type protection. Furthermore, the drug market was illegal, thus there were no legal competitors who could have stepped in. And yet the Calabresi failed to control the market. There are at least three key differences between the two cases. First, in Verona the dealers had emerged from the same local milieu as the consumers, felt a common connection to the radical behavioral revolution of the 1960s, knew each other well, and relied initially on trust but then, as the number of market actors grew, rules of fair bargaining and cooperation in their exchanges. They did not need a third-party enforcer of deals. The makeup of the market actors is markedly different from the poorly educated and unemployed immigrant workers living in squalor in Turin and needing the Calabrese fixer to find employment.

Second, in Verona—as in other instances—the mafia found it impossible to create bottlenecks to channel the supply of drugs into the city.[136] The Calabresi could not offer local dealers access to particularly attractive new sources of supply, as Turkish and Sicilian mafiosi did not enter into exclusive deals with one distributor. In Bardonecchia, by contrast, construction firms arrived from Calabria to offer employment to the immigrant workers.

Third, dealing in drugs is not an activity tied to a fixed place, as in the case of construction. Construction sites provide a focus for violence, as did bars during Prohibition in the United States.[137] The Veronesi were able to elude mafia attempts at controlling their activity, moving distribution to different areas while continuing to sell to customers with whom they had developed long-term relations of cooperation. Local dealers did not need or demand Calabresi protection in the illegal market.

Conclusions

In light of the different outcomes of the 'Ndrangheta attempts at transplantation in the two regions, I can draw some general considerations. Table 3.4 summarizes the key factors that the two cases share and those that distinguish them (it also includes columns that will be filled as I cover the other cases in this book).

Supply. Immigration impacted the two locales differently. Verona experienced significant arrivals, like Turin, Rome, and Milan, but in contrast to the case of Turin, immigrants found employment in the expanding local economy. No pocket of poorly housed immigrants far away from their structures of support existed in Verona at this time. A second difference is that immigrants were from the region of Veneto, rather than from the South.

The comparison between Bardonecchia and Verona reveals that in both cases, mafiosi from Calabria were forced to resettle in these regions, but only in Bardonecchia did they succeed in realizing their long-term criminal goals. Moreover, other parts of Piedmont and northern Italy experienced an influx of a similar or higher number of individuals forced to migrate due to the soggiorno policy, yet mafias did not emerge everywhere. A supply of specialized criminals (as distinct from generalized migration) is not enough to produce successful transplantation. As for ex ante motivations to expand, I found no evidence that the incoming mafiosi arrived in order to obtain special resources, invest in the local economy, or colonize a new market. Mafiosi did invest *after* they had been forced to migrate there, but this was not the reason that they migrated.

Local conditions. A high level of interpersonal trust and civic engagement is present in both cities. It is hard to tell conclusively whether trust was

TABLE 3.4

Factors Facilitating Mafia Transplantation, Bardonecchia and Verona

Factors facilitating mafia transplantation/cases	Bardonecchia	Verona	Budapest	Rome	New York City (1910–30)	Rosario (1910–30)	Shenzhen/ Guangzhou
Generalized migration	Yes	No					
Mafiosi migration (willing/unwilling)	Yes (unwilling)	Yes (unwilling)					
Supply of mafiosi	Yes	Yes					
Local conditions							
Level of trust/civic engagement	High	High					
Presence of local illegal protectors	No	No					
Size of locale	Small	Large					
New and/or booming markets*	Yes	Yes					
Demand for mafia services	Yes	No					
Transplantation	Yes	No					

* The markets considered are construction (Bardonecchia and Rosario), drugs (Verona and China), property rights (Budapest and China), oil (Budapest), alcohol (New York City), gambling (New York City and China), and prostitution (China).

depleted as a consequence of the success of the 'Ndrangheta in Bardonecchia. Surely, voting in referenda and the European elections (where the
constituency covers the entirety of northern Italy) continued to be high,
and mobilization took place in order to defend the mafia rather than oppose it.

One might ask if the effectiveness of law enforcement could account for
the diverging outcomes. There is no evidence that the police and judiciary
were less efficient in Turin Province than in Verona. In both cases, I found
instances of occasional corruption within law enforcement. Indeed, in the
case of Verona, a corrupt police officer was behind the murder of a colleague
who was investigating cargo thefts. The judiciary in both locales put pressure
on the mafia, instructing several trials since the 1970s. (As for the existence
of local protectors, no homegrown mafia existed in either Bardonecchia or
Verona, unlike cases that I will explore later in this book.)

Verona is a significantly bigger city than Bardonecchia. The penetration
of politics is, ceteris paribus, easier the smaller the locale. According to his
own estimate, Lo Presti controlled five hundred votes in the Piedmontese
town. That portfolio of votes was enough to elect a sizable section of the
city council. The same five hundred votes would have had a less dramatic
impact in Verona, where the Communist Party alone could count on fifteen thousand card-carrying members. The structure of the economy also
differed. Verona was an export-oriented economy, and thus we would expect it to be less susceptible to mafia efforts to offer services of cartelization. The Bardonecchia economy experienced an economic boom in a
local market, where mafia services aimed at reducing competition would
have benefited market incumbents in significant sectors (see the "new and
booming market" condition in table 3.4).

In short, a combination of factors account for the outcome in the Piedmontese town—that is, large-scale migration from outside the region combined with illegal employment in a localized booming market of a small
town and the presence of a small supply of 'Ndranghetisti forced to reside there. The migrant workers accepted illegal employment, and thereby
deprived themselves of trade union and more generally state-sponsored
protection. If they had acted differently, they would have remained unemployed. Construction firms benefited from the muscle offered by the
'Ndrangheta in pushing out competitors. A demand for criminal protection allowed the 'Ndrangheta Mazzaferro clan to offer its services and

entrench itself in a faraway territory. Contrary to what some authors might have predicted, the levels of trust and social capital among the population at large did not in themselves prevent transplantation.

A booming illegal market does not always generate a demand for criminal protection. In Verona a mafia failed to take root in a large illegal market, where by definition traders cannot turn to the state in case of disputes. This reflects a combination of three factors. First, traders and consumers knew each other, and had entered into long-term relations of cooperation. A third-party enforcer of deals was not necessary; a customer who defected simply would not be served the next time around. Second, the Calabresi had no particular connection to drug suppliers and could not force local dealers to use their sources. Third, selling drugs is a more mobile type of economic activity than erecting a high-rise building. To the extent that the Calabresi tried to force dealers operating in a given area to hand over a cut to them, the latter would simply have moved elsewhere.

Let me offer a final word on the relationship between the outpost and homeland in Bardonecchia. There is no evidence that the Calabrese bosses were paying a salary to Lo Presti or other mafiosi in Bardonecchia. However, the outpost was not fully independent, as indicated by the fact that it did not have the power to carry out initiation rituals. New recruits had to travel back to the homeland to join the organization. What accounts for this relatively close relationship? The explanation lies in the pre-eminence of money-laundering: Calabrese firms operating in Bardonecchia were a conduit for investing money obtained by the 'Ndrangheta in Calabria. Since capital was coming directly from the cosca in Calabria, the group of origin retained a relatively strong connection with the outpost.

FOUR

The Russian Mafia in Rome and Budapest

THE SOLNTSEVSKAYA

Solntsevo is a rundown, working-class district of Moscow, located in the western and southwestern parts of the city. Lying outside the MKAD, Moscow's equivalent of Washington's Beltway or London's M25, the inhabitants of central Moscow would never venture into this depressed zone of the outer city, and many would not even consider it part of the Russian capital.[1] The intrepid traveler who still wants to visit Solntsevo must spend no less than an hour on the orange metro line that leaves from the center of town and then, once they have reached the end of the line, board a city bus. The area used to host a pleasant spread of dachas until the Soviet authorities decided to construct several impersonal high-rise buildings. Possibly in recognition of the fact that skyscrapers obscure the sun, the district was named after the Russian word for sun (*solntse*) when it was officially established in 1938. As in other instances where the object does not fit the moniker, the English rendering of Solntsevo is Sunnyside.

This district has given its name to arguably the mightiest organized crime group to emerge from the wreckage of the Soviet Union, often referred to as the "Solntsevo fraternity" (*Solntsevskaya bratva*). The founder of the fraternity, allegedly, is Sergei Mikhailov, a respected businessperson and patron of the Orthodox Church. Nowadays, you can see pictures of him wearing a tweed jacket and tie, perfectly shaved and groomed, with serious yet quizzing eyes glaring into the camera. He was born into a modest working-class family in February 1958 and raised in Solntsevo. As a young

Five-story apartment houses on Glavmosstroy Street, Solntsevo, Moscow. Photo credit: Artem Kostyukovsky.

man, Mikhailov trained to be a maître d'hôtel at the Sovietskaya Hotel in central Moscow while cultivating his other passion: wrestling. In 1984, he was found guilty of insurance fraud (he stole his own motorbike) and spent several months in custody. After receiving a conditional jail sentence, he returned to Solntsevo, and started setting up sports clubs and organizations to which he recruited the tough, unemployed, and aggressive young men living in the district.[2] He joined forces with a former prison inmate, Victor Averin, to create his own gang, and named it after the district. It was only with the spread of the new post-Soviet market freedom that the Solntsevskaya became a significant player in the Russian underworld. In order to fend off a major challenge from Chechen groups, Mikhailov joined forces in 1989 with Sergei Timofeev. Nicknamed "Sil'vestr" after Sylvester Stallone for his muscular build, Timofeev was the leader of the Orekhovskaya gang comprising mainly young sportsmen and wrestlers. By the mid-1990s, the Solntsevo had grown in strength. A Federal Bureau of Investigation (FBI) report in 1995 described it as the most powerful

Sergei Anatol'evich Mikhailov (b. 1958), the founder, allegedly, of the Solntsevskaya bratva in Moscow. He is now a respected businessperson and patron of the Russian Orthodox Church. Photo credit: News Agency Thompson Reuters.

Eurasian organized crime group in the world in terms of wealth, influence, and financial control.[3] The core of its business was protection, or what in Russian is termed "roof" (*krysha*).[4]

Estimates of the size of the brotherhood (possibly exaggerated) range from five to nine thousand members. The group comprises no fewer than ten semiautonomous brigades (*brigady*), which operate under the umbrella name of Solntsevskaya. The Russian police claim that it controls various banks along with about a hundred small and medium-size enterprises. Although little is known of the inner workings of the group, former members have claimed that the organization is governed by a council of twelve individuals, who meet regularly in different parts of the world, often disguising their meetings as festive occasions. The Solntsevskaya maintains a common fund (*obshchak*), which is reinvested into the legal economy through a number of banks that work for the organization, with members of the organization's council overseeing the investment decisions. At one point in its history, this mafia set foot on the Italian peninsula.

THE SOLNTSEVSKAYA IN ITALY

Fano is a sleepy beach resort on the Adriatic Sea, in the Italian region of Marche, a few kilometers from the more prestigious cities of Pesaro and Urbino. Among its few historical claims to fame is having been invaded by Cesare Borgia, the man who tried to create a state of his own in central Italy in the late fifteenth century and was the main subject of Niccolò Machiavelli's *The Prince*. The city was bombed heavily during the Second World War by Allied troops, while the Nazis destroyed its historical towers and bridges (the Gothic Line stopped here). The center of the town still retains its pleasant character, with the spread of cafés and hangers-on one would expect on a warm day in a town in this part of the world. Besides tourism and small-scale fishing, family-run firms producing shoes, hosiery, furniture, and home furnishings abound, frequently supplying their products to big European brands. Professors at the local university contend that a special "Marche model" of economic development characterizes the area.

Fano is also where two mobsters, Monya Elson and Yossiff Roizis, had come to live in the 1980s and 1990s. Their arrest in 1995 started a chain of events that led to several investigations in the United States and Italy, revealing the presence of the Solntsevskaya in Rome. Monya Elson, a native of the Jewish ghetto in Chisinau (Kishinev), the capital of Moldova, had migrated to New York City in 1978, claiming Jewish preferential status. When he arrived in the United States, he continued to exploit his Jewish identity. He would dress up as an Orthodox Jew and, with an accomplice, walk into a jewelry shop, asking to see expensive diamond stones. While his accomplice blathered in Yiddish, distracting the shop owner, Elson, sporting a paste-on beard, side curls, long black coat, and black hat, switched the diamonds with cubic zirconia. He soon graduated to more serious crimes, including extortion and murder. His rise in the Russian underworld brought him into contact and then conflict with a prominent Russian drug dealer, and then with Viacheslav Ivan'kov, nicknamed "Yaponchik," the Solntsevskaya boss who had escaped to New York.[5] In order to avoid being murdered, he fled to Fano, where a Ukrainian with a U.S. passport, Yossif Aronovich Roizis, had been living since the mid-

Pallbearers carrying entrepreneur and *vor-v-zakone* Vyacheslav Ivan'kov aka Yaponchik's casket to his grave in the prestigious Vagankovskoye Cemetery, Moscow, on October 13, 2009. Photo credit: RIA Novosti News Agency.

1980s. Roizis had started an import-export business of furniture between Italy, Brooklyn, and Russia. Allegedly, Roizis and Elson had met in Budapest at a gathering of associates of the Solntsevskaya.

The Italian police were keeping an eye on Roizis, who had previously been charged with drug offenses (but never convicted) and was receiving money from exotic locations, including New York and Russia, into his account at the Banca Popolare dell'Adriatico di Pesaro, not quite a renowned investment establishment. The U.S. institution at the center of the unexplained money transfers to Roizis was the Bank of New York, eventually the subject of an investigation that made headlines around the world in the late 1990s when two Russian émigrés working at the bank—one was a vice president— illegally moved more than US$7 billion via hundreds of wires. Nine people were eventually prosecuted.[6] At the same time, Elson was wanted in New York for murder and, at the prompting of the FBI, the

Sharply dressed mourners entering the church for Ivankov's funeral. Photo credit: RIA Novosti News Agency.

Italian police closed in. In the early hours of March 8, 1995, they stormed through the door of Roizis's apartment and arrested the two men.

Shortly after his arrest, Roizis began to cooperate with the authorities. In a startling development, he informed them that, in a small seaside resort just outside Rome, a prominent member of the governing body of the Solntsevskaya, *Ivan Yakovlev,* had been in residence since October 1994 (some documents relating Yakovlev to Elson were found in Roizis's apartment). A special unit of the Italian police was quickly assembled and started an undercover investigation of this cell of the Solntsevskaya in Rome, lasting three years (1995–97) and resulting in a three-volume report that was to be used during the trial. The document contains hundreds of pages of transcripts of telephone conversations between Italian and Russian criminals, checks on money transfers, international financial operations involving banks in London, Budapest, Vienna, New York, and Rome, property speculations in Italy, and individual files on some forty-five people. For each individual, the file contains information concerning their various aliases, passport details, residencies, travels, ownership of real estate, and information collected from other police forces. These people include members of parliament in both Italy and Russia, political leaders in Russia such as a governor, lawyers, executives of various banks in Rome, Moscow, and Saint Petersburg, a general of the Italian army, the former deputy head of one of Italy's oil and gas concerns, former KGB officers, a colonel in the North Korean army, the Russian government's undersecretary of state for energy, police officers, and embassy staff in Rome. The companies involved include car and computer manufacturers as well as Russian oil companies. This source paints an elaborate picture of the operations and objectives of the group.

The end point of this investigation was October 1996, a few weeks after the murder narrated in the introduction of this book, when Sergeev, a business associate of Yakovlev, also operating in Rome, was gunned down in Moscow. The Italian police wrapped up the investigation and sent the results to the prosecutor. The main players were subsequently arrested. It transpired at the trial that the police did not have the correct authorization to collect evidence, especially wiretapping evidence. This technicality prevented the prosecutors from using the material that had been collected, and the court case collapsed.[7] The Russian protagonists of this story were nevertheless expelled from Italy and later resurfaced in Moscow. Thus the reader must remember that the people discussed here have not been convicted of any crime in Italy. In order to protect their identity, all names have been changed. Some place names have also been changed.

As for chapter 3, I start by reviewing whether Rome was ever a destination for Russian immigrants. During the 1970s, the Italian capital was a transit zone for Russians of Jewish origin on their way to the United States.[8] At this late juncture in the Cold War the Soviet leader, Leonid Brezhnev, sought to improve links with the West, in particular the United States. In a move bitterly opposed by U.S. president Richard Nixon and U.S. secretary of state Henry Kissinger, the U.S. Democratic senator Henry Jackson succeeded in linking the status of "most-favored nation" to the issue of Jewish immigration. In 1975, U.S. president Gerald Ford signed the Jackson-Vanik Amendment into law. Brezhnev obliged the senator and started to allow a number of Russian Jews to emigrate.[9] In a hideous twist, the Soviet government made sure that its worst criminals were among the "Jews" allowed out of the country. The route that the migrants took was rather complex. Normally, they would go to Vienna and then be moved to other distribution centers. One such transit camp was located in Ladispoli, a town thirty kilometers from Rome on the Via Aurelia, the highway built originally in Roman times that links the Italian capital to Pisa, now known also as Strada Statale 1. The camp was run by the Lubavitch movement and the American Jewish Joint Distribution Committee. While in Rome, the Russians applied for a visa to the United States.

In the late 1970s and 1980s, there were several thousand Russians in the Ladispoli camp at any one time.[10] Exasperated by the long delays, they organized protests directed at the U.S. embassy. They also ventured out of the camp and engaged in small commerce. Once a week, the camp residents would go to Rome, squeezing on to the local buses and converging on Vittorio Square in the Esquilino neighborhood, not far from the railway station, and on Sundays they would go to Porta Portese. Throughout the 1980s, the famous Porta Portese flea market had a so-called Russian area (*la zona dei Russi*), where refugees would sell objects smuggled out of the Soviet Union. The area has since been taken over by Chinese sellers.

Monya Elson was one of those Russian Jews who transited through Ladispoli in 1978, after a brief spell in Vienna, equipped with a visa for entry into Israel. He was in the town for three months where—in his free time—he pick-pocketed the locals in order to buy designer clothes for his wife and daughters.[11] A newspaper investigation dated 1977 confirms that Italians were exasperated by the petty crime undertaken by some of the refugees and records instances of racist slurs directed at them.[12] Camps such as the one in Ladispoli proved to be excellent recruiting grounds and networking centers, where gangsters on their way to Brighton Beach met gangsters bound for Antwerp, Brussels, or London. Once they arrived at their new destination, they had a ready-made set of friends to whom they could turn for advice as well as an international network.[13] By 1991, the United States stopped awarding the status of refugee to Russian Jews, who could now apply to move to the United States directly from Moscow. This type of migration left virtually no trace in Rome, but the physical proximity of so many criminals had far-reaching consequences, never recognized at the time.[14]

The post–Cold War phase of Russian migration to Rome involved few individuals. Immigrants residing in the city in 1997 numbered no more than 800 in a city of more than 2.5 million people. The following years saw a similarly low number of arrivals to the Eternal City. For instance, in 2005 no more than 1,000 Russians were registered in Rome, fewer than the numbers of some 40 other nationalities, suggesting a rather stable trend. What they had in common with the earlier migration is that they, along with other East European immigrants, chose to live in the small towns off the Via Aurelia, where housing is cheap. In fact, when Yakovlev arrived in Italy he moved to *Margherita Laziale* (population just over 14,000, according to official 1995 data), a town not far from Ladispoli, with few Russian residents.[15] He rented a large villa tucked away on a side street, and lived there with his wife, two sons, and a rottweiler.

Yakovlev was a senior figure in the Solntsevskaya, regularly invited to attend the Supreme Council of the organization, such as the one that took place in November 1993 in Miami with the other eleven bosses. Born in the Russian Far East and a guest of Soviet prisons in the 1970s, Yakovlev was running a crew attached to this crime group in Moscow. Most crucially, he had been a close ally of Timofeev, who was gunned down in September 1994 together with one of his lieutenants (a man called Kruglov).[16] Indeed, one of the most trusted associates of Yakovlev in Rome had worked as Timofeev's driver for several years. A war was clearly under way among the high echelons of the organization. A well-built man with short graying hair and blue sullen eyes glaring at the camera for his passport photo, Yakovlev had a choice: stay in Moscow and fight, or send a strong signal of neutrality toward the winning faction. As is often the case in the criminal world, the decision to move away could be such a signal. Remarkably, Yakovlev and his entire crew surfaced in Rome a little more than a month after the death of Sil'vestr. According to conversations intercepted while already in Italy, Sil'vestr's supporters were afraid to meet the same fate as their old leader. *Fedya Sidelnikov*, speaking from Moscow where he planned to attend the funeral of a man gunned down in the war, tells Yakovlev, "They will kill all Seriozha's people." "For instance, they have just killed [XXX], who had done nothing and nobody knows why he ended up dead. . . . Even the police says that if all the followers of Sil'vestr (the *Silvestrovskie*) die, there will be peace."[17] In a rare display of criminal bonding,

Yakovlev's interlocutor, against the advice of the boss, states that he wants to attend XXX's funeral, even if it might be dangerous: "I have to go, he was a true friend and a cell mate."[18] In a subsequent conversation, the boss discusses a newspaper report claiming that he "had escaped from [the Far East] and was hiding in Italy." He wonders why such a piece of news had appeared: "Is this a message? Do they still want to kill me?" As for his standing in the Moscow underworld, the wife of the boss tells her son: "I think Ivan is worth nothing nowadays in Moscow." Thus, mafia internal squabbles are at the origins of Yakovlev's presence in Rome.[19]

Although Italy did not have a significant Russian population, it did have the largest Communist Party in Europe (though the party was never in government). Some of the party faithful had married Soviet citizens and spoke some Russian. Crucially, one of Yakovlev's future Italian accomplices had worked for several years at the party headquarters in Rome and had a Russian wife.[20] This is a background factor that eventually facilitated Yakovlev's work in Rome. A view that emerges among the group members is that Italy was an easy country to move to. "Here [in Italy] you can do whatever you want, it is not Europe," quips a longtime collaborator of the boss.[21]

Yakovlev already knew at least two Russians in Italy. Boris Sergeev, who was to become central to Yakovlev's operation in Italy, was a businessperson with contacts with the Solntsevskaya who dealt in oil products originating in Chechnya and had been involved in some money-laundering operations while living in Vienna. He moved near to another town on the Lazio seaside in the early 1990s and set up a number of companies located at an address in Rome where Yakovlev's firms would come to be registered. As narrated in the introduction, he was ultimately murdered in Moscow in 1996. Another collaborator of Yakovlev's, *Bogdanovich*, had relocated to Italy before Yakovlev, in 1991, and lived in Ladispoli. A small-time crook, Bogdanovich spoke Italian and would become a trusted gofer of the boss.[22]

Among the Russians who moved to Italy with Yakovlev were *Sidelnikov* and his wife. Yakovlev's closest and most trusted associate, he had been a bodyguard of the Solntsevskaya founder and first leader. His wife, *Raisa Artamova*, was managing the common fund ("the pot") in Italy for the group.[23] Yakovlev's crew, which remained based in Moscow, included *Rostovtsev*, a former KGB officer who was fluent in Italian and had close contacts with the Italian embassy in Moscow as well as with the political elite in Russia, and had been collaborating with Yakovlev for eight years; he was involved in arranging visas and passports as well as trips to Moscow by Italian contacts of Yakovlev. *Vlasik*, also based in Russia, was a businessperson who had worked for Yakovlev as the "clean face" of the organization and was a financial wizard. Eventually he was killed.[24]

A key local helper was *Giorgio Facchini*, a former low-level official at the Rome headquarters of the Italian Communist Party who was married to a Russian, *Alina Kamenskaya*. At the time of his employment in the Communist Party bureaucracy, Facchini organized trips and cultural exchanges between Italy and the USSR. After being dismissed by the party in the mid-1980s, he continued to be involved in tourism and cultural exchanges throughout the 1990s. Another critical player in Yakovlev's Italian crew was *Giovanni Pepe*, Facchini's assistant. Finally, mention should be made of *Riccardo Brenno*, former manager of a sizeable Italian company. He emerged as the most high-profile Italian involved with the group—a man whose connections extended to the highest echelons of the business and political elite of the country. Table A4.1 in the appendix to this chapter summarizes some characteristics of the main players.[25]

Was there a sudden expansion of either legal or illegal markets at this point in Margherita Laziale or Rome more generally, like in Bardonecchia and Verona? I found no evidence of this. The construction boom had taken place in the 1950s and 1960s in the seaside town, and no new significant construction was under way in the 1990s. As for illegal markets in Rome, prostitution and drug trafficking were dominated by, respectively, Nigerians and Brazilians, and local Italian gangs.[26]

What, then, did Yakovlev do in Margherita Laziale? In order to answer this question, I embarked on a systematic content analysis of all the segments of conversations intercepted by the police (a "segment of conversation" is a fragment of a conversation that has a meaningful beginning and end). After coding each segment, I decided to divide the topics of conversation into four main categories: investments in the legal economy, the acquisition of resources, protection activities, and maintaining internal order. "Investments in the economy" refer to attempts to reinvest the proceeds originating from the Solntsevskaya core activity in Russia in a variety of other businesses. "Resource acquisition" refers to the acquisition of specific input resources to run the group, such as information, equipment,

TABLE 4.1

Distribution of Tasks Discussed in Segments of Conversations

	Tasks by segment of conversations	
Tasks	Frequency	Percent
Investments in the economy (E)	620	52.2
Resource acquisition (RA)	262	22.1
Maintaining internal order (MIO)	235	19.8
Protection activities (PA)	67	5.6
Total	1,184	99.7
Other	3	0.3
Total	1,187	100.0

or labor. "Protection activities" refer to efforts to control markets and offer criminal protection. Finally, "maintaining internal order" refers to the
activities of monitoring, intimidation, and punishment of both local fixers
and Russian members.

Table 4.1 presents the data. Slightly over half of the segments of the
conversations concern investments in the economy. Resource acquisition
and maintaining internal order are the next two most important tasks discussed, while discussions of protection activities come last.

Let's now turn to what appears to be the main task undertaken by the group
in Rome: investing money in the legal economy. A significant amount of
time, scheming, and traveling was devoted to identifying investment opportunities, mainly in Italy, and exporting goods to Russia. The source of
the money to be used in these ventures was clearly Russia. The most basic
money laundering technique was to set up a vast network of individuals
traveling from Russia to Italy carrying cash. Yakovlev and his associates
would take the money, buy the products, and send them back. The Italian police point out that the system may appear rudimentary and of little
consequence, but in fact it is used by various Russian criminal organizations, and may involve thousands of people and the transfer of hundreds of
millions of dollars.[27] A more sophisticated system to introduce money into
the Italian economy was through bank transfers to various companies—all

based at the same address in Rome—that had been set up by Yakovlev's associates in Italy. Money laundering occurred through Russian and, outside Russia, mainly Austrian banks connected with the Solntsevskaya.[28]

The money coming from Russia was invested in a vast array of import-export ventures. The Russian actors in this story, in particular Yakovlev, contacted hundreds of Italian companies and businesspeople, offering to buy their products. The police file records no fewer than a hundred such deals. The deals ranged from purchasing sparkling wine to buying frozen meat, wood, furniture, wheat, steel, pharmaceutical products, Olivetti computers, food products (including fish), Armani suits, works of art, gold, helicopters, and antennas. The Russians had plans to buy a fishery in Tuscany—a scheme that failed. From Italy they also negotiated the establishment of a gambling boat in Korea, another failed venture, and the purchase of goods in Venezuela. The group controlled a small arms shop in Moscow and arranged for several shipments of firearms to be sold there. The Russians seemed to be indiscriminate in their import activities. Normally, they would make an appointment with the firm in question, often pay in cash, and arrange for the delivery of the goods to Russia.

The highest-profile Italian businessperson who worked with Yakovlev was Brenno. The boss said about him:

> Brenno is the former deputy head of [an important Italian company].
> He had some problems with the law, but now he is a free man. . . .
> He was sentenced to four years, but he lives at home, he works, he is
> all right. Whatever happens, he can fix everything with a phone call
> in every part of the world. I know him very well, and he has many
> friends, all Andreotti people.

When he traveled to Moscow to negotiate import-export deals for the group, Brenno was given the royal treatment. The boss ordered a Russian Duma member to be Brenno's chaperone in the Russian capital: "[He] is coming Sunday. Go get him at the airport, take good care of him, take him to the best restaurants, champagne, obviously. Give him an armed escort and a 'cow' for the night. You will see, he is a very serious man. [Prime Minister Viktor S.] Chernomyrdin was keeping his head down when they met."[29]

Some of the transactions were wholly illegal in nature. One significant activity was the illegal export of oil from Russia to various countries, including Italy.[30] The group was also involved in a scam for which the Russians are well known: the attempt to sell radioactive material, especially so-called red mercury, on the international black market. Such a product did not exist, at least in the form described to the prospective buyers. A member of the North Korean army fell for the trick, and several conversations refer to this sale.[31]

The common feature of these ventures was that the money used to pay Italian suppliers came from criminal activities outside Italy, in breach of Italian law. From several conversations it transpires that the money being imported illegally into Italy, and more generally at the disposal of Yakovlev for investment in the legal economy, was the fruit not only of the criminal activities of Yakovlev's crew in Moscow. For instance, in one conversation Yakovlev referred to other Russian criminal groups as having contributed money to the rather significant investment in a fishery. Similarly, it emerged that the money entrusted to a Russian businessperson close to the group, Vlasik, to invest in Korea, belonged to at least three different groups: "In this thing [business venture], there is money invested belonging to people from Magadan to Moscow. We must put Vlasik immediately on trial."[32]

In order to carry out their business deals, the Russians, sometimes with their Italian helpers, traveled extensively through northern and central Italy and stayed in hotels in Lombardy, Veneto, Marche, Piedmont, Tuscany, and Emilia Romagna. They also went to Switzerland several times. Among these trips, some were to Pesaro and the Fano area to negotiate the purchase of furniture using some of the contacts of Elson and Roizis.

While Yakovlev was investing money originating in several groups in Russia, these gangs' representatives traveled regularly to Italy to inspect their investments, to the point that Yakovlev decided to rent a house for his guests. Visitors included members of the Izmailovo and the Kurgan mafia groups along with leaders of other Russian mobs. When they came, Yakovlev made sure they were provided with prostitutes, often Russians. One of his helpers said on the phone, "I am on my way to Venice to bring prostitutes to our guests, because our friends cannot stay without hookers a single day!" Another pastime was attending sporting events, such as the final of the Champions League between Juventus and Ajax in May 1996, or a Davis Cup match between Russia and Italy, also in 1996. On that occasion, the group was partying with one of the Russian players, allegedly providing him with illegal substances.

Yakovlev devoted almost 50 percent of his conversations to investments in the economy, and Sergeev, Yakovlev's business partner who was later killed, devoted 67 percent of his conversations to this task. In contrast, Sidelnikov, Yakovlev's enforcer, hardly spoke about this item. Sixty-two and 97 percent of the time Pepe, the Italian fixer, and Brenno, respectively, dealt with investments in the economy. Another indicator of whether the activity was directed at Italy or Russia is the country of origin and country of destination of the call. Seventy-five percent of the calls originated in Italy, while Russia was the country of origin for 16 percent of the calls. Italy received 65.5 percent of the calls, and Russia got 23.5 percent. This suggests that most of the talking was done within Italy, with some significant conversations made to and from Russia, since goods were eventually going to reach that country.

These data point to a rudimentary division of labor within the group, with some actors, such as Brenno, almost exclusively dedicated to helping the group fulfill the aim of finding investment opportunities, while others, as we will see below, were more evenly spread across the tasks they discussed. A third subgroup focused exclusively on other tasks.

To what extent were the Russians in Rome to acquire input resources for their operations in Russia? Some authors discussed in chapter 2 suggested that one effect of globalization for legitimate firms is to open outposts abroad in order to acquire resources that are not easily movable, such as minerals, or labor. Intangibles such as knowledge, innovation capabilities, and management or organizational skills are also among the resources being sought. For illegal firms, resource seeking could refer to intelligence and information, labor, and technical equipment like arms, hideaways, and spying technology. Did Yakovlev go to Rome to acquire resources to use for his Russian operations? Once I had read the content of the conversations relating to this task, I discovered that the actors were referring to resources that were instrumental in running the crew *in Italy* rather than input resources for the group back in Russia. The group spent a lot of time trying to open bank accounts, and to obtain Italian citizenship through fictitious marriages, forged drivers' licenses, and guns. In order to achieve these aims, they engaged in the corruption of local officials.[33]

At least nine fictitious marriages involved key members of the group. The local fixers for the group would find Italians willing to marry Russian nationals for a sum varying between US$15,000 and US$20,000. For instance, both Yakovlev and his wife married Italian citizens, although they continued to live together.[34] The few guns that the group used were smuggled into Italy by some of the female members. These guns were for their own personal use rather than for sale on the Italian market, and came from Russia; they were not a resource acquired in Italy for the Russian operation.

Overall, 22 percent of all conversation segments were devoted to resource acquisition. The Italian fixers of the group and Bogdanovich, the close collaborator of Yakovlev who spoke Italian and had been in Margherita Laziale since 1990, were those mostly involved in conversations about resource acquisitions, well above the overall average (with Bogdanovich at 55 percent, Facchini at 52 percent, Facchini's Russian-speaking wife at 45 percent, and Pepe at 23 percent). The keeper of the common fund spoke mainly about maintaining internal order (62 percent), but her second most important task was resource acquisition (31 percent). The boss was well below the average, with 11.2 percent, while Sergeev was near the average, with 19 percent. Some 80 percent of conversations that had resource acquisition as their main topic were made *within* Italy, and only 16 percent between Italy and Russia.

The key aspect of resource acquisition is that resources were used to ensure the group functioned properly in Italy instead of being invested in operations in Russia. This is contrary to the view that mafias open outposts abroad in order to take advantage of attractive labor or raw material markets. The data show that a rudimentary division of labor emerged, with the Italian fixers and a Russian go-between involved in acquiring resources, while the "enforcers" and "businesspeople" scored quite low or very low on this measure. As one would expect, most of the conversations were within Italy because the resources to be acquired were in Italy.

Since protection racketeering is the Solntsevskaya's core business, we should expect the group to engage in such activity if its motivation for migrating to Italy were to expand its core activity (the market-seeking motivation discussed in chapter 2, pp. 20–21). To the contrary, none of the recorded conversations referred to protection activities in Italy. They instead offered a fascinating insight into racketeering in Moscow and, to a lesser extent, other cities such as Prague. The calls were frequently prompted by a delay in payments or interference from other racketeers. For instance, the boss threatened the owner of a shop in Moscow who was late with a payment of US$25,000. In another case, a Moscow wholesale dealer of food products—under Yakovlev's protection (to whom he paid US$200,000 a month)—was being harassed by some officials who had requested a million rubles. Clearly his protection was far from tightly sealed, and naturally the boss was worried by this attempt to harass one of his protégés. In a similar situation, in July 1996, the boss received a call from Prague; the caller explained that he had been harassed by certain "gypsies" who were demanding protection money from him. The man in Prague recounted that when asked who his protector (vor-v-zakone) was, he named Yakovlev. Tellingly, the Czech gypsies replied that such a protector should be there to look after his associate rather than remaining several thousand kilometers away. (As Machiavelli taught us, the prince has to reside among his people.) The boss at the other end of the telephone line was duly cross.[35]

No conversation referred to any attempt to create a protection racket in Italy. The only information recorded by the police on this dimension was a criminal charge brought against Bogdanovich in 1991, three years before the arrival of Yakovlev in Rome. Bogdanovich was briefly arrested for attempting to extort money from two other individuals from the former Soviet Union. The case collapsed in court, and Bogdanovich was acquitted.

The two actors who were most involved in discussing protection activities were Yakovlev (14 percent) and Sidelnikov (22 percent), well above the 6 percent average for the group. Also, most of the calls were between Italy and Russia (83 percent), and only one call was within Italy, suggesting that the activity in question was located outside Italy, and the Russians in Rome needed to call home to manage this aspect of their criminal activities.

Any crime boss has the task of maintaining internal order, ensuring that his underlings do not disobey or report him to the authorities, and more generally that members of his crew do not cheat. The mere threat of violence should be sufficient to ensure compliance. This was the case with Marco Ferrari, a Roman petty criminal, who had "misbehaved" and even threatened to report Yakovlev to the police unless the boss repaid some money he owed him. The reaction of the Russian criminal and his deputy was swift: they scared him to the point that Ferrari recanted and apologized profusely. Ferrari was then eased out of the organization rather than physically punished, possibly because such punishment would have attracted the attention of the Italian police.[36]

One would imagine that the ability of such a powerful organization as the Solntsevskaya to inspire fear and obtain compliance would be sufficient to ensure obedience from its accomplices. Yet mafia-type criminal organizations might have to use more violence than one would expect. Vlasik, a Russian in his mid-forties with a mild stutter, had been entrusted by Yakovlev with a considerable sum to invest in a deal in Korea. It transpired that the money originated in several Russian groups, not just from Yakovlev's own crew.[37] Although Vlasik must have known the risk that he was taking, he embezzled the funds and tried to disappear. "It is a bloody pain to think that among us only Vlasik is able to carry out financial operations," notes the boss. "And that is why he takes advantage of us—retorts his interlocutor,—but I will show him what a badly beaten up guy looks like and make him understand that he will be next."[38] Vlasik was eventually tracked down in Korea and escorted back to Italy, where he was held in captivity and tortured for some weeks. Later he was put on a plane to Moscow, accompanied by a "jailer." While in Russia, Vlasik managed to escape and gave himself up to the police. The punishment was only delayed; he was later killed.[39]

Twenty percent of the conversations dealt with internal order. The upper echelon of the group had more conversations about this topic than average: Yakovlev had a value of 28 percent, while Yakovlev's two enforcers had values of around 45 percent (with Sidelnikov at 44 percent, and Vladimir Sidorov at 45 percent). Most remarkably, it transpires that women were directly involved in discussing issues related to maintaining internal order. For instance, Yakovlev's wife, Marina (with a value of 53.3 percent), directly threatened Ferrari, whose wife was Russian, for disobeying Yakovlev ("we will chop your head off"). Ferrari's wife calls back, begging for forgiveness, admitting that they had been wrong and one needs to pay respect to the boss, "because he has been in prison for 15 years." Alina Kamenskaya (38 percent), the wife of Italian fixer Facchini, on several occasions advocated appropriate punishments for those who had misbehaved toward Yakovlev.[40] Artamova, the keeper of the common fund, engaged in many conversations related to maintaining internal order (62 percent). The women around Sergeev, who would be killed in 1996, also spent a considerable amount of time talking about internal order. Kostina, his "official" Italian wife who worked as his interpreter and overall helper in Italy, had a value of 58 percent, while Sergeev's real wife, Nadia, with whom he lived, had a value of 33.3 percent.

On the whole, severe acts of violence were rarely carried out in Italy, and murders were committed only in Russia. This suggests that the group did not want to attract the attention of the police in Italy.

Figure 4.5 presents the tasks discussed in all the conversations over almost a year—from January 1996, when the Italian police started systematic phone intercepts, to October 1996, when Sergeev was killed. The only correlation that is statistically significant is between resource acquisition and investments in the economy ($r = 0.758$, $p = 0.011$, $N = 10$). That is, discussions of investment opportunities in the economy covary with discussions of acquisition of resources, suggesting a relation between the two sets of tasks. This further confirms that discussions on resource acquisition were closely connected to those about money laundering and illegal investments in the Italian economy. In contrast, references to protection racketeering do not seem to be cyclic and are unrelated to other tasks. As mentioned above, racketeering was carried out in Russia by members of the group—a task unrelated to their presence in Italy.

As in other cases discussed in this book, a prominent mafioso reached a faraway land as the product of an unintended consequence; a war in Moscow pushed Yakovlev to Rome. He withdrew from the conflict at the price of losing some control over his racket at home. While in the Italian capital, he maintained contacts with the new leadership and helped them invest some of their money in the West (recall that in the mid-1990s the Russian banking system was under severe strain, the ruble was not a safe currency, and Russia defaulted on international loans in August 1998).[41] Thus, the activities of the Italian outpost were squarely in the realm of investment seeking although one cannot state that this was the motivation to open the outpost.

The organization was not looking for any particular resource to use in running its core business in Russia of protection racketeering or even

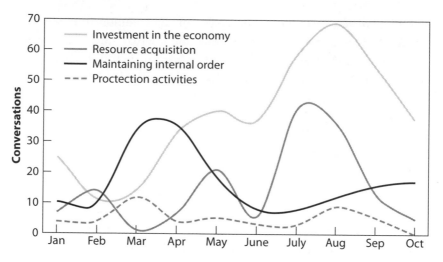

FIGURE 4.1 Tasks discussed in conversations, January to October 1996

related businesses, such as prostitution or drug trafficking. Nor was Italy a place where a firm-owned subsidiary could act as a conduit for valuable local knowledge to be used in Russia. Again, this marks a departure from the behavior of legitimate firms taking advantage of globalization.

The organization was not planning to enter the market of any rival organization. In one of his conversations, the boss made it clear that the Italian capital had been selected because it harbored no major criminal organizations, such as the Sicilian mafia.[42] Indeed, if market expansion had been a motivation, violence would have ensued, while the Italian outpost was careful to avoid drawing any attention to itself. The group had been able to evade the notice of the police in Rome. Only a tip-off from the Russian mobster arrested in Fano alerted the authorities to the existence of such an entity in Rome.[43]

Yakovlev would at the same time invest money originating from several Russian groups in the legal economy while continuing to run his protection rackets in Russia. This explains why a proportion of the conversations of the Russians in Italy involved matters related to the racketeering activities of Yakovlev back in Russia.

Clear signs of the internal division of labor emerge. Besides the boss, the only official role in the group is that of Artamova, who controlled the group's budget. But an informal structure becomes evident from the patterns of the conversations. Some of the Russian enforcers who had joined Yakovlev in Italy were mainly involved in (talking about) enforcing internal order within the group and protection racketeering back home. Women were highly involved in conversations over internal matters, including punishment. As one would expect, Italians with a local knowledge of Rome mainly helped in acquiring resources for the group to operate in Italy. Italians also were relatively more concerned with investments in the economy, as the group was dealing with Italian entrepreneurs. The boss was heavily involved in most tasks (with the exception of resource acquisition), but especially in overseeing investment decisions and reporting back to Russia. In a separate paper, I explore further issues related to the internal division of labor through the use of correspondence and social network analyses.[44]

How did Yakovlev's Italian adventure end? The entire crew, including guests from Moscow, was celebrating the birthday of the boss in a posh resort in early 1997. They had booked an entire floor of the most expensive hotel in town. The guests had arrived with several thousand U.S. dollars each, as birthday gifts for the boss. The only object of value to be put in the hotel's safe, however, was a precious Russian Orthodox bible. Yakovlev kept his boys (*rebyata*) on a short leash; he made them go to bed at 6:00 p.m. but forced them to get up at 3:00 a.m. to engage in endless discussions, while his crew was half asleep and half drunk. It is possible that Yakovlev was about to perform an initiation ritual for a new member, since a black cloth with verses in old Russian engraved in gold and scrolls containing Russian Orthodox prayers were later found in his rooms.

Several officers disguised as waiters and hotel staff observed the group for a few days. When the order arrived, in the early hours of the morning, they made the arrests. The entire operation took no longer than five minutes, without disrupting the wealthy clientele's sleep. After his arrest, the boss made a point of paying the bill in full, in cash. The next day his photos were all over the papers. Italian readers could see a man with cropped white hair, a tattoo in the hollow of his right hand, waving his fingers at the cameras, his eyes screaming with rage, furious yet nonplussed by the arrest.

The story presented here involves the most powerful mafia group operating in Russia at the time, and implicates a vast section of the Italian political and administrative class. And yet the group failed to take root in the country where it had chosen to relocate. After the arrest of the key players and their repatriation to Russia, the police and prosecutors told me that the group had left no traces in Rome.[45] Organized crime is not always successfully transplanted in a different territory. In some cases, it is enough to eliminate a few central actors to disband a network. As the group did not offer any particular service to the local criminal markets, no demand for it existed and no other group replaced it. The failure of transplantation does not mean that the crime group is weak in its territory of origin, though. After being rebuffed in Rome, Yakovlev and his crew returned home and continued their activities there. In the home country, this mafia group still extracts protection money and governs a territory.

The Solntsevskaya in Hungary

The story of the Solntsevskaya penetration of Hungarian society revolves around a Ukrainian-born businessman, Semën Yudkovich Mogilevich, who moved to Budapest in 1991 and was arrested in 2008. Mogilevich, who is bald, weighs some three hundred pounds, and is a chain smoker ("Davidov's cigarettes"), holds a degree in economics from Lvov University. He came to international attention when the FBI accused him of involvement in the Bank of New York scandal mentioned previously (p. 70). He had solid connections with the Solntsevskaya's leaders, Mikhailov and Averin, who had both chosen Budapest as the site of one of their residences in Eastern Europe.[46] Were they part of a larger migration of ordinary Russians—and possibly Ukrainians—to Hungary? Between 1990 and 2005, Russian and Ukrainian nationals never reach 1 percent of the total population. Romanians, Serbians, Germans, and Polish nationals are all more numerous, and significantly so (See table A4.2 in the appendix to this chapter).

On the other hand, the police claim that specialized criminals from Russia were in quite good number following the early 1990s. It appears that the initial presence of a 'supply' of Russian criminals in Hungary was due to an accident of history, namely the vast contingent of Red Army soldiers and security officials stationed in the country. Reportedly, more than 1,000 Russians deserted the Red Army just before they were due to return home in 1991, and many of them went on to set up crime groups. In 1998 the police estimated that "200 criminal gangs, mostly Russian controlled, have established themselves in the country, with a couple of dozen dominating."[47] According to U.S. and Hungarian officials, many of the criminal bosses had a background in the KGB and the Soviet army.[48]

Contrary to the situation in Rome, at the time of the Solntsevskaya attempts to move into Budapest, the country as a whole was undergoing a transition from a state-planned to a market economy. Hungary had begun restructuring state-owned enterprises before the end of the Communist regime, and by 1985 two-thirds of all state enterprises had been granted self-governance through enterprise councils. By the end of the 1990s, between 80 and 85 percent of the gross domestic product (GDP) was privately owned. The emerging market economy could also rely on laws and regulations that had been in place even during the Communist regime. A commercial code, never formally repealed during the Communist period, had existed since before the Second World War, in turn based on a law passed in 1875. Moreover, reforms that began as early as 1968 and continued, with interruptions, up to 1988 had reduced the role of the state in the economy and given greater autonomy to enterprises. The Act on Business Organizations of 1988 consolidated previously fragmented corporate law and was amended throughout the 1990s to reflect the changing commercial environment.[49]

The transition to the market led to a significant expansion of the economy. The value of the GDP at 2006 prices went from 2,498.3 billion Hungarian forints in 1991 to 23,795.3 billion forints in 2006. The real wage index (1990 = 100.0) grew from 93 in 1991 to 121.7 in 2007.[50]

Still, the Hungarian transition has not been entirely free of problems. Hungary underwent what scholars have labeled "spontaneous (or informal) privatization," led by managers who were able to acquire stakes in state companies in the absence of legislation that fully protected shareholders or clearly defined property rights. László Urbán, an economist, writes that "informal privatization ranges on a scale from outright theft of potentially useful physical assets of a SOE [state-owned enterprise] through different forms of simple corruption to more sophisticated appropriation of assets through the creation of new corporations."[51]

Notwithstanding the relatively probusiness atmosphere of Hungary during its socialist period, a fully developed legal framework was not yet in place by the time the transition got under way. Writing in the late 1990s, György Csáki and Gábor Karsai point out that there are several legal and institutional problems that hinder the effective operation of Hungarian enterprises. Certain laws and modifications (for example the reform of the real estate law and the contract law) are still lacking. Conceptually, the majority of existing economic regulations is not sufficiently developed and includes a number of internal contradictions as well as contradictions with other laws.[52]

The state apparatus proved slow and ineffective in servicing the new market players. The real estate register was inaccurate and outdated, and the process of company registration was slow. In the early 1990s, the poorly computerized Hungarian real estate registers was inadequate to deal with the demands for the production and modification of information. Throughout the 1990s' boom in company creation, company registration faced the same challenge. Thus, Csáki and Karsai observe, "There is no up-to-date company data with respect to the assets and financial position of market players. The problems caused by overloading, as well as by the widening circle of corruption and other abuses, only make matters worse."[53]

Such inefficiencies decreased public confidence in the legal system, and economic crimes increased. In the 1990s tax avoidance became widespread, and the breaching of contracts, value-added tax fraud, and false bankruptcy petitions were considered minor transgressions.[54] According to a survey conducted in 1998, some 80 percent of the respondents agreed that "in order to get by, it was necessary to break the rules."[55] As crime against property increased significantly during the transition, the criminal justice system proved to be, in the view of Csáki and Karsai, "almost entirely powerless in the face of the spread of economic criminality," and the capacity of the civil law courts was "not satisfactory."[56]

Court proceedings were "lengthy," and delays in the pronouncements of verdicts were "frequent," making the execution of verdicts "often impossible."[57] The introduction in 1994 of an act meant to speed up the execution of court orders did not change matters much; the only major change was the increased costs of and payments to the private executors.[58] Police corruption has also been described as "pervasive."[59] Not surprisingly, the level of the informal economy was vast, at approximately 31 percent of GDP in 1994.[60]

Has the imperfect transition to the market economy generated a demand for criminal protection? Géza Katona, former chief of the Investigation

Department of the National Police, links the initial shortcomings of the Hungarian transition to a market economy to the rise in the demand for mafia-related activities, in a lucid analysis that is worth quoting at length:

> A new arena has been created by organized crime during the 1990s: the so-called violence industry. It is quite normal for a newly established market economy to face serious capital shortages. The financial foundations of the private enterprises are usually very shaky and unstable. In such a situation the role of the state in the enforcement of private law becomes extremely important. The court's rapid, reliable, and effective enforcement of contracts, bankruptcy, and debt collection are crucial for the new economic actors. In this respect, the Hungarian state has miserably failed in the last few years. Civil law cases drag on for years, and the enforcement of judicial decisions is unreliable. The state has failed to establish a well-functioning legal and institutional system, to set up an effective legal framework for the private economy, or to pass an effective law on bankruptcy. . . . [It] has also failed to create and administer a reliable system for registering real property. This negligence has created a paradise for those who make use of others' well-meaning, law-abiding behavior. It is not surprising that businessmen, some law-abiding and others not, try to defend themselves and find other non-legal or semi-legal ways to defend their interests, without legal support from the state. The defects of state law enforcement have opened the field to organized crime, and their "violence" organizations have simply taken control of this area.[61]

Katona concludes by pointing out that organized crime has played a major role in the area of the extrajudicial settlement of disputes; indeed, it has virtually "taken over" this sphere.

Katona identifies a second area of opportunity for criminal organizations to control a market: the oil sector. After 1989, the former state oil trade monopoly ceased to exist while new regulations for the oil sector were still absent. Virtually anyone could establish a firm to sell oil; since the state failed to screen firms seeking official registration; meanwhile, due to the departure of the Soviet troops, vast storage facilities had become available. At the same time, the Hungarian government, in an effort to shield farmers and the poor from the full impact of high inflation and rising heating bills, introduced a dual-price system for heating and diesel oil. One side effect was the creation of artificial opportunities for money-making operations.[62]

In contrast to the virtual absence of mafia-related violence in Rome, the level of such brutality was high in Hungary. The *Washington Post* reported on December 21, 1998 that

> by 1996, violence began to spill onto the streets here. The Hungarian police have recorded 140 mob-related bombings, grenade attacks and killings since 1991, most in recent years. In November 1996, alleged mob leader Jozsef Prisztas was gunned down and killed on a Budapest street. In August 1997, shots were fired into a disco, wounding one woman. Last February [1998], a business magnate with alleged mob ties was assassinated with an automatic weapon as he sat in his car at a traffic light. A grenade was hurled at a bar the following month. And in June, shots were fired into a shop, injuring one person. Mobsters killing mobsters, however, engendered a certain so-what attitude among the public, officials said.[63]

Between 1991 and 1998, there were more than 100 gangland murders and 170 explosions in Hungary.[64]

An oblique reference to the Solntsevskaya appeared in the *Boston Globe* on November 29, 1998, which reported on a "Russian-speaking gang believed to be the most powerful and dangerous in Hungary." The article continued: "This mob, law enforcement sources said, has a presence in the United States."[65] I now turn more specifically to the activities of this group in Budapest.

Through Mogilevich, the Solntsevskaya created an intricate network of companies and factories in Hungary, laundering and investing a significant amount of money in the legal economy, mainly in arms production and the oil business. In 1995 Mogilevich bought Magnex 2000 (a magnet manufacturer in Budapest), the Army Co-op (a mortar and antiaircraft gun factory), Balchug (a firm that produces and sells office furniture), and Digep General Machine Works (an artillery shell, mortar, and fire equipment manufacturer). Mogilevich had been involved in the oil business since the 1980s, creating Arbat International, a petroleum export-import company of which he owned 50 percent (the other shareholders were Ivan'kov, Mikhailov, and Averin), and Arigon Ltd., which sold oil products to the Ukrainian railway administration and was allegedly managed by Mikhailov's wife. Most recently he has been connected to Eural Trans Gas, an obscure Hungarian company holding a contract with Gazprom to provide gas from Turkmenistan to Ukraine.[66]

The Solntsevskaya did not limit itself to investment in the legal economy but tried to defraud the Hungarian government and push competitors out of the oil market. In short, the government had passed a law subsidizing some gas consumption for home use, creating opportunities to arbitrage between the subsidized price and the market one. Several loopholes in the law made it easier for criminal elements to enter this market.[67] Some believe that the loophole might have been intentional. According to one view, the Hungarian secret services were also players in this market, exploiting the opportunity generated by this law in order to buy arms to help the Croatians in their war against Serbia during the Yugoslavian conflict in the 1990s. Although I have no way to confirm this interpretation, it is well known that Croatia armed itself in the lead-up to the war and that some weapons came from Hungary. Belgrade amassed evidence that Croatia's defense minister was importing arms from warehouses in Hungary.[68] In any case, the unintended consequences of a well-meaning policy that created easy opportunities to defraud the state and enforce criminal monopolies over supplies of oil constituted a second crucial factor fostering the growth of Russian groups in Hungary. It is widely believed that the warfare within the Hungarian underworld, which took place in the 1990s, and involved both Russian and Hungarian groups, was due to conflict over how to allocate lucrative state oil and gas contracts.[69] According to a BBC documentary on Mogilevich's activities, Zoltán Seres, one of his Hungarian partners, was "the victim of the Russian-Hungarian turf wars which have followed the oil rackets."[70] A businessperson involved in oil fraud, Tamás Boros, said during confessions made to the police in February 1997 and May 1998 that "company owners who had not imported oil through the Russian Mafia boss Semyon Mogilevich were threatened and blackmailed."[71] Boros was killed, together with three other victims, in a car bomb explosion in central Budapest in early July 1998.[72]

The Solntsevskaya has expanded beyond the oil business, runs protection rackets and prostitution rings in Budapest, and has tortured and murdered local opponents.[73] (Averin is suspected by the Hungarian police of the murder of a man in Budapest, Andrey Mochin. Also, he allegedly acted as an intermediary in the kidnapping of another man, Abner Kandov.) According to police sources cited by *Népszava* in 1998, a Hungarian daily, some eight hundred companies in Hungary have direct links to the underworld.[74] Although it is hard to discern the exact nature of the relationship between these firms and the underworld, mafia groups typically offer criminal protection to firms that cannot turn to the state. Partial evidence of this was revealed at the "bomb factory" trial of former Stasi agent Dietmar Clodo.[75] At the trial, several defendants named Leonid Goldstein Steigura as the second-in-command of Mogilevich's operation in Budapest and the real owner of the bomb-making facility run by Clodo. More importantly, a killer for the group, Nándor Erdélyi, claimed that criminals in Budapest had to pay a 50 percent "fee" to Steigura in order to be allowed to operate.[76] Furthermore, at the same trial it emerged that Steigura had planned Mogilevich's murder, possibly in an attempt to increase the autonomy of the group from the original, Moscow-based mafia.

Additional evidence of the ability of this Russian crime group to impose its protection on traders based in Hungary came to light in November 2003, when four men were arrested by the police with the FBI's help. They were charged with having forced their protection on as many as a thousand small businesspeople and shop owners, for a total income of some US$10 million. Police claim that the leader of the group, a Ukrainian Israeli Greek citizen, was working for Mogilevich.[77] As recently as March 2007, officials in Hungary believed that Russian-speaking groups were well entrenched in the country. The 2006 yearly report of Hungary's National Security Authority states that "it is still the case that Hungarian and Russian-speaking organized crime groups are the dominant forces in Hungary." Among other sectors, Russian organized crime groups are entering Hungary's booming construction material trade, the report says.[78]

Although the evidence is sketchy, it appears that the Solntsevskaya and Russian criminal groups more generally have established themselves in Hungary—contrary to the outcome that we observed in Rome. The Russian mafia is simultaneously trying to exercise a monopoly over certain sectors of the economy, such as the oil business, and offering criminal protection to both businesspeople in the gray economy and criminal entrepreneurs. It has penetrated into the economy and has sustained its activity for a long period of time.

Conclusions

The comparison between Rome and Budapest allows us to identify key factors at work in Mafia transplantation (table 4.2).

A number of elements are shared by both cases, suggesting that they do not explain the divergent outcome. In both cases generalized migration from Russia was negligible. Also, Russian mafiosi were in Rome and Budapest due to forced migration (Rome) or accident (past Soviet presence). The crucial difference between Rome and Budapest was the presence in the latter of new and booming markets (legal and illegal) that were not adequately protected by state institutions, thereby generating a demand for nonstate forms of protection. This is the key variable that leads to long-term entrenchment.

The emergence of vast market opportunities unregulated and unprotected by the state offers incentives for mafiosi from different territories to exploit local opportunities by offering criminal protection. Hungary experienced both the inability of the state to clearly define and protect property rights, and the presence of lucrative opportunities to obtain selective access to valuable markets, such as oil and gas, through the use of violence (Bardonecchia experienced only the latter, lucrative opportunities in the construction business). This concatenation of factors increases the likelihood of mafia transplantation. Such a conclusion goes against supply-side explanations of both the origin and diffusion of mafias—that is, against the idea that the presence of a supply of criminally minded people is sufficient for a mafia to develop in a new territory. If mafiosi exist in an area where no significant unprotected market exists, I contend that they will simply be unemployed mafia enforcers.

The Hungarian case indicates that circumstances conducive to mafia transplantation can be the product of state failures to equip a country fast enough with the institutional features of a market economy, such as a well-functioning legal system as well as clearly defined and enforced property

TABLE 4.2

Factors Facilitating Mafia Transplantation, Bardonecchia, Verona, Budapest, and Rome

Factors facilitating mafia transplantation/cases	Bardonecchia	Verona	Budapest	Rome	New York City (1910–30)	Rosario (1910–30)	Shenzhen/ Guangzhou
Generalized migration	Yes	No	No	No			
Mafiosi migration (willing/unwilling)	Yes (unwilling)	Yes (unwilling)	Yes (unwilling)	Yes (unwilling)			
Supply of mafiosi	Yes	Yes	Yes	Yes			
Local conditions							
Level of trust/civic engagement	High	High	Low	Low			
Presence of local illegal protectors	No	No	No	No			
Size of locale	Small	Large	Large	Large			
New and/or booming markets*	Yes	Yes	Yes	Yes			
Demand for mafia services	Yes	No	Yes	No			
Transplantation	Yes	No	Yes	No			

* The markets considered are construction (Bardonecchia and Rosario), drugs (Verona and China), property rights (Budapest and China), oil (Budapest), alcohol (New York City), gambling (New York City and China), and prostitution (China).

rights. The unintended results of a well-meaning policy that created easy opportunities to defraud the state and enforce criminal monopolies over supplies of oil constituted a second crucial factor fostering the move of Russian groups to Hungary.

Still, the Italian authorities have reason to worry about the ease with which Russians were able to launder money in the country. Italy has rather inflexible instruments to deal with this crime. Whenever financial authorities come across irregularities and suspicious activities, they can only initiate a superficial investigation and then turn the evidence over to a prosecutor's office, where thousands of similar files await the attention of the judiciary.[79] The jurisdiction over financial crimes in Italy belongs almost entirely to the criminal prosecutor, and both financial institutions and prosecutors have to uphold the *segreto istruttorio*: the duty to keep the identities of persons under investigation secret. This provision stops the authorities from exposing businesses that engage in sharp practices or become conduits of money laundering, hence eliminating reputational sanctions. Other jurisdictions (such as the United Kingdom) allow the financial authorities to conduct parallel investigations, which turn out to be faster, and also involve civil sanctions and incentives for collaboration on the part of the businesses involved. As the cases of Bardonecchia and Budapest show, it might well be that criminal markets open up while a foreign mafia is residing in the new territory and engaging in money-laundering activities. At that point, conditions conducive to long-term entrenchment would obtain.

Appendix

WIRETAP RECORDS

The police investigation into the Solntsevskaya crime group started in 1995 and lasted three years, from 1995 to 1997. By January 1996, the police were consistently listening in on twenty-four phone lines (cell phones and terrestrial lines). A total of nineteen people used such lines. The protagonists of this story talk about incriminating matters on the phone, including the use of violence and torture along with the murders that they plot and later carry out. If they had talked strategically on the phone, we would expect them not to reveal so much and to omit information that under any legislation could result in a lengthy sentence. Furthermore, the police validated the content of some conversations by tailing several individuals and checking their movements within Italy as well as to and from Italy.

For the purpose of this chapter, I have carried out a systematic content analysis of the conversations that were recorded by the police in order to establish the topics discussed and the tasks undertaken by the group in Rome. With the assistance of Paolo Campana, I created a file with all the conversations recorded by the police for the period 1995–96. For each conversation, we coded the topics discussed (each conversation could include several topics). The total number of topics for all conversations comes to sixty-nine. We also identified the task that the actors were discussing. Drawing on the theoretical discussion outlined in chapter 2, we identified four tasks: resource acquisition, investment in the economy, involvement in protection rackets, and maintaining internal order. Taken together, these tasks cover all the conversation segments, save for three (see table 4.1). Most of the conversations (97.5 percent) took place without an interpreter between the two speakers.

We made several decisions regarding these data. The conversations are informal, and jargon is often used. The informal nature of the conversations implies that hidden meanings are transmitted. An automatic form of coding, such as counting words, would not register such meanings. Hence, we decided to read and code each conversation manually. We also coded segments of conversation. A segment of conversation, as noted earlier, is a fragment of a conversation that has a meaningful beginning and end. In order to reduce coder bias, we undertook intercoder reliability tests for the tasks, which resulted in a high and statistically significant correlation coefficient between the two coders. (The two coders read a sample of the conversations [N = 20], identified the tasks and topics, and checked the level of intercoder reliability. The correlation coefficient between the two coders resulted in 0.95, p = 0.001.) This degree of concordance enhances our confidence in the reliability of the results.

Third, while studying the files, we decided to use only the conversations from January 1996 to October 1996 (N = 758). This is because the wiretapping started in earnest in January (only two conversations were recorded in 1995). In December 1995, phone lines and cell phone numbers were still being put under surveillance, and the police recorded few conversations.[80] The end point is late October 1996, a few weeks after Sergeev was killed.

We also coded quantitative information on the group and extracted network data. The police intercepted no fewer than 164 individuals over the period of the investigation. Of the 164 individuals involved in criminal conversations, 115 (more than 70 percent) were men, and the overwhelming majority were either Italian (50 people, or 30 percent) or born in the former Soviet Union (107 people, or 65 percent). Additional nationalities were Polish (2) and Korean (2); the nationality of 3 individuals is unknown. The place of birth, however, may be a poor indication of where the actors actually operated at the time of this investigation. We could reconstruct this type of information for 161 of the 164 actors. These data confirm that most of the individuals operated in either Rome (47.6 percent) or Moscow (20.5 percent). The median year of birth is 1957 (thirty-nine years old in 1996). This suggests that the group was made up of rather experienced individuals—an age profile similar to the Sicilian mafia.[81]

We created three network data sets: a global network of 164 actors; a directed global network where we recorded who initiated the call (as we could not find this information for all calls, this data set contains only 138 actors); and a longitudinal directed network, which includes 138 actors, with the direction of the call split at three points in time (I–III/96, IV–VI/96, and VII–IX/96). Finally, we matched several attributes (gender, language(s) spoken, nationality, and tasks) to the actors by creating an attribute file. In a series of future journal articles, we will present the results of this more sophisticated analysis.

Table A4.2 shows official data from the population censuses on foreign residents in Hungary since 1990 as a percentage of the total population. The data in the first column refer to people whose mother tongue is other than Hungarian.

The data in table A4.2 suggest that many other groups besides Russians and Ukrainians have settled in Hungary, and that their numbers are negligible compared with the total population. In 1991 almost 40,000 people spoke German as their mother tongue, or some 0.3 percent of the total population. Other languages more widely spoken than Russian and Ukrainian were Croatian (17,577 people), Slovakian (12,745), and Roma-

TABLE A4.1

Summary Characteristics of Key Players, Russian Mafia in Rome

Name (changed)	Nationality	Background	Function
Yakovlev, Ivan	Russian	Crime	Boss
Pepe, Giovanni	Italian	Journalism	Local fixer
Sergeev, Boris	Russian	Business/crime	Russian businessperson close to the Solntsevskaya, murdered in 1996
Bogdanovich, Oleg	Russian	Crime	Boss's bodyguard and gofer
Facchini, Giorgio	Italian	Politics	Local fixer
Sergeeva, Nadia	Russian		Sergeev's wife
Kamenskaya, Alina	Russian		Facchini's wife
Brenno, Riccardo	Italian	Business	Business associate of the group
Kamenskii, Vadim	Russian		Facchini's son
Artamova, Raisa	Russian		Sidelnikov's wife, keeper of the common fund
Pepe, Elena	Italian		Pepe's wife
Sidelnikov, Fedya	Russian	Crime	Boss's right-hand man
Yakovleva, Marina	Russian		Boss's wife
Sidorov, Vladimir	Russian	Crime	Boss's right-hand man
Kostina, Sonya	Russian		Sergeev's Italian wife
Sergeev, Denis	Russian		Sergeev's son
Rostovtsev	Russian	KGB	Based in Moscow, keeps contacts with Italian embassy and the political elite in Russia
Vlasik	Russian	Business	Business partner, murdered in 1996
Sergeeva, Ekaterina	Russian		Sergeev's daughter
Manin	Russian	Politics	Russian politician
Yakovlev, Alex	Russian		Boss's son
Ferrari, Marco	Italian	Petty crime	Associate of the group
Rossi, Donatella	Italian		Office secretary

nian (8,730). Polish (3,788) is just below the level of Russian. According to the 1995 data column, Romania, Serbia, Germany, and Poland all have more nationals in Hungary than the Ukraine, and the number of Russians is negligible. In 1995, Ukrainians accounted for 0.034 percent of the entire population. If we add the Russians, the combined percentage amounted to 0.036 percent in 1995.

Table A4.2
Total Population and Foreign Citizens Residing in Hungary by Country, 1990–2005

	1990*	1995	1996	1997	1998	1999	2000	2005
Total population		10,245,677	10,212,300	10,174,442			10,138,844	10,006,835
Romania	8,730	68,439	65,705	61,579	62,130	57,357	57,343	41,561
Serbia and Montenegro	2953	15,297	16,173	15,449	14,250	15,223	15,571	12,664
Ukraine	674	3,501	4,432	5,625	7,184	9,898	11,016	8,947
Germany	37,511	7,427	7,802	8,277	8,985	9,396	9,631	7,493
Poland	3,788	4,628	4,521	4,297	4,471	4,386	4,144	2,279
Russia	3,902	277	1,124	1,708	2,502	2,809	3,002	1,893
Slovakia	12,745	231	461	600	968	1,571	1,717	1,576
Croatia	17,577	305	532	688	929	1069	1,162	917
Austria	***	616	694	872	1,031	990	1,053	694
China	204	3,469	4,276	6639	7,809	8,306	8,861	5,819
United States	410**	1,700	2,008	2,420	2,835	3,132	3,261	1,636
Africa	229	2,081	2,210	2,488	2,659	2,594	2,559	1,233
Australia and Oceania	**	573	717	734	750	812	779	507
Total foreign****		138,101	139,954	142,506	148,263	150,245	153,125	110,028
Total population	10,381,959	10,245,677	10,212,300	10,174,442			10,138,844	10,006,835

Notes: * Data refer to people who declare that they speak a given language as their mother tongue
** People who give English as their mother tongue; for 1990, Australians are counted under the United States.
*** Austrian nationals are counted as German speakers in this column.
**** Total includes more countries than those listed in the table.

Sources: Központi Statisztikai Hivatal (Central Statistics Office), available at http://portal.ksh.hu/pls/ksh/docs/eng/xstadat/xstadat_annual/tabl1_06iea.html; http://www.nepszamlalas.hu/eng/volumes/06/00/tabeng/1/prnt01_11_0.html.

FIVE

Lessons from the Past: Sicilian Mafiosi in New York City and Rosario, circa 1880–1940

A tough young man with neither prospects nor any intention of working in the sulfur mines or fields of his hometown, Siculiana, in the Agrigento Province of Italy, Nick Gentile—also known as Zu Cola (1885–unknown) and author of the first insider's account of the American mafia—preferred to try his luck abroad. A well-oiled network allowed him to reach the United States and land in New York City in 1903 at the age of eighteen, with an address in hand, 91 Elizabeth Street, in one of the city's Sicilian colonies. His U.S. contact, who directed immigrants from Siculiana and the nearby villages to their place of employment, sent Gentile to do railroad construction in Kansas City, a six-day train journey from New York. In a few years, Gentile did away with his work clothes, sporting expensive suits and darting scowling eyes in the pictures that survived.[1] A fellow Sicilian, Gaetano Pendino, from Alessandria della Rocca, a small town some forty kilometers from Siculiana, chose instead to migrate to Argentina, where he arrived in 1888 at the age of thirty-five. After working as a bricklayer and builder, he eventually established himself as the boss of the mafia in Rosario. This mafia, however, lasted only a relatively short period of time. Scholars who link the emergence of the mafia in New York City to Italian migration ignore the fact that in the same period many Italians, including those of a criminal bent, migrated to several other destinations. Yet not everywhere Italians went did a stable and long-lasting criminal organization with features similar to the Sicilian Cosa Nostra emerge. After sketching the contours of the mafia in Sicily in the nineteenth century, this chapter outlines the parallel history of Italian migration and mafia activities in New York City and Rosario, and offers an analytic account of the diverging outcomes.

THE MAFIA IN SICILY

The first clear sign that a Mafia existed in Sicily dates from the 1830s. In 1838, the procurator general of Trapani wrote that "in many villages, there exist fellowships [*unioni*] or fraternities" led by a boss. Each fraternity had a common fund, and the members included ordinary people, landowners, and even priests. One service that they performed was to retrieve stolen property, in particular cattle. The official perceptively dubbed the societies "small governments within the government," suggesting that by this time they were already an established extralegal form of governance, in competition with the state.[2]

After unification (1861), the "Southern Question" became a burning political issue for the new Italy. The government struggled to impose the rule of law on Sicily, where insecurity and "banditism" were rife, and it feared rebellions and secessionist movements inspired by the defeated Bourbons and the Catholic church. Dissatisfied with an official report on the state of affairs in the island, a twenty-nine-year-old Tuscan aristocrat, Leopoldo Franchetti, set out for Sicily in 1876 to undertake independent research on the *Condizioni politiche ed amministrative della Sicilia*. Franchetti's study ranks among the classics of nineteenth-century social science, on par with Alexis de Tocqueville's *Democracy in America*. Among his numerous insights, he wrote that members of the mafia belonged to all classes and occupations, including the middle class, and were autonomous from other social and political entities, such as the state. He also suggested that the mafia's single most important activity was ensuring selective access to key resources, in a context where the state was unable to offer fair and universal rules. More specifically, Franchetti documented the existence of cartels among producers backed by the mafia. In one case, a society of millers (*la società dei Mulini*) was said by Franchetti to be under the protection of "powerful Mafiosi." Members of the society kept the price of flour artificially high, and the capo mafia ensured that everybody followed the agreement and did not free ride on fellow society members by producing more than the agreed-on quota.[3]

FIGURE 5.1 Map of Sicily

By the end of the nineteenth century, some organizational features of this secret fraternity had been identified. A book published in 1886 and based on police documents dating back to 1860 describes in detail the structure of some early *cosche* (individual, autonomous "families"), the division of territory, and the mechanisms of coordination among them. Rather than a single giant organization stretching across the entire island, the mafia was composed of cosche, located in western Sicily, who recognized each others' right to exist, and had devised means to coordinate activities and settle interfamily disputes. A police report compiled in 1898 and 1900, the *Rapporto Sangiorgi*, names eight mafia families operating in Palermo and the nearby villages at the time. It identifies the bosses and the underbosses, and includes personal details on many of the rank-and-file members. The document recounts the initiation ritual, code of behavior, and many markets that the mafiosi had penetrated, and confirms that a coordinating body linked the cosche of Palermo to those operating on the city's outskirts. According to the report, some 218 individuals had joined this society. Scholars often marvel at the striking continuity of the mafia's organizational structure from its origin in the first part of the nineteenth century to the time of the revelations during the Maxi trial in the 1980s.[4]

From the mid-nineteenth century, many Sicilians, including members of the mafia, were on the move. In the remainder of this chapter, I will trace their migration to New York City and Rosario, Argentina. Most crucially, only in the North American city did a mafia that resembled the Sicilian one emerge. Below, I explain why.

The Italian American Mafia in New York City

New York City was a key destination for the first wave of European immigrants— mostly Irish and Germans—who arrived in the 1840s, in the wake of the potato famine in Ireland. Jews from Eastern Europe landed in the 1880s, while most of the Italians reached their new *patria* in the period between 1876 and 1915. The number of Italians in New York City rose from just over 12,000 in 1880 to just over 145,000 in 1900 (see table A5.1). By 1910, immigrants and first-generation Italian Americans accounted for 500,000 New Yorkers—a tenth of the city's population. When the First World War broke out, 370,000 Italians lived in New York City.[5] Between 1876 and 1930, some 80 percent of Italian migrants to the United States had originated from southern Italy (see table 5.3 below). Italians reached New York City within a short time span and arrived relatively late in the city's own development, when other ethnic groups had already established themselves. The majority of them joined the unskilled labor force.[6]

Nested within the flow of Italians to New York City were people who had mafia skills and had been initiated into cosche back home. Many were running from the reach of state organs. For instance, Ignazio Lupo became embroiled in a dispute in his store in Palermo in 1898, which ended with Lupo murdering a man. He went into hiding and, on the advice of his parents, fled Italy, reaching New York, where he joined a gang of counterfeiters headed by Giuseppe Morello (see below). Similarly Joseph Bonanno narrates that his father, a man of honor back in their hometown of Castellammare del Golfo, moved to Brooklyn in 1908 in order to avoid prosecution (later returning to Sicily in 1911). The same applies to Giuseppe Joe Masseria, who apparently fled his hometown to avoid murder charges.[7]

Some mafiosi were running away from other mafiosi. The corpse of Antonio Deodati, a Sicilian counterfeiter, was found in 1865 in the woods near Greenwood Cemetery, Brooklyn, having suffered pistol shots to the head. Italian authorities, in a report cited by the *Times* (London), on June 21, 1875, claimed that Deodati had fled to New York City in order to escape a mafia feud, but was "overtaken by an assassin, especially sent out after him, and horribly murdered."[8]

One political development prompting some mafiosi to run off to the United States was Benito Mussolini's accession to power in 1922. In October 1925, Mussolini appointed Cesare Mori as a special prefect to Palermo, giving him vast police powers and an army of elite agents to eradicate the "honored society." Dubbed the "Iron Prefect," and aided by some landowners and businesspeople, Mori rounded up and imprisoned scores of clan bosses as well as innocent bystanders. Bonanno—the future boss of the Bonanno family in New York City—writes in his autobiography that in 1924,

> a tempest would tatter my sails and toss my ship in unknown waters. Now undisputedly in control of the national government, Mussolini sought to eradicate all dissent and to install a totalitarian regime. . . . Men of my Tradition reviled Mussolini, once he showed his true colors, ... [and] were imprisoned in droves, often on the flimsiest charges. They were tried and sentenced with utter disregard for their civil liberties.[9]

In fact, mafiosi were far less antifascist at first, and even planned to support a fascist party list in the 1924 elections.[10] By late 1925, though, Mori's policies had begun to have some effect and forced many mafia members to escape. Antonio Calderone (b. 1935), the Catania underboss, writes in his memoirs: "There was nearly no mafia left after the war. Sicilian families had been shut down by prefect Mori."[11] Some of Calderone's relatives escaped to Tunis, where by the 1930s a mafia outpost was fully operational.[12] The boss of Tommaso Buscetta's family in Palermo took shelter in France instead. Bonanno explains that "many [men of my tradition] were forced to flee to America" as a consequence of Mori's action in Sicily.[13] David Chandler, in his book *The Criminal Brotherhoods*, suggests that no less than five hundred mafiosi escaped Mussolini's regime by immigrating to the United States, although such a figure is most likely an exaggeration.[14] In conclusion, a contingent of Sicilian mafiosi was present in North America.

PROTECTIVE UMBRELLAS

Did Sicilian mafiosi find in New York City a land rich in criminal opportunities that would allow them to re-create the control of markets and territories they had in their homeland? I now turn to a brief description of New York City, and the opportunities to control markets and enforce protection rackets. In the mid-nineteenth century, the city was already one of the world's greatest metropolises. By 1860, it handled two-thirds of all U.S. imports and one-third of its export trade, and ranked first in the country in all but seven items of exportable goods.[15] In transportation links and banking, New York towered over the rest of the country. By 1890, its population was almost double the 1860 figure. Manhattan dominated the women's and men's clothing trade, and ranked first nationally in the number of factories, their capital valuation, gross domestic product, and number of employees. A great deal of its economic achievements depended on the continuing availability of cheap immigrant and nonunionized labor working in appalling conditions.[16]

The new wave of Italian and Jewish immigrants in the 1880s settled near their compatriots, mainly in the low-rent, run-down areas of the Lower East Side (their arrival encouraged the Irish and German residents to leave). In the Fifth Ward Neapolitans lived mainly on Mulberry Street, while the Genoese and Sicilians settled, respectively, on Baxter and Elizabeth Streets. Northern Italians were to be found in the Eighth or Fifteenth Wards west of Broadway.[17] The Italian neighborhood of Five Points was "at the time perhaps the worst slum in the world."[18] The West Twenties (starting around West Twenty-third Street) was the hub for gambling dens, brothels, and late-night saloons. A police captain labeled this area the "Tenderloin," while a less-endearing name, "Satan's Circle," originated with enraged preachers. In a lengthy article published in 1909, *McClure Magazine* called Satan's Circle "the recognized metropolis of American criminals."[19] Vice also flourished somewhat south of the Tenderloin, in the Battery, Five Points, and Bowery, close to where the Italians lived.[20]

The illegal markets of sex and gambling were sizable. In 1897, New York had some 30,000 public prostitutes. By 1900, there were more than 250 brothels in Satan's Circle, and over a thousand poolrooms and card rooms in Manhattan. These services were illegal, but who was protecting them? The most profitable illegal markets since the mid-nineteenth century in the city were protected by an alliance of corrupt politicians and police officers. This was the time when "political machines" dominated U.S. cities—a system that ensured the distribution of jobs and favors in exchange for votes. The most influential organization in New York City was the Society of Tammany, the Democratic political club on East Fourteenth Street. In each election ward, a "captain" was responsible for making sure that votes would flow toward Tammany's candidates. Often, the captain employed gangs of petty criminals who would vote more than once (they were known as "repeaters"). In exchange, the captain ensured that jobs, contracts, and permits were handed out to the politically well connected, although the ward captain frequently provided genuine help to the newly arrived destitute residents. Yet merit was hardly a concern for appointing somebody to public office: often people with a criminal record were selected to work as court clerks, while judges and prosecutors routinely accepted bribes. Between 1886 and 1902, Tammany was headed by a former street brawler and petty gangster who had been tried for murder.[21]

Police recruitment was in the hands of ward leaders and activists, who would recommend a potential recruit directly to police commissioners, bypassing the uncertain and demanding application to the Civil Service Board, an independent body that appointed officers on merit. During the last decade of the nineteenth century, individuals following the former route had a nine-in-ten chance of being successful, while those applying through the latter had a one-in-eight chance. Not only did recruits have to be connected to local politicians but they also had to pay in the region of $250 to $300 (a full year's pay was $600) to join, and substantially more to be promoted (a captaincy cost somewhere between $12,000 and $15,000).[22]

"Big Tim" Sullivan (1862–1913) was at various points district leader of the wards that comprised the Five Points and Satan's Circle. As historian Mike Dash has vividly shown, the Democratic machine led by Sullivan not only manipulated polls but also enforced a strict protection racket, collecting money from saloons, brothels, and gambling establishments in exchange for protection from law enforcement. Sullivan used new immigrants, including Italians, as enforcers for his get-the-vote operations, but racketeering was done by the political-police alliance. Police officers on the ground extracted payments and kicked a portion of their take "up" to senior officers and their political allies. In other parts of the city, "clubbers" also helped employers keep peace with labor, and ensured that workers would be intimidated and harassed when going on strike and marching through the city. Arrests were often arbitrary and a source of graft; it was common practice for police on the beat to arrest people and have them locked up at the nearest station house. The charge would then be dropped, and the bail money went into the pocket of the arresting officer, their precinct captain, and the bondsperson (in 1909, 262,000 arrests had been made in New York City, compared to 111,000 in London, despite its larger population). Corruption was so widespread that officers would not bother to investigate robberies unless the victim offered a reward. Thieves were permitted to operate within carefully defined territories on the condition that they handed back the proceeds of certain robberies on demand, so that the police officer could claim to have recovered the stolen merchandise. On the other hand, owners of brothels and gambling dives obtained a degree of safety for their money. Police Commissioner William McAdoo observed: "A corrupt police captain doesn't have to force payments. They will thrust money upon him and those under him. These men and women feel that when they pay their money they are going to be protected."[23]

A damning investigation into the system of graft in the state Senate—the Lexow Committee of 1894–95—set in motion some key reforms. Building on the committee report, the city administration reduced discretion for recruitment into the police force, bringing to an end the practice of paying a fee to join. To a degree, this reform reduced the intimate ties between the police and politicians, but it was not enough to stop the grafting. Freed from their political overlords, the New York police simply began to keep the income from corruption for themselves. According to the *New York Times'* calculations published in 1900, the owners of the city's largest gambling clubs paid as much as $12,000 a year for protection; smaller operators were required to part with nearly $2,000; poolrooms stayed open in exchange for $300 a month and craps games for $150. Millions were handed over to the police every year, in "taxes" that were—according to the newspaper—as fixed in size and regularity as the "laws of Medes and Persians."[24] Similarly, brothel owners paid heavily for police protection, and, if they failed to do so, found themselves mercilessly raided.[25]

By 1910, a combination of effective reforms and a few driven individuals led to the virtual end of grand graft. The reformist district attorney, William Travers Jerome (a cousin of Winston Churchill who had worked for the Lexow Committee), joined forces with the mayor, Judge William Jay Gaynor, elected in 1910, to enact and see through far-reaching reforms. First, the mayor appointed a like-minded police commissioner, Rhine lander Waldo. He went on to put an end to arbitrary arrests by the police; for trivial matters, police officers now were to issue a simple summon, otherwise every arrest was to be based on legal evidence and the suspect was to be taken before a magistrate on the day of the arrest. The aim was to dry up a major source of bribes for the arresting officer and precinct captain. Gaynor encouraged the prosecution of police officers who raided premises without the proper warrant and advised gamblers that they should resist arrest if the police did not show the correct paperwork. Then, observing that the New York Police Department regularly broke up strikes as well as dispersed meetings organized by socialists and anarchists, he instructed officers to protect pickets and marchers, so long as the protesters obeyed the law. This was at a time when militancy was on the rise. For instance, in 1909, some seventy thousand "shirtwaist" women had gone on a strike led by Clara Lemlich. Gaynor's biographer writes: "During 1910 immigrant workers . . . fought out a long, bitter strike, and Gaynor kept the police, who before notoriously sided with the employers, out of the dispute."[26] These measures worked. By the end of 1910, arrests had fallen by one-third, police behavior had noticeably improved, and some of the force's most unrepentant grafters had been summarily dismissed. In addition, trade union activities were growing.[27]

Mayor Gaynor went further: he centralized policing, so that officers on the beat did not have the power to raid establishments. Police officers made a lot of money by threatening to shut down bars and taverns that violated Sunday closing laws (there were nine thousand saloons and eighteen hundred hotels serving liquor in New York). For a bribe, the officers could be persuaded to look the other way. The mayor's solution was twofold: first, he called the Liquor Dealers' Association and ordered its members to stop paying protection money. He then issued

William Jay Gaynor (1848–1913), mayor of New York City (1910–13), hit by a bullet. Source: Frederic Lewis, photographer/Hutton Archive/Getty Images.

instructions ordering police officers to stop entering licensed premises or speaking to their owners. Detectives were forbidden to make on-the-spot arrests or report violations of the law to their captain. Rather, they were to file an affidavit for each violation with the district attorney, where intelligence would be collated and indictments prepared. Remarkably, the plan worked. Violations of the Sunday closing law fell to a mere handful within two weeks. By the beginning of 1911 saloon graft had been practically wiped out for the first time in living memory. One bartender, who had worked thirty-five years in the New York liquor trade, marveled that he had never known a time "when the laws were so nearly enforced in their intent as they are today. Mayor Gaynor has done away with the collector who used to come around from 'the man higher up.'"[28] The city newspapers were effusive in their praise.[29]

The mayor applied the same logic to the policing of gambling and prostitution. Until then, the suppression of vice had been the responsibility of New York's fifty or so precinct captains, each of whom would gather intelligence and order raids in their own district. The mayor transferred responsibility for policing brothels and gaming clubs to headquarters, forbidding precinct cops from mounting raids and opening up the possibility of gathering intelligence from all five boroughs. Thus, corrupt captains could no longer offer ironclad protection. Gaynor hoped that this would make it easier to curb graft as well as deal with the most influential madams and gamblers, some of whom controlled premises all over the city.[30]

Such innovations were complemented by the creation of special police squads, based at the headquarters and reporting directly to the commissioner. These squads would conduct raids that had hitherto been carried out at the precinct level and—properly led and supplied with detailed information—might well succeed in closing down establishments that had enjoyed police protection. Most of the targets for the raids were selected by the police commissioner or mayor, acting in response to tip-offs received from members of the public who were—it seems more than likely—in many cases rivals of the gamblers on whom they informed. This system made it virtually impossible for unscrupulous officers, bent on continuing to extort gambling dens and brothels, to offer effective protection, as they had no power to stop raids or be informed beforehand that a raid was being set up. Further reforms to reduce waste and improve accounting practices were introduced by Gaynor's successor, elected in 1914.[31]

Early Italian Criminality

At first, Sicilians with a criminal inclination, and even members of Sicilian cosche, did not embark on activities that indicated an ability to control markets or specialize in protection, contrary to what they did in Sicily.

In other words, there might have been mafiosi, but there was as yet no mafia because the police was performing this function. For instance, Italians were involved in counterfeiting from at least the 1860s. One gang of counterfeiters, all originating from Messina, was exposed in 1865 in connection with the Deodati murder. Another significant murder connected to this trade—that of Antonio Flaccomio, who was stabbed to death in 1888 at the corner of St. Marks Place and Third Avenue by a counterfeiter named Carlo Quatertaro—led Chief Inspector Thomas Byrnes to declare that Sicilians "banded together in a secret society known as the Mafia" were the culprits.[32] Morello (1867–1930) and his brother-in-law, Lupo, led one prominent counterfeiting gang based in East Harlem. The forgeries were manufactured in upstate New York. Morello and Lupo then sold them to wholesalers at thirty to forty cents on the dollar for distribution throughout the country. By 1899, Morello was an influential figure in East Harlem, along with his brothers Tony and Vincent and their half-brother Ciro Terranova. Counterfeiting generated great alarm among U.S. authorities, since it was undermining confidence in the currency, and significant resources were devoted to stopping it. These efforts were successful, and by 1910 massive police repression led to the virtual death of this criminal activity. The participants themselves understood that the costs of engaging in this trade were high. As late as 1963, novices taking the mafia ritual oath in New York were still required to promise not to take part in counterfeiting.[33]

Italians were also stealing horses at the turn of the twentieth century in New York City. In 1908, more than a hundred complaints reached police headquarters from people whose horses and wagons had disappeared, causing insurance rates to rise. A year later, a network was discovered, "working on a scale unknown even in the days of 'horse lifting' in the West," the *New York Times* reported in October 1909.[34] The stolen animals were taken to a stable where they were kept before being sold. The police identified 334–337 East 108th Street, in Italian Harlem, as the hub of the ring. And yet there were no territorial disputes between different gangs of horse thieves, and in any case the business died when motorized public transport and automobile usage increased.[35]

At the turn of the century, a crude technique of random extortion known as "Black Hand" came to define the perception of southern Italian immigrants in the mind of the U.S. public. The standard Black Hand

Giuseppe Morello (1867–1930), a prominent counterfeiter in New York City. Photo credit: David Critchley.

crime consisted of sending a letter to businesspeople and shopkeepers in Italian neighborhoods warning them of dire consequences if they failed to pay up. Invariably, the picture of a black hand fringed by a knife and skull was imprinted on each letter. The Black Handers did not attempt to control markets, territory, or even the name Black Hand, although some gangs formed and celebrated rituals. Soon, every crime committed by Italians was credited to the Black Hand, and press excitement encouraged both the real practice and the emergence of fakes. Continued press coverage led to more and more letters being sent. The Black Hand brand proliferated in several U.S. cities, but it did not correspond to any specific organization. Eventually it died out, perhaps for lack of a connection to a specific mob able to prevent other lesser entities from using the same logo (Black Hand); when inefficient groups used the label, victims realized that they could safely avoid paying. [36]

In conclusion, before Gaynor's reforms, Italians were involved in a variety of crimes—counterfeiting, horse theft, and crude extortion—but they had not yet managed to reproduce the control of markets and territories typical of Sicily in New York City.

THE BIRTH OF THE MAFIA

Paradoxically, the end of widespread police corruption instigated by Gaynor's reforms and more generally by the Progressive movement led to the birth of the mafia. Police reform had left a void to be filled by new actors. As policing was being centralized, an organization able to coordinate illegal activities was much needed. For instance, a mafia could prevent rival gamblers from informing on each other and enforce an informal license system. It could put pressure on local police officers on the beat not to pass information to headquarters. Around this time, Italians started to protect brothels and gambling establishments. In a few years, Lucky Luciano would be indicted for controlling no less than eighty brothels in Manhattan. The protection that Gaynor's reforms afforded to trade unions led some employers to turn to mafiosi rather than corrupt police officers. The former leader of the notorious Five Points Gang, the Italian Paul Kelly (Paolo Vaccarelli), moved into labor racketeering at this time. Some workers too turned to extralegal help. In 1913, an Italian gang that had been implicated in crude Black Hand extortion offered its violent services to workers (not employers, in this case) in the garment industry. Mafiosi rather quickly started to offer their services to market operators who wanted to keep some competitors out of a given industry or expel troublesome insiders, and enforce cartels among a limited amount of producers, as they did in the case of millers in Sicily I discussed at the beginning of this chapter. Gaetano "Tom" Reina (the future boss of the Lucchese family), Tommaso Gagliano (also a future boss in the same family), and Jack Dragna were implicated in the murder of a poultry dealer in 1914, Barnet Baff. The dealer had volunteered information to the district attorney's office on a cartel of eighty-seven other dealers. Industry insiders who wanted to punish the defector had orchestrated the murder. Italians infiltrated other industries, such as barbershops, the garment industry, and the docks. Over the subsequent decade, they continued to organize cartels, such as the Bronx lathing and plastering industry, the fiefdom of the Lucchese family since at least 1928. Although some Italian criminals could be found operating in illegal markets at the apex of Tammany, they typically were not the protectors, but rather the operators of brothels and shady saloons. It was only after the reforms described above that their role changed.[37]

A major impetus to the expansion of the Italian American mafia was the creation of yet another vast illegal and unprotected market. Legislation intended to prohibit the "manufacture, sale, or transportation of intoxicating liquor" culminated in the approval by the U.S. Congress of the Eighteenth Amendment to the Constitution in January 1919. By the end of 1919, thirty-six states had ratified the amendment. Prohibition and its enforcement machinery, the Volstead Act, came into effect at midnight on January 16, 1920. This "noble experiment" (in the words of President Herbert Hoover) was part of the same Progressive movement that had succeeded in reducing grand graft and police corruption in the first decade of the twentieth century.[38]

An illegal market estimated to be worth some two billion dollars a year was born overnight.[39] The bulk of the alcohol that reached consumers was either produced abroad and smuggled into the country (the so-called high seas or rum-running operations), or produced illegally in the United States and transported on land. As a rule, higher-quality merchandise was produced abroad while domestic producers manufactured the cheaper-grade liquor.[40]

Those who imported liquor from abroad formed international networks of cooperation. The Canadian-U.S. border (some thousand miles long) was one point of entry for land smuggling operations. Thus, several U.S. traffickers teamed up with Canadian distillery conglomerates and liquor distributors. Another method of getting the goods to the East Coast market was by means of ocean vessels anchored offshore in international waters, on "Rum Row," as the stretch of coast on Long Island and northern New Jersey came to be known. The ships would sell their cargo to the owners of high-speed "feeder" boats, who would then bring the merchandise to beaches on Long Island and northern New Jersey.[41]

The alcohol coming in from Rum Row would be loaded onto trucks and sent to depots located in Manhattan. The market was fraught with dangers. Hijackers of vessels were a serious problem for sailors bringing cargo from abroad. Herbert Asbury (the author of *Gangs of New York*) recalls in his 1950 study of Prohibition that "these seagoing hijackers, in fast boats, swarmed along the Row and robbed everybody they could catch and overpower. They prayed principally on the small craft, some of which carried huge sums of money, jumping them if possible on their way out to the Row."[42] Alastair Moray, a Scottish rumrunner with literary aspirations who kept a diary of his years in this business, concurs: "There is a good deal of what is known as 'hi-jacking,' inshore and out here too; in plain English, 'highway robbery.'"[43] Most of the sailors were armed with revolvers, rifles, and the occasional machine guns, and would not dare to go on deck unarmed during the night. Bill McCoy, possibly the best-known captain on Rum Row, aimed machine guns and rifles at any unknown boat that approached his ship, and allowed only one person aboard at a time.[44]

The route from the Long Island beaches to the City was also dangerous. Hijackers would regularly stop the trucks, hold up the drivers, and steal the cases. A man known as Big Eddie led a notorious gang of hijackers. "The New York police," writes Asbury, "said that he and his gang hijacked many truckloads of liquors on the roads of Nassau and Suffolk counties, the principal highways into New York from the lower end of Long Island."[45]

Jewish and Italian gangsters—such as Arnold Rothstein, possibly the most enterprising bootlegger on Rum Row—took it on themselves to offer two services to this market: the protection of truckloads, and a place where buyers could meet sellers. Luciano and Frank Costello together with Roth-stein created squads to protect the procession of vehicles carrying liquor on the way to the warehouses. Each truck had a driver up front and two armed guards in the back, ready to fire if attacked. The recruits for this job were Italian and Jewish youths from the Lower East Side.[46]

Early Italian mafiosi were also responsible for the creation of the equiva-lent of a Stock Exchange for booze, the so-called curb exchanges (after the name of the New York Stock Exchange, originally called the Curb Ex-change), where bootleggers met buyers. The first curb exchange emerged in September 1920 in the area bounded by Canal, Bowery, Prince, and Mulberry Streets, right in the middle of a territory controlled by Joe "the Boss" Masseria (see below) and just a block away from police headquarters. Bootleggers and buyers met almost every night from 9:00 p.m. to 1:00 a.m. to deal cases of rye whiskey, Scotch whiskey imported from England, bourbon, Canadian scotch, Canadian rye, domestic Gordon's gin, Bur-nett's bonded gin, Italian vermouth, French vermouth, and Dubonnet (the list is courtesy of the local police).[47]

In order to avoid police detection, a slightly different meeting place was selected every night. The curb traders, writes the *New York Times*, met in "yards of tenement houses, usually in the rear of saloons."[48] The prod-ucts, continues the *New York Times* article, "were sold by purveyors on the 'curb,' either in single cases or by the load. While the sales were effected on the 'market,' . . . the liquor itself was not handled at the 'curb,' but was obtained on orders at various rendezvous in different parts of the city, and in New Jersey, Long Island, and Connecticut points."[49] For instance, on March 20, 1921, the police raided a garage at 144 Mulberry Street. About one hundred people ("recognized by the agents as bootleggers") were gath-ered there, but only samples of liquor were seized.[50]

Curb trading was more efficient than the system employed previously. In the previous system, all liquor was stored in cellars and tenement apart-ments, so it was easy for the police to spot the trucks coming and going, and thus arrest the drivers. Now, the liquor was hidden out of the city and directly dispatched to the buyers. "The brokers," officials told the *New York Times*, "do not handle any liquor themselves, nor is any money dis-played on the market, . . . so [officers] have difficulties in getting any evidence."[51] Most significantly, these individuals were private protectors independent of bootleggers and restaurateurs. An informant told the *New*

York Times that "a considerable number of them were agents, who received commissions both from the bootleggers and the purchasers." These individuals were tasked not only with providing physical protection but also ensured that promises made on the curb were kept. The strong-arm men were local youths from the Italian neighborhood: "The sudden prosperity of some of these agents has been the source of considerable comment on the part of the police and residents of this bootlegging zone. All are young men whose homes are in nearby tenements."[52] This segment of the market was not run as a cartel of the suppliers (the bootleggers) and consumers (the saloon keepers) but rather the mafia offered a universal service to both the sellers and buyers. It was more profitable for the mafia to be paid a fee by all market participants than to force some out.

Curb exchanges were not limited to lower Manhattan. A "whiskey curb exchange" was reported to be operating in New Jersey already in November 1920. When police started to raid the curb exchange in Little Italy, the market moved uptown, and Prohibition officials admitted that "it is increasing its operations. . . . The new curb is said to be on Fortieth Street, near Broadway, and most of the 'brokers' who did business in the old market, on Mulberry Bend, have shifted their activities."[53]

Masseria, who was to become the head of the most influential New York syndicate in the 1920s, lived above a saloon on Forsyth Street, right in the curb exchange area. His early criminal career included extortion, kidnapping, and burglary. Together with associate Tommy Pennochio, Masseria was the organizer of this portion of the market, independently from both the bootleggers and buyers of liquor. Another significant player in the curb exchange was Salvatore Sabella, who had worked and had been arrested at the curb exchange. The boss of an existing Italian group, Salvatore D'Aquila, wanted a cut from this business. One famed street battle erupted on May 8, 1922, within a block of the police headquarters in the curb exchange territory, between D'Aquila and Masseria men. The struggle between the Masseria and D'Aquila families ended when, on August 11, 1922, D'Aquila's main killer was assassinated by Masseria. At this stage, Masseria gained considerable prestige and started to undermine D'Aquila both in New York and other cities. Eventually D'Aquila himself was gunned down, beside his car, on October 10, 1928, after driving his wife and children from the Bronx to consult a doctor. Following his death, the D'Aquila family would ally with Masseria.[54]

Mafia historian David Critchley notes that Masseria's role in the curb exchange market enabled him to expand "from his lower east side territory and secured a lock on an important portion of the Italian-American underworld extending from Brooklyn to the Bronx, operating primarily through Salvatore Lucanio and West Side-based Vito Genovese."[55] Bonanno, an enemy of Masseria, concurs that, at the height of Prohibition, Joe the Boss was the dominant leader.

By 1928, the Coast Guard had grown more effective at intercepting this illegal traffic at sea. A series of treaties with other countries also allowed the Coast Guard to search and seize within one hour's running distance of the U.S. coast, while its fleet was greatly improved by 1928. Rum Row had declined in importance by this time as a source of imported liquor.[56] Local booze producers flourished as a result of such decline. Italians were quick to enter this section of the market as well. Salvatore Maranzano, the mafioso who would fight the Castellammare War against Masseria in 1930 for control of the Italian American mafia, came to prominence by protecting illegal distilleries. Already a mafioso of consequence in Sicily, born in 1886, he arrived in New York most likely in 1925 via Canada. He entered the Schiro family and soon took control of the *borgata* (the word borgata is equivalent to cosca, although it is normally used to refer to U.S. mafia groups only). Maranzano had invested in a number of distilleries in Pennsylvania and upstate New York. The operations were typically run by a local manager and part owner who was not a member of the mafia; Maranzano and his gang provided protection for this network of producers of illegal products. He ensured that supplies arrived as well as that the whiskey was stored in safe houses and then shipped on to the buyers. He dealt with the police and settled disputes that arose among the various players. Bonanno, who worked for Maranzano, recalls that hijacking of delivery trucks was a common occurrence and one of his jobs was to retrieve stolen trucks. In one instance, a violent shootout led to a significant police investigation.[57] Italian mafiosi were now deeply involved in the largest illegal market of the time and a rough distinction between producers (bootleggers, the stills' managers), buyers (saloon owners), and protectors (mafiosi) was emerging. This was a far cry from writing extortion letters or stealing horses. Surely the goods were reaching the consumers: the mayor of Berlin, while visiting the city in the fall of 1929, asked the mayor of New York, "When does the Prohibition law go into effect?"[58]

Prohibition provided an enormous boost to both the personnel and power of Italian organized crime. The risk of punishment was low, the gains to be made were enormous, and there was no social stigma attached to this trade. One by-product of the massive profits was that syndicates could easily bribe the judiciary and politicians in New York City, reversing the attempt at curbing corruption initiated by Mayor Gaynor in 1910.[59]

ORGANIZATIONAL MATURITY

Italian criminal groups existed in New York City before Prohibition: the Morello gang of counterfeiters in East Harlem; a group led by Nicolò (Cola) Schiro, mainly formed by immigrants from Castellammare del Golfo and based in Brooklyn; and the borgata around D'Aquila, also in Brooklyn. How were these groups related to the Sicilian mafia? Although American mafiosi were not agents of the Sicilian ones, the homeland still exerted some influence on such U.S. outposts. Between 1910 and 1920, there were three different routes into a U.S. family. One was previous membership in a Sicilian cosca. Nick Gentile—who had entered the Porto Empedocle one before migrating to the United States in 1903—was admitted into the Philadelphia family in 1905. He then moved to Pittsburgh, where after a brief and successful campaign against the despised local gang of Neapolitan descent, he murdered the boss and became a capo. Such a route was open as late as 1925, when Maranzano was accepted into the Schiro family right after arriving in New York City "because," writes Bonanno, "of his position in Sicily."[60] It was customary for would-be members to carry a letter from Sicily testifying to their position in the cosca back home. When Morello was captured in 1909, the secret service discovered such "letters of admittance." Gentile confirms in his memoirs that would-be mafiosi from the old country needed a "letter of reference" from Sicilian bosses in order to be admitted into a cosca, and any change of family had to be approved by the boss back home. A second route was birth in a Sicilian town that was known to be under the sway of the mafia, and thus where Sicilian mafiosi could "vouch" for a prospective U.S. member. Third, coming from a well-known mafia family could ease admittance. This appears to be the way Bonanno entered the Schiro mob: his father had been a leader back home. Still, in contrast to Sicily, mafiosi in the United States could move

quite freely from one family to another, as Gentile did, and dual membership (Sicilian and American) was possible.[61]

As a consequence of Prohibition, the New York mafia families consolidated and grew in number (table 5.1). Masseria, who had played a crucial
role in the development of the curb exchange, was the boss of a new family
firmly located in Brooklyn and the Bronx as well as in Manhattan and, following the murder of D'Aquila, the D'Aquila family had become an ally.
Joe the Boss also had contacts with mafia syndicates in Chicago, Detroit,
and Cleveland (Capone was his ally in Chicago). Maranzano, who had
taken control of the Brooklyn Schiro family, greatly strengthened it to the
point that it became Masseria's main competitor in the war that broke out
in 1930, the Castellammare War. The Reina (later Lucchese) had absorbed
the bulk of the Morello borgata in the 1920s. By the late 1920s, a second new family had emerged, the Profaci, later called Colombo. Thus, the
number of established mafia groups in New York City grew to five and also
swelled their ranks. The Castellammare War was a conflict between the
two main leaders at the time, Masseria (allied to D'Aquila) and Maranzano
(allied to Reina; Profaci remained neutral). Although Maranzano won the
war, he was soon gunned down, due to the fear that he would want to
exert excessive control over the other groupings. As a result of the war,
the new leaders created a commission— a forum where key decisions were
discussed and enforced. Individual families retained their autonomy, and
over the subsequent decades, the commission tended to intervene mainly
when an individual family was unable to choose a successor and plunged
into internecine violence. Contrary to a widespread conception suggesting
that the Five Families were created after the Castellammare War, they were
already in place by the late 1920s. What did change after the conflict was
the identity of some leaders. For instance, because of the war, Luciano and
Bonanno were elevated to the rank of boss. These Five Families exist to
this day.[62]

By the late 1920s, U.S. families were growing in importance in the
eyes of their Sicilian counterparts. For example, when a significant dispute
arose between two Palermo mafia factions in 1928 over how to split a payment from a company that had obtained a public contract thanks to the
mafia, a U.S. delegation was sent to put an end to the dispute, as testified
to by Dr. Melchiorre Allegra in his 1937 deposition: "I was told that three

TABLE 5.1

Timeline of Italian American Crime Families, 1910 Circa to Present, Core Territories and Key Events

Timeline:					
c. 1910	Masseria (Brooklyn, Bronx, East Harlem, and Manhattan)	D'Aquila (Brooklyn and Manhattan)	Morello (East Harlem and Manhattan)	Schiro (Brooklyn)	Profaci (Brooklyn and Staten Island)
c. 1920		D'Aquila (Brooklyn and Manhattan)	Morello (East Harlem and Manhattan)	Schiro (Brooklyn)	
Late 1920s	Masseria (Brooklyn, Bronx, East Harlem, and Manhattan)	D'Aquila-Mineo-Mangano (Brooklyn and Manhattan)	Reina-Gagliano (East Harlem)	Schiro-Maranzano (Brooklyn and Manhattan)	
1931	Castellammare War: Maranzano boss; Masseria killed				
1931	Murder of Maranzano (September 10, 1931) Creation of the Commission				
1931–	Luciano-*Genovese*	Mangano-*Gambino*	Gagliano-*Lucchese*	*Bonanno*	Profaci-*Colombo*

Notes: The names of the Five Families, as they are known today, are in italics. Luciano, Mangano, Gagliano, Bonanno, and Profaci were the bosses in 1931 as well as members of the Commission, which included representatives from Chicago and Buffalo.
Sources: Bonanno with Lalli 1983; Critchley 2009; personal communication, December 19, 2009.

special delegations composed of mafiosi residing in the US arrived [in Palermo] with the ultimately unsuccessful aim of finding a solution to the dispute."[63]

The U.S. groups were also becoming autonomous, rescinding any dependency on the Sicilian homeland. By the end of the war that pitted Masseria against Maranzano, and led to the death of both leaders in 1931, dual Sicilian and U.S. mafia membership was forbidden. Furthermore, membership of a Sicilian cosca was no longer a sufficient qualification to join a U.S. family. Buscetta dates the full separation between the two entities at around 1950.[64]

Because of the Castellammare War, the families had turned to new sources for recruitment. In order to increase their ranks to fight the war, families started to look beyond Sicilians and, anathema to a Sicilian mafioso, admitted Neapolitans, the most famous being Joe Valachi, who testified against the mafia in 1963. Over time, typical new recruits came to be youths of Italian descent who had grown up in the inner-city neighborhoods of New York City. The candidates would be observed for a while and then, if deemed worthy, schooled for full membership. This is a sure sign that the U.S. mafia had become an autonomous organization.[65]

Italian American families had not yet acquired a publicly recognized name. Until the 1960s, each borgata was called after the name of the boss at the time or the territory that they inhabited (for example, the Luciano-Genovese faction was known as the West Side to insiders). Thus how did the Gambino, Genovese, Bonanno, Colombo, and Lucchese families come to acquire stable names by the 1960s that have survived to this day? Table 5.2 offers an important clue. In October 1963, Valachi, a soldier in the Masseria Luciano borgata, gave a televised testimony to the Permanent Subcommittee on Investigations of the U.S. Senate Committee on Government Operations (best known as the McClellan Committee). In October 1963 the bosses happened to be Gambino, Genovese, Bonanno, Colombo, and Lucchese. The testimony transfixed the U.S. public, and the families were from then on assured a place in the U.S. psyche with the names of the bosses at that particular time. As in other instances, an external source conferred a recognizable identity on a phenomenon that already existed but was struggling to consolidate. In order to be recognized, mafiosi themselves started to call their organizations by names that they had not quite chosen.

TABLE 5.2

The New York City Mafia Bosses by Families and Key Events, 1930s–80s

Timeline:	Genovese	Gambino	Lucchese	Bonanno	Colombo
			Familes		
1930s	Salvatore Lucania ("Charlie Lucky" Luciano), 1931–46	Vincent Mangano, 1931–51	Tom Gagliano, 1931–53	Joseph Bonanno, 1931–68	Joe Profaci, 1931–62
1940s	Frank Costello, 1946–57				
1950s		Albert Anastasia, 1951–57			
			Gaetano Lucchese (Thomas Lucchese), 1953–67		
	Vito Genovese, 1957–69	Carlo Gambino, 1957–76			
1960s					Joseph Colombo, 1962–71
October 1963			Valachi hearings		
1964–69			Bonanno war		
			Carmine Tramunti, 1967	Natale "Joe Diamond" Evola, 1968–73	
	Tommy Eboli, 1969–72		Anthony "Tony Ducks" Corallo, 1967–87		
1970s	Frank "Funzi" Tieri, 1972 Anthony "Fat Tony" Salerno, 1972–87			Philip Rastelli, 1973–85	Vincent Aloi, 1971 Carmine Persico, 1971–96
		Paul "Big Paulie" Castellano, 1976–85			

Notes: The dates refer to the tenure of each boss. The names of bosses at the time of Valachi hearings are set in bold. Tom Gagliano might have died in 1951.

Let me conclude this section on the birth of the Italian American mafia. Mafiosi arrived in New York City before a mafia was present, in a fashion not dissimilar from the arrival of members of the ʻNdrangheta in Bardonecchia and Verona in the 1960s. The push factor was the unintended consequence of prosecution in Italy along with the attempt of mafiosi in Sicily to avoid mafia disputes and punishment, as was the case with Yakovlev's move to Rome in the 1990s and those of triad members to China in the 1990s (see chapter 6). Some of course just came as part of the generalized migration to North America, in search of a better life. In the nineteenth century, the most profitable markets were already protected by a combination of corrupt police officers and local politicians. The arrangement is not unlike the "protective umbrellas" operating in China (see chapter 6). Italians in the United States did congregate in crime groups and even performed admission rituals, while the Sicilian homeland had a say on admission and moves among families, and operated as a certification agency on reputations. The Italian Americans involved themselves in ordinary crimes, such as counterfeiting, horse theft, and crude extortion.

In the first decade of the twentieth century, leaders of the Progressive movement to reform city politics were successful in curbing grand corruption. Prostitution, gambling, and late-night drinking as well as labor relations were suddenly left unprotected. A central argument of this chapter is that the unintended consequences of police reform gave the mafiosi a golden opportunity to become entrenched as suppliers of services of dispute resolution and protection.

In addition, the Progressive movement succeeded in banning alcohol consumption and manufacturing in 1920. Thus, another vast unprotected market was created shortly after the reform of the police. Mafiosi stepped in to protect truckloads entering the city from Rum Row and large stills in upstate New York. They were also instrumental in the creation of spaces where suppliers could meet distributors and prices could be set. The Italian mafiosi were independent of either suppliers or distributors, offering their services to both. Contrary to a common perception, Prohibition did not create the Italian American mafia.[66] Rather, mobsters had already penetrated some key markets in the previous decade. During and after Prohibition, the Italians continued their involvement in other illegal markets, such as prostitution and gambling.[67]

The Five Families as we know them today had already been formed by the mid- to late 1920s. They had also already started to assert their independence from the Sicilian homeland, as demonstrated by the fact that dual membership in the two organizations came to be forbidden and the major source of recruitment became, from the late 1920s onward, local youths of Italian descent. The final nail in the organizational edifice of the Italian American mafia was the Valachi testimony in 1963. While it fixed the spotlight on the organization, it also gave each family a stable and recognizable name that persisted after the demise of the particular boss.

Italian Mafia in Rosario

Italians set foot in Argentina earlier than in New York City, arrived at a more even pace, and were the most numerous migrant group. Significant influx to the shores of Río de la Plata had started already in the mid-eighteenth century. By 1855, Italians were the largest migratory group in Buenos Aires and other urban centers in the provinces of Santa Fe and Entre Ríos. Most of them lived in the La Boca neighborhood of Buenos Aires, where they already constituted almost a quarter of the capital city's population. Italians continued to form the bulk of overseas migration to Argentina in the last decade of the nineteenth century and until the First World War. According to the Third National Census of 1914, almost a million of them resided in Argentina, making up 20 percent of the population of the capital.[68] While those going to New York City arrived relatively late in the city's own development, when other ethnic groups had already established themselves and the majority of them joined the unskilled labor force, in Argentina the first wave of Italians was able to enter the professions and more generally join the local elite.

The regional background of Italian immigrants to Argentina was also different from the background of those who emigrated to New York City. In the Latin American country, 41 percent came from northern Italy, 47 percent from southern Italy, and 12 percent from central Italy (see table 5.3), while some 80 percent of the migrants to the United States had originated in southern Italy.[69]

And yet one has to be mindful of the changes over time. Arrivals to Argentina from southern Italy jumped from 28 percent of the total Italian immigration in the 1870s to 55 percent in the first decade of the twentieth

FIGURE 5.2 Map of Argentina-Rosario

TABLE 5.3

Regional Origins of Italian Immigrants to Argentina and the United States, 1876–1930

Period	Percentage from northern Italy	Percentage from central Italy	Percentage from southern Italy
Argentina			
1876–78	66	6	28
1884–86	66	9	25
1894–96	44	16	39
1904–6	32	20	48
1907–9	31	14	55
1910–14	31	14	54
Total, 1876–1930	41	12	47
United States			
1876–78	41	11	47
1884–86	12	3	85
1894–96	7	5	88
1904–6	9	12	79
1907–9	9	14	78
1910–14	11	14	75
Total, 1876–1930	11	9	80

Source: Klein 1983, 309.
Note: "The regional divisions used here are those in effect before 1919—that is, northern Italy includes Piedmont, Liguria, Lombardia, and Veneto; central Italy includes Emilia, Toscana, Marche, Umbria and Lazio; southern Italy includes the remaining peninsular divisions plus the islands" (Klein 1983, 309).

century. By the end of the nineteenth century, migration from northern Italy declined (especially from Liguria and Lombardy), while arrivals from other central (Le Marche) and southern regions (Abruzzi, Campania, Calabria, Basilicata, and Sicily) increased in relative terms. In the first decade of the twentieth century, many Sicilians, mainly from Caltanissetta, Catania, and Agrigento, moved to urban Argentina. Their professional background also changed: the number of farmers (*agricultores*) declined, while the numbers of day laborers (*giornalieri*) and artisans increased.[70]

After Buenos Aires, Rosario attracted the greatest number of immigrants, mainly from Europe. Italians started arriving in the first half of the nineteenth century and represented the highest percentage of the city's foreign residents, followed by the Spaniards (who were almost as many as the Italians in 1926), French, Russians, and British.[71] The composition of the Italian contingent in Rosario did not diverge from the national trend. The majority of Italian immigrants recorded in 1870 was from Liguria, Piedmont, and Lombardy, and was made up of mostly shopkeepers and shop assistants, craftspeople, or those employed in the services sector. This first wave was upwardly mobile, in a social setting that did not have an entrenched Argentinean aristocracy. The later influx represented less-qualified workers (agricultural laborers and day laborers), who found jobs in the construction of urban infrastructure and did not achieve the same economic success. According to estimates by economic historian Carina Frid, the Sicilian population reached its peak in Rosario in 1900–1914, when it represented between 15 and 20 percent of Rosario's Italian population for a total ranging from 8,500 to 10,800 of the 54,401 Italians residing in Rosario in 1914.[72] An analysis of marriage records in the Fifth District of Rosario in 1905 (n = 582) shows that 19 percent of the total number of those getting married originated from Sicily, followed by Piedmontese (18 percent). Other regions were less represented.[73]

A number of the Italian residents in Rosario (including the leaders of its mafia) had been born in Agrigento Province in Sicily. According to a conservative estimate, the Agrigentini in Rosario were just below one thousand in the period 1900–1905. At the end of the nineteenth century, this part of Italy experienced substantial departures to both North and South America. Some villages in the northern part of the Magazzolo Valley (Alessandria della Rocca, Cianciana, Bivona, Raffadali, Santo Stefano Quisiquina, and Burgio) were almost emptied (see fig. 5.1). The valley was an inhospitable land, where most people worked in the fields or sulfur mines. The inhabitants were mainly bricklayers, shoemakers, and unskilled workers. Some found employment in construction, while others went to reside in—and work in the fields of—the agricultural towns of Arroyo Seco, Serodino, and Villa Gobernador Gálvez outside Rosario (see fig. 5.2).[74]

Was there a "supply" of people with mafia skills in Rosario, as there was in New York City? The Rosario mafiosi were from Sicily, originating from the Magazzolo Valley. José Cuffaro and Esteban Curabà, heading a group of *paesani* involved in kidnapping and blackmailing from the mid-1910s, had been born in Raffadali, near Agrigento. Gaetano Pendino, a Sicilian

Juan Galiffi (1892–1943), the charismatic crime boss of Rosario in the 1930s, known as "Al Capone Argentino." Photo Credit: Osvaldo Aguirre. Historias de la mafia en la Argentina (Buenos Aires: Aguilar, 2000).

from Alessandria della Rocca, chose to migrate to Argentina, where he arrived in 1888 at the age of thirty-five and eventually became the boss of the mafia in Rosario. Santiago Buè and Carlo Cacciatore, members of Francisco Marrone's group (see below), came from the same town in Agrigento Province, and were at once cousins and brothers-in-law. Some Sicilians later involved in crime in Rosario originated from Catania Province, but their role was more limited.[75]

The most charismatic crime leader of the 1930s was Juan Galiffi, dubbed by the press "Al Capone Argentino" and made into Argentinean public enemy number one. Born in Ravanusa (Agrigento) in 1892, he arrived in Argentina in 1910 and first settled in Buenos Aires. Galiffi claimed to be a barber and trader. His career as a businessperson was rather successful. He associated with a Milanese who owned a vineyard in the province of San Juan. Soon after, he forced his Milanese partner out and became the sole proprietor of the firm Vinos Galiffi as well as the owner of a furniture workshop. His criminal career started in the 1910s as a thief in Santa Fe, Córdoba, La Rioja, and Salta provinces. In the early 1920s he married the daughter of a criminal from the town of Gálvez (240 kilometers from Rosario), where he rented a café (*fonda*). He was accused of robbery and disposing of stolen goods (fencing), though he managed to avoid prison. By the mid-1920s, he had moved to Rosario, where the police suspected him of being a mafia boss as well as involved in several kidnappings and the 1932 murder of a *La Crítica* journalist. Galiffi was also suspected of counterfeiting, extortion, and fixing horse races.[76]

A new generation of mafia leaders arrived in Rosario in the latter part of the 1920s, as a consequence of the fascist repression in Italy. Their arrival upset the local equilibrium and led to violence. The most important newcomer, via France, was Marrone, known as "Don Chico" or "Chicho el Chico" (although he used an exotic name at first—Ali Ben Amar de Sharpe). According to a statement made in 1938, Don Chico arrived in Argentina in 1930 with messages to deliver to Galiffi from Palermo. More specifically, a defendant (who was the first person that Marrone contacted in Argentina) claimed that Marrone "had a mission to accomplish" on behalf of the Sicilian mafia, to ensure that his fellow Palermitani were not taken advantage of by the Sicilians from Agrigento.[77] As soon as he arrived, he tried to muscle his way to the top of the local underworld. He orchestrated the death of three old-timers allied to Galiffi in a villa in San Lorenzo (twenty kilometers from Rosario). The massacre generated great police interest and concern among other Italian criminals, sowing the seeds of further violence. Marrone's epoch was short lived, however. In April 1932, Galiffi convinced him to attend a meeting at his house in Buenos Aires, where Marrone was assassinated.[78]

LOCAL CONDITIONS

I now turn to review the local economic conditions of the city in order to explore whether a demand for protection might have been present in specific markets. Rosario in 1850 was a trading post of no more than three thousand inhabitants in the southeastern Santa Fe Province. It was famed in the late eighteenth century for its locally bred mules as well as the silver, copper, and hides that it received from the interior and forwarded to Buenos Aires. From the late 1830s, its port was banned from foreign trade

by a decree of Juan Manuel de Rosas, the first strongman of independent Argentina. Yet Rosario's marginal economic role was to end in August
1852, when a politically weakened Rosas ended Buenos Aires's legal monopoly on international trade. The port was now allowed to receive ocean-
going ships. Another lucky development took place a year later, when the
province of Buenos Aires seceded from the rest of the country (it rejoined
a decade later) and Rosario became for a brief period the capital-cum-
port of the Argentine Confederation. As a consequence, Rosario's trade
and population tripled between 1852 and 1858, and received a significant
number of Italian immigrants, mainly from Liguria and Piedmont, who
would eventually form the economic and social elite. As the city's leading
historian Juan Álvarez noted, there were two great epochs in Rosario's history: "that with the river closed, which meant poverty and backwardness,
and that with the river open, which meant prosperity and culture."[79]

In the mid-1870s, Rosario as well as the rest of the country went through
an economic depression, stopping economic growth and reducing immigration to half of what it had been earlier in the decade. By the 1880s, though,
the recession ended, and stable links with international capital and commodity markets led to an impressive burst of direct investment along with
the arrival of nine hundred thousand immigrants to Argentina between
1880 and 1890.

The economy of Rosario from this period onward was mainly based on
grain production, and land plots tended to be large. Agricultural development was impressive: grain production tripled between 1883 and 1895,
and at least 150,000 seasonal laborers worked in the fields. In contrast to
western Sicily, where land plots were small, medium-scale rural properties
of one to three hundred hectares were common in the province after the
1860s; land tenancy developed in some districts of southern Santa Fe, as
large-scale land proprietors (mainly cattle breeders) rented out part of their
land for agricultural production. In 1890, an economic crisis ruined many
small private producers and agricultural colonies, hastening the trend toward the consolidation of landownership. The price of land increased,
making it even harder to buy after 1890. According to economic historian
Michael Johns, Rosario lived off the value of its rich hinterland. "Moving
commodities, primarily grain, was Rosario's main economic function."[80]
The massive expansion of agriculture led also to the creation of factories
mainly connected to agriculture production, rail links, and housing.[81]

Unlike in Sicily, where *banditismo* was rife after Italian unification, there was no threat to the transportation of products from the interior to the port. The bands of *Indios* that could have intercepted the goods and robbed the farmers had been exterminated by the vicious campaign conducted by Rosas in 1833 in the province of Buenos Aires. In the second half of the nineteenth century (1858–84), the local provincial government ensured that the rich landowners had nothing to fear from these and other potential bandits. In addition, trade unions were slow to organize in Argentina. Unionization started at the end of the nineteenth century, while the first strikes took place in 1902–3, led mostly by anarchists from northern and central Italy. A wave of strikes hit Argentina in the period 1907–10, but the police ruthlessly repressed them. A leader of the Radical Party in Rosario concluded a speech in 1906 by attacking the government's violent repression with these words: "Here in the City of Rosario . . . the police declared the workers outside the law. Under the pretext of searching for presumed delinquents, they have closed down union headquarters, they have searched homes at all hours of the night, masses have been imprisoned, and what is more despicable, workers declared innocent have been held for 18 hours and beaten up in police stations." There was no Mayor Gaynor to protect protesters.[82] Contrary to New York City, in Rosario there was no demand for an illegal protection agency to supply muscles against employees. The official organs of the state took care of that.

The economic crisis that coincided with the First World War caused numerous small farmers, land tenants, and businesses to default on their credits. Yet no demand for informal dispute settlement in the countryside emerged, mainly thanks to a peculiar system for settling disputes—an informal tribunal known as Paz del Trigo.[83] After 1918, Rosario experienced another brief economic boom that came to an end with the worldwide crash of 1929. The city then relinquished its role as a leading commercial center and has relied on grain exports ever since. Argentinean democracy suffered a blow in 1930, when a military coup took place. Although a civilian government was reinstated in 1931, the Partido Radical and the Communist Party were outlawed, and electoral frauds helped a general win the presidential elections. This period in Argentinean history is known as the Infamous Decade and marks the beginning of the end of Argentinean democracy. By 1943, another coup was staged.

THE CONSTRUCTION SECTOR

There was a point in the history of Rosario when a demand for extralegal protection might have emerged: the construction boom of 1904–11 offered Italian criminals the opportunity to enforce a cartel of firms, excluding competitors in a lucrative market, as the `Ndranghetisti did in Bardonecchia in the 1960s. I now explore this little-known episode. Pendino operated a construction firm from 1895 until around 1913, at a time when the sector was employing between 8 and 12 percent of the entire labor force. Figure 5.6 records the number of building permits granted by the city of Rosario between 1890 and 1910. It shows an increase between 1894 and 1895 and a steady growth from 1904. The boom came to an end by the beginning of the First World War.

The housing boom was driven by the construction of new *conventillos* (tenements) and the transformation of houses into rental units—a profitable investment. Indeed, according to estimates by Johns, rents on houses and labor costs were possibly the highest in Argentina.[84] Labor in the construction industry was organized through merchants who supplied workers (bricklayers, painters, carpenters, and unskilled laborers) to construction firms. The merchants organized workers from the same area of origin in Italy and even offered them accommodation. Italian laborers, bricklayers, and builders had also formed their own association in 1895, the Sociedad Cosmopolita de Obreros Albañiles, which comprised around five hundred members out of a total workforce of seventy-five hundred. Except for the years of economic crisis (1890–95), the demand for bricklayers and construction materials was high, and it increased particularly after 1904. As the industry began to boom, workers mainly originating from central and southern regions, such as Le Marche, Calabria, and Sicily, were hired.[85]

In order to ascertain whether new construction firms owned by southern Italians had entered the market, I collected information on building permits from 1890 to 1910. Table 5.4 shows the share of the market in the preboom and boom periods.[86]

Between 1890 and 1904, four firms had a significant share of the market. Rizzi and Prioni were both run by families from the North (respectively, Liguria and Lombardy). Little is known about Bongiovanni, except that it operated only until 1899. Curti was from Agrigento and a relative of Pendino. Indeed, it is likely that Pendino chose to migrate to Rosario because

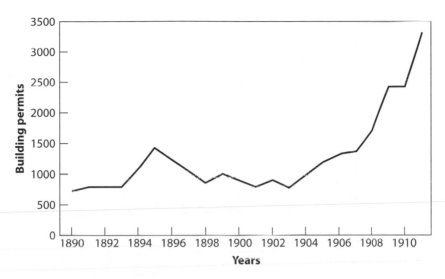

FIGURE 5.6 Building Permits, Rosario,1890–1910
Source: Lanciotti 2004, 229.

he hoped to find a job through his relative. All four firms are documented as operating since at least the early 1890s. I have also listed Micheletti, although it had only 3.2 percent of the market in this period, because it became a significant player later. An established firm, Micheletti was closely connected to the Catholic church in Rosario and remained a prominent constructor even after the First World War. The rest of the market was quite fragmented. Fifty-nine firms (out of eighty-five) had less than 1 percent of the permits. Only ten companies had more than five contracts.

As the market expanded in the next period, the number of firms grew (N = 189) and the established firms lost quotas. Micheletti, Rizzi, Prioni, and Curti were now the top four firms, with 22.8 percent of the total permits. The remaining ones gained little share in new projects. In the 1905–11 period, 157 firms applying for permits had less than a 1 percent market share, out of a total of 189 firms. Pendino's firm had 1.1 percent of the construction permits in this period. Large traditional companies such as Maspoli and Co. won profitable public contracts, including the construction of the Italian Hospital of Rosario, the Opera Theater as well as the North, South, and Central Markets.[87]

Rosario's construction market shares some key similarities with Bardonecchia's. They include a sudden boom, the presence of both workers

TABLE 5.4

Percentage Shares of Licenses Obtained by Five Firms to Build New Dwellings, Rosario, 1890–1907

Firm/year	1890–1904	1905–11
Rizzi	10.7	5.8
Prioni	9.6	5.1
Bongiovanni	6.8	—
Curti	6.0	4.5
Micheletti	3.2	7.3
Total	33.1	22.8

Source: Archivo de Obras Particulares, Municipalidad de Rosario, Rosario.

and entrepreneurs from so-called mafia regions (Calabria and Sicily, respectively), and a clear attempt by individuals linked to the mafia to establish themselves in the market.[88] Masons were organized in a trade union of notable size, making communication and coordination easier. Why, then, did the mafia fail to penetrate this market? Surely the most profitable public projects of this time required contacts within the political elites, and traditional companies secured those contacts. Yet the market boom revolved around the construction of houses for the middle and lower middle class in the suburbs as well as the working-class neighborhoods—a sector of the market that could have been cornered by mafia firms. Also, in such a long period, firms connected to the mafia could have secured public contracts, as they did in both Sicily and New York City, and Rosario gangs had contacts with the political elite of the period, as mentioned below.

Despite some crucial similarities, differences exist that ultimately explain the diverging outcomes. A structural difference is the sheer scale of the market: many more operators were at work in Rosario than in Bardonecchia[89] A mafia finds it extremely difficult, if not impossible, to create cartels when the market actors run into the hundreds. Most crucially, the mafiosi did not have a lock on the labor supply. Recall that in Bardonecchia Lo Presti was the sole supplier of unemployed workers to local companies, which hired their workforce in defiance of existing legislation. Lo Presti ensured services of dispute resolution between workers (hired illegally) and construction firms (which benefited from such informal arrangements, but could not use the law when disputes arose). In Rosario, firms could bypass a mafia fixer and hire workers through several *padroni* who had no connection to the Agrigentani. Two generous sources of labor were available: the rural folk who moved to the city during the agricultural off-season in search of work in the housing industry, and continued migration from Italy.[90] Since migration from Italy was conducted through "chains"—namely, immigrants arrived because relatives and acquaintances had arrived before them—the supply of labor was diversified. Workers from several parts of Italy, such as Le Marche along with various parts of southern and northern Italy, would arrive in Rosario and be directed to employment through their regional networks. None had complete control over the supply, as Lo Presti had in the case of Calabresi working in Bardonecchia. Since workers in Rosario were hired legally, within a general framework of informality and flexibility, there was no demand for extra-legal dispute settlement. To the extent that disputes arose, bosses could turn either to the law or existing informal systems of dispute resolution (It does not follow that workers were better protected in Rosario than in Bardonecchia).

ITALIAN CRIMINALITY

The mafia failed to penetrate a booming new market (construction). In addition, trade union activism was repressed by brutal state intervention, thus there was no demand for mafia groups to do so, and no significant illegal market existed in the city. Some of the mafia activities do suggest an attempt to offer services of dispute resolution and protection, however the demand was never enough for the mafia to become a viable and long-term criminal group. Pendino acted as an informal judge within the Sicilian community of Rosario, moderating differences and trying to settle disputes. Along with his associate Curabà, Pendino represented the *mafia limpia*. A member of Marrone's gang (see below), testifying before a judge in 1939, described them as "people who had ascendancy over their countrymen and settled their disputes."[91] A police document dated 1899 contains a description of the new crime of *vendetta*: the use of violence to settle disputes within the Italian community without turning to the authorities. The murder of Francisco Randisi, an unemployed day laborer from Raffadali who was assassinated in 1909 while leaving a boarding-house used by Sicilians, was considered a vendetta murder, as was the murder of Cayetano Saracco in 1903. In a town fifty kilometers south of Rosario (Arroyo Seco), Maria Ferraris was murdered in 1910. The police discovered that the murder had been ordered by her husband and carried out by people linked to Pendino. Vendetta episodes continued to feed the collective imagination and the police chronicle. In some cases, the authorities concluded that such crimes were the product of an internal mafia feud, as in the case of the homicide of Nicodemo Furforo, which took place in Arroyo Seco in 1911. Furforo was suspected of informing the police about a plot to assassinate a shopkeeper.[92]

Italians also provided muscle and personal protection for politicians or their clients during the elections. The local mafia groups sided with the provincial government, which supported the Unión Cívica Radical Anti-personalista, a faction of the larger Unión Cívica Radical (1891), founded in 1924. They acted as bodyguards, intimidated the political opponents of incumbent government officeholders, and helped secure election victories in small towns and cities in the interior of Santa Fe Province. Mafia boss Galiffi in the mid-1920s carried out several acts of intimidation against the local opponent of the Unión Cívica Radical Antipersonalista in the town of Gálvez (there is no evidence that Galiffi had a political agenda of his own).[93]

The political elite did return favors. The first indirect evidence of such connections emerged in the first decade of the twentieth century, when twenty Sicilians from Agrigento Province requested Argentinean citizen-ship and were supported by Lisandro de la Torre, a candidate for the Liga del Sur, a reformist party that represented the interests of traders and rural producers south of Santa Fe. Among the Sicilians was Pendino, who was considered at the time the boss of the local mafia. More direct evidence of favors emerged when Carlos Centeno, lieutenant governor of the Unión Cívica Radical Antipersonalista, repaid gangs connected to Galiffi by en-suring the reduction of the prison sentences they received for committing a murder. The Antipersonalisti also approved Galiffi's request for citizen-ship in 1925 (Galiffi by that time had been operating in the criminal un-derworld in Santa Fe). Arturo Amato, a Radical Party leader and police adviser, became one of the defenders of Galiffi in the first case against him for robbery and blackmailing, while Claudio Newell, a lawyer and politician with the Radical Party, defended associates of Galiffi. The Santa Fe political elite favored the election of judges amenable to "listening" to political officials. The criminal activities of these Italians were protected in the 1920s and 1930s by the weakness and impunity generated by the same judicial system of Santa Fe Province.[94]

And yet the Rosario mafia was never able to offer services that were demanded by a large enough sector of the local population. For the most part, it engaged in an Argentine version of the Black Hand (Mano Negra) blackmail practices, train robberies, and kidnapping for ransom. The victims of blackmail and threats were in most cases fellow Italians who worked in small businesses, or were craftspeople, shopkeepers, and commodity traders. José Martiré, a potato trader who resided in the suburbs north of Rosario, refused to yield to frequent blackmail and had an incendiary bomb thrown at his house in 1911. Even a prominent member of the underworld, Pendino, was on the receiving end of an arsonist attack in 1907. Although a Mano Negra group led by three men originating from nearby Catania was arrested in 1912, blackmailing continued throughout the 1920s, in contrast to New York City, where this type of crime died out by 1915.[95]

The Cuffaro gang, the most renowned in the 1910s, is credited with carrying out the first Argentine train robbery. Thanks to a tip from a guard who worked in the Central Railway, the gang attacked train number 20 on its way from Tucumán to Buenos Aires. The exploit made the headlines, while the police were duly criticized for their incompetence. As a direct result of the public outrage, the investigation unit of the Rosario police was reorganized and its leadership removed.[96]

By 1914, criminals of Italian origin had turned to a new crime: kidnappings for ransom. The first well-known case was that of the son of Antonio Bevacqua, a coal merchant. His kidnapper, Nicolás Ballestreri, one of the first capos to engage in ransom kidnappings, demanded an exorbitant sum, but did not receive it and so killed the hostage. Kidnappings for ransom continued in the 1920s and 1930s in Santa Fe Province and Buenos Aires, and generated significant social alarm. The victims were professionals, traders, industrialists, and landowners. One of the most brazen acts on the part of the mafia was the kidnapping and murder in 1932 of Silvio Alzogaray, the Rosario correspondent for La Crítica who had covered crime in the city. Several theories were floated in the press as to why such a murder was carried out. One suggests that Alzogaray had tried to extort money from mafia boss Galiffi in exchange for compromising documents, while another theory purports that the journalist had started to uncover police corruption in Rosario.[97]

The abduction and murder of Abel Ayerza—a medical student and son of a wealthy Catholic doctor whose family was connected to the Agustín P. Justo's government—in October 1932 stirred public opinion in an unprecedented way. The case inspired two plays at the time, *La Maffia* and *Don Chicho*, and two movies, *Bajo las garras de la mafia* (1933) and *Asesinos* (1933), and influenced the Senate debate on the new Criminal Code. Rumors ranged widely, and included suggestions that the incident was a staged kidnapping. The discovery of the young man's body on February 21, 1933, led public opinion to focus on the failure of the police and generated calls for the culprits to be severely punished. At the funeral, one orator blamed unregulated foreign immigration for the rise in violence in the country. The boy's kidnappers, linked to Galiffi's gang and of Italian origins, were apprehended in April of the same year (the boy was held captive by the Di Grado family, which owned a fruit and vegetable store in Rosario).

After the murder of Abel Ayerza in 1933, Galiffi fled to Montevideo. He then decided to return to Argentina in 1934 in order to prove his innocence, but was betrayed by his associates, arrested, and accused of the kidnapping of Marcelo Martin (a professional snatched in 1933). After a brief time behind bars, Galiffi was expelled to Italy in 1935. There he continued his low-level criminal life. Accused of counterfeiting, in 1939 he was imprisoned in Milan, where he died in 1943. Galiffi's arrest and expulsion weakened the Rosario mafia, which was also under renewed pressure from the government and the press because of the Ayerza murder (the mafia was also accused of consorting with anarchists). The majority of the ringleaders received prison sentences, while others were expelled from the country.[98]

Galiffi's shadow, however, still haunted the collective imagination; rumors suggested that he had returned illegally to Argentina and that his followers rallied behind his daughter, Agata Galiffi. Agata's green eyes earned her the nickname of "Gatta" (cat), while her decision to leave her husband and move in with a lover fascinated the local press. Up until her arrest in 1938, she was heavily involved in criminal affairs. She had been present at the murder of Don Chico in her father's house and, after Juan had fled to Italy, she continued to organize currency and stock counterfeiting operations.

Agata Galiffi (1916–67), the olive-skinned and aspiring actress was the daughter of Juan Galiffi, the Rosario mafia boss. Known as "Flor de la Mafia," she followed in the footsteps of her father and masterminded the Banco de Tucumán robbery. Photo Credit: Osvaldo Aguirre. Historias de la mafia en la Argentina (Buenos Aires: Aguilar, 2000).

The police regarded her as a capo in Rosario and a key player in the Argentine underworld. In 1938, she was arrested while discussing a plan to rob a bank in the city of Tucumán; the gang had drilled a tunnel almost a hundred meters long with the aim of switching good banknotes kept in the bank's safe with fakes. Sentenced to prison in 1939, Agata was released in 1948 and went on to work as a nurse in Rosario, Buenos Aires, Villa Constitución, and Caucete (a small town in San Juan Province), where she managed her father's property until her death in 1967. By 1940, the Italian mafia had died out.[99] Galiffi is now one of trendiest clubs in Rosario, "prácticamente un icono de nuestra ciudad," writes one of its five thousand friends on its Facebook page, advertising two dancing halls, karaoke, and a VIP space for its best customers.

In conclusion, Italians migrated to Rosario in two broad phases. The first wave of migrants was from the North, some joined the professions while others became large landowners and entrepreneurs. The profile of the migrants in the second phase is quite similar to those who migrated to New York City and were mainly low skilled, and found employment in agriculture as seasonal laborers and in the construction industry. Among the immigrants from Sicily, some had a mafia background, but the local conditions did not offer opportunities for these mafiosi to become established in the long run.

As in Bardonecchia, the construction market boomed and individuals connected to crime tried to penetrate it. The size of the market, much larger than in Bardonecchia, and the presence of a varied source of cheap labor that was not controlled by the mafia led to the ultimate failure of this criminal organization to control a key sector of the economy. As for illegal markets, and in contrast to New York City, in Rosario there was no equivalent of Prohibition. In addition, the police repressed labor militancy, thereby drying up a source of activities in which the mafia in New York was prominent. It is intriguing to note that the Partito Radical seemed to make use of mafiosi—the very party that would be banned after 1931. This suggests that electoral democracy would in some circumstances offer opportunities to mafias—a theme that I will return to in chapter 7. Rosario mafiosi thus engaged from the start in crimes such as theft, counterfeiting, the Mano Negra, and to a degree unknown even in the early years in New York City, kidnapping. A rudimentary organizational structure and the presence of charismatic leaders were not sufficient to entrench this mafia in Rosario. There were some mafiosi, but never a mafia.

Conclusions

Rather than summarizing the reasons for the divergent outcomes of Rosario and New York City, I want to try to take stock of the results that have accumulated across the six case studies (table 5.5). As for "supply," generalized migration from mafia territories is usually present when transplantation succeeds, with the exception of Budapest. Yet migrants from mafia territories do not invariably produce a mafia, as testified to by the case of Rosario discussed in this chapter. Clearly, a supply of mafiosi must be present for transplantation to take place, and thus the long list of "Yes" in the "Mafiosi migration" row in table 5.5. What is rather counterintuitive is that I found no instances where mafiosi rationally decided to move in order to open an outpost abroad. They were usually pushed out by state policies, mafia feuds, or in some cases covered in this chapter, poverty. (In the case of Hungary, the initial supply of foreign individuals inclined to form criminal groups was composed by Red Army defectors). Yet, when forced to move, mafiosi do not choose their new location at random: unless they are told by the courts where to go, they usually join relatives, trusted friends or previous contacts. Contrary to the view that high levels of trust prevent transplantation, this book's findings indicate that such outcome is possible even in highly civic territories, such Bardonecchia. Table 5.5 also suggests that local protectors must not be present for a mafia to transplant successfully. The case of New York City before 1910 is telling: while the police themselves were enforcing protection rackets, the Sicilians had no hope. Paradoxically, when a movement to reform city politics and the police was successful at curbing corruption, a demand for protection developed.

Transplantation goes hand in hand with a demand for criminal protection. New and booming markets tend to generate such a demand. For a mafia to be successful and exert a role, though, it must be able to solve problems in such markets that have not already been solved autonomously by local actors, as in the case of Verona. For instance, the Italian American mafia supplied a service highly valued by market operators: protection of the truckloads and stills, and a place where buyers and sellers could meet. Construction booms can generate such a demand when a mafia has monopoly access to cheap labor that can be hired illegally. Once firms and workers step outside the frame of legality, a demand for alternative forms of dispute settlement emerges. On the contrary, in Rosario local firms managed the same boom by hiring employees legally and bypassing anybody who could have exclusive control of the workers. Rather than liquid and floating in a virtual world, the markets covered in this book are all localized in a specific territory; there is no instance of a mafia offering protection to computer hackers or traders in sophisticated derivatives. Mafiosi might use the Internet for conducting frauds or invest their money in the Stock Exchange, but they do that as customers, not as protectors. Certainly, some structural factors can make it easier for mafias to become entrenched: the smaller a locality, the easier it is to control it. Yet a mafia can develop in a metropolis when an illegal market is large enough, as in the case of Prohibition. Ultimately, a demand for mafia services emerges out of transformations in the economy that local actors and regulators have not been able to govern. When foreign mafiosi are present and can offer genuine protection to some, transplantation is set to take place.

TABLE 5.5

Factors Facilitating Mafia Transplantation, Bardonecchia, Verona, Budapest, Rome, New York City, and Rosario

Factors facilitating mafia transplantation/cases	Bardonecchia	Verona	Budapest	Rome	New York City (1910–30)	Rosario (1910–30)	Shenzhen/ Guangzhou
Generalized migration	Yes	No	No	No	Yes	Yes	
Mafiosi migration (willing/unwilling)	Yes (unwilling)	Yes (unwilling)	Yes (unwilling)	Yes (unwilling)	Yes (unwilling)	Yes (unwilling)	
Supply of mafiosi	Yes	Yes	Yes	Yes	Yes	Yes	
Local conditions							
Level of trust/civic engagement	High	High	Low	Low	Low	Low	
Presence of local illegal protectors	No	No	No	No	No	No	
Size of locale	Small	Large	Large	Large	Large	Large	
New and/or booming markets*	Yes	Yes	Yes	No	Yes	Yes	
Demand for mafia services	Yes	No	Yes	No	Yes	No	
Transplantation	Yes	No	Yes	No	Yes	No	

* The markets considered are construction (Bardonecchia and Rosario), drugs (Verona and China), property rights (Budapest and China), oil (Budapest), alcohol (New York City), gambling (New York City and China), and prostitution (China).

Appendix

Table A5.1

Foreign-born Italians in New York City and Rosario, 1860–1930

Year*	New York City's Italian population	Italian-born as a percentage of New York City's total population	Rosario's Italian population	Italian-born as a percentage of Rosario's total population
1860	1,464	0.1		
1870 (1869)	2,794	0.3	2,120	9.0
1880 (1887)	12,223	1.0	11,955	23.0
1890 (1895)	39,951	2.6	25,546	28.0
1900	145,433	4.2	25,679	23.0
1910	340,765	7.1	37,414	20.0
1920 (1914)	390,832	7.0	45,357	18.0
1930 (1926)	440,200	6.4	79,920	19.6

* The year of Rosario's census is in brackets.

Sources: For New York City, Baily 1983, 300; 1999, 58. For Rosario, Frid de Silberstein 1992; Cuarto Censo Municipal de Rosario 1926.

SIX

The Future of the Mafias? Foreign Triads in China

THE NEW CHINA

I crossed into China in September 2009. My companion and I had boarded the East Rail Line in downtown Hong Kong heading toward Lo Wu, the last stop before the People's Republic of China. The trip takes no more than forty-five minutes, and there is hardly any time to enjoy the vista. The train races through the center of Hong Kong, allowing the passenger just a glimpse of Mong Kok, the suburb where most of the brothels and karaoke bars run by the triads are located, and quickly covers the several miles of the agricultural, sparsely built land in the new territories, before reaching the border. After our passports were checked on the former British colony side, we set out on foot to cross a modern overpass, equipped with conveyor belts for speedy arrival to the other side. The bridge stands over the Shenzhen River separating Hong Kong from the Middle Kingdom (the name of China in Mandarin). As we approached the other side, I looked at the riverbank through the thick glass. I was reminded by my companion that not long ago Chinese nationals trying to cross this stretch of water would have been shot at by border guards, just as the East Germans who tried to climb the Berlin wall. Today, the business elites of Hong Kong, Taiwan, and other capitalist economies are undertaking the journey in the opposite direction.[1]

Once we got across, we were in Shenzhen, a metropolis of twelve million with a skyline littered with as many skyscrapers as New York City (as far as I could judge), hypermalls, and factories. The city lies on the eastern shore of the Pearl River delta. To the north was our next destination, Dongguan, where I was going to conduct several interviews. A fast train service then connects Dongguan to Guangzhou, the capital of the Guangdong region, the third city in which I spent time last winter.

Until 1979, Shenzhen as such did not exist; it was a fishing village named Bao'an, with 310,000 residents. This part of the world was transformed in more than just name when Deng Xiaoping decided to open China to the world economy in 1978. The new policy called for the creation of special economic zones where the government offered tax benefits, relaxed regulation, invested in better infrastructure, and reduced bureaucratic obstacles in order to attract foreign investors. The central government selected several cities in the Guangdong, Fujian, and Hainan provinces as the sites of China's experiment with a market economy among them Shenzhen and Dongguan.[2]

Deng's reform produced unprecedented economic development and unemployment. China's GDP grew by 8.8 percent between 1978 and 1991 on average every year (Guangdong's GDP grew by 12.8 percent on average in the same period). The economic boom spurred a construction spree and rapid urbanization. Roads and superhighways were built to serve the ever-increasing number of cars, and construction of some ten to twelve million housing units is begun every year (Chinese citizens can now apply for personal loans and mortgages). Capital inflow was mainly coming from Taiwan, Hong Kong, and the United States. After Taiwan lifted the ban on its citizens visiting China in 1987, the first to invest in the mainland were small and medium scale manufacturers. By 1991, Taiwan was the second-largest investor in China after Hong Kong. In the meantime, around 170 million peasants were officially classified as surplus labor in 1990. This number swelled to 200 million in 1994 and then approximately 300 million in 2000. The northeast was the most seriously affected area. Starting in the 1980s, the Chinese government also reduced military personnel on a large scale.[3]

The increase of surplus labor in the rural areas led to China's "internal immigration"—millions of people fled to cities to seek employment. Mostly they left the western and central provinces to find employment in the more economically developed eastern provinces, such as Guangdong, Zhejiang, Fujian, Jiangsu, and the cities of Beijing and Shanghai. Some

FIGURE 6.1 Maps of China

Shenzeng construction site. Photo Credit: Federico Varese.

two hundred million people were on the move. At three times the number of people who emigrated from Europe to the United States over a century, this represents the largest migration in human history. One finds them employed in factories, restaurants, cleaning services, babysitting, garbage collection, and the sex industry. (Several reports suggest that they are responsible for increasing crime rates.)[4]

Young, immigrant women service the entertainment and night economy of Shenzhen, as I discovered during the first evening that I was in the city, when we were invited by scions of rich Hong Kong businessmen to join them for a night of partying. Trendy, unattached, and foreign educated, these partygoers travel (with bodyguards) to Shenzhen every weekend and keep apartments next to upscale saunas. My evening's entertainment included a massage, dinner, drinks, and games at the most expensive sauna in town. Rather incongruously, the sauna was decorated with gilded festive ornaments hanging from the ceiling celebrating the sixtieth anniversary of Communist China in a setting that encouraged anything but communist frugality. The night ended at one of the hippest discos, Baby Face, where we were greeted by the manager and quickly surrounded by hostesses, all immigrant women. Although prostitution was not on display at the disco, other clubs and saunas have such a reputation. And so do entire districts. The phenomenon is so widespread that certain parts of Shenzhen and Dongguan have been dubbed "concubine villages" or "second-wife villages" (*er nai cun*), where for a few hundred pounds a month middle-aged men from Hong Kong and Taiwan keep a young (immigrant) woman as a long-term mistress. One such neighborhood is the New Garden Village in Dongguan, a long row of drab apartment buildings and shopping centers, frequented by heavily made-up female shoppers.[5]

Movements of Triad Members to China: The Supply

Have triads from Hong Kong and Taiwan also followed the swarm of businesspeople, wealthy partygoers, and immigrants from the poorest parts of China, and transplanted to the regions that have opened up to Western capital? The first sign of foreign triad activities on the mainland dates to the early 1980s. In 1982, the Shenzhen police arrested 76 Hong Kong criminals with triad backgrounds. By 1992, 338 triad members were behind bars in Shenzhen. In the next two years, the Guangdong police arrested an additional 11 members of the Hong Kong triads.[6]

A key motivation for the brothers (triads members) to cross into China was to avoid police scrutiny and antigang crackdowns in Hong Kong and Taiwan. For instance, crime expert Bingsong He writes that

> police found that over 30 criminals that were wanted by the Hong Kong and Taiwan police came to hide in Shenzhen and engaged in criminal activities between 1992 and 1994. . . . While sheltering in Shenzhen, they not only continued their criminal operations, but also actively recruited new members and spread their criminal skills. For example, shortly after he escaped to Mainland China following an armed robbery, He Suti, a member of Hong Kong "Victory" Triad group, was involved in three stolen cars cases within three months.[7]

Since police in Hong Kong were making it increasingly difficult for triads to carry out their functions, such as reunions, parties, and funerals, the brothers went to China. The Sun Yee On, a Hong Kong triad, started to perform ceremonies in Guangdong in 1999. The most significant one discovered by the police took place in April 2000, when three senior members of the Sun Yee On performed the Zhazhi ritual in Shenzhen. During the ritual, six Blue Lantern–level members were promoted to Red Pole, a senior position in the group. Shenzhen was also used as a convenient location to plan crimes far from the interference of Hong Kong antitriads squads. For instance, the kidnapping of the son of one of the richest Hong Kong businessman took place in 1996—a joint plot by a Hong Kong triad and Chinese gangsters in Shenzhen.[8]

Taiwanese mafia leaders and foot soldiers have also been escaping police crackdowns and hiding abroad since at least the 1980s. Indeed, a major effect of antitriads operations in Taiwan was to push gang leaders overseas and internationalize the Taiwanese underworld. The first major operation, named "Clean Sweep," took place in 1984 and lasted several months, leading to the arrest of thousands of criminals. Those who managed to escape fled Taiwan and sought refuge in Thailand, Japan, and the Philippines. Those who were caught were housed in two reform camps in remote areas of the country. After living together for almost three years, they came to know each other well. According to a Taiwanese middle-ranking boss, Clean Sweep did not solve the crime problem; "actually," he maintains, "it allowed *jiaotou* [organized crime] figures from across Taiwan to come together and establish a network. After their release, if one asked for help from another, it was unlikely that it would be refused."[9] Indeed, the Celestial Alliance, which was to become one of the most formidable and resilient mafia groups in Taiwan, was formed in those prison camps. The 1984 crackdown had a second unintended consequence: it disrupted the orderly division of territories among bosses, and allowed for ruthless, inexperienced aspiring criminals to emerge and claim profitable territories and businesses. When the brothers were released from the camps in 1988 and wanted to reassert power over their turfs, the authorities witnessed an escalation of gang violence. As a result, a new antimafia operation—"Operation Thunderbolt"—was launched in 1988. This time the targets were better prepared than in 1984; they were ready to flee, with their main destination being China. As He put it, "Many Triad groups members in Taiwan who were on the run or had escaped from jail came to Mainland China, changed their names, rented houses, got married and settled down."[10] Most of them chose Guangdong and the

Fujian region, which is located opposite Taiwan, some 150 miles across the Taiwan Strait (the dialect spoken in southern Fujian is the same as the one used in Taiwan). Although the first Taiwanese triad arrived in China in 1987, a massive exodus started only after Operation Thunderbolt, when some three hundred organized crime figures left Taiwan for China. Among them were Wu Tung-tang of the Celestial Alliance as well as one of the leaders of Bamboo United, White Wolf (Chang An-lo), who moved to Shenzhen in 1988 and to this day lives there. Crime chronicles in both countries recount the stories of many brothers who moved to this part of the world, including one who arrived in Shenzhen via Argentina. Between 1992 and 1994, no less than thirty criminal leaders from Taiwan were hiding in Shenzhen.[11]

In 1996, a third major antitriads operation was launched in Taiwan, set off by the stabbing of one lawmaker, the kidnapping of another, and the outbreak of a major bid-rigging scandal—all involving triad members. As in previous antitriads sweeps, the major organized crime figures fled the country, with most of them heading to China. By 1999, more than a thousand members had settled in China, mainly in Dongguan, Guangzhou, and Shenzhen in Guangdong Province, Xiamen and Fuzhou in Fujian Province as well as in Shanghai and on Hainan Island, and they traveled freely to Singapore, Thailand, and the Philippines. By the beginning of the new century, Bamboo United had a presence in Guangdong and the Pearl River area, the Celestial Alliance in Fuzhou and Xiamen, and the Four Seas in Shanghai and Haikou.[12]

The Chinese authorities generally do not pursue fugitives and former criminals unless they commit crimes. In fact, they view their presence as an opportunity to attract foreign investment. Ultimately, as long as these gangsters bring investments to the mainland, they are welcomed as businesspeople by the Chinese authorities. And investments they did bring. In May 1992 a boss of Hong Kong 14K triad group, Huang Jianming, entered China and started a program of investments of 14K funds into Shenzhen, beginning with a restaurant. By 1998, he had acquired thirty-five properties. Similarly, the Sun Yee On invested in a multiplex to be built in Shenzhen (Nanshan District). Taiwan's Pine Union gang also bought real estate. Nuoquan Chen, a former high-ranking member of the Wo Shing Tong triad society, bought a hotel in Shenzhen (his hometown), where he recruited local youngsters and formed his own gang, the Flying Eagle. According to an investigation conducted in Shenzhen in 1999, among the fifty-two restaurants and entertainment businesses owned by overseas citizens, thirty-two were associated with outside triads, making up 62 percent of the total. In Fuzhou, Taiwanese triads formed joint stock companies, invested in shares, and hired local agents to open firms and purchase real estate. They established businesses in the service and entertainment sectors. For instance, Wu Tung-tang, the leader of Celestial Alliance Sun Branch, owns a luxury hotel in Fuzhou.[13]

A major concern of previous chapters was to identify a supply of people who belong to a mafia group moving into new territories. Even a small number of the latter can be highly significant because such specialized criminals are well equipped to set up criminal groups. Although the numbers of hardened criminals might be relatively small, they have the potential to recruit among the new unemployed or underemployed immigrants. The data above suggest that a supply of members of the Hong Kong and Taiwanese triads was present and tried to create groups in mainland China. They moved due to renewed police pressure in their homeland (this was the historical nemesis of a set of events that took place in 1949, when Chinese underworld leaders had escaped to Hong Kong and Taiwan after the Communist victory in order to avoid execution).[14] Once in China, they found a land rich in commercial opportunities and invested some funds in the new market economy. Has the presence of these individuals led to the entrenchment of foreign mafias in China? Surely, new markets—legal and illegal—have suddenly emerged and expanded: construction, manufacturing, gambling, prostitution, and drug trafficking. Such developments in the economy lead to disputes among market actors, and the emergence of a demand for services of dispute settlement and protection. Who is fulfilling such a demand? My aim is to establish if foreign or local triads or members of the state apparatus offer criminal protection to these market operators.

I draw on twelve in-depth field interviews and a detailed examination of seventy-four mafia cases extracted from four Chinese-language sources.[15] For the most recent period (2008–9), I selected official press reports released by the Ministry of Public Security. All publications adopt the official Chinese definition of an organized crime group: "an organization with an underworld nature." To qualify, a group must show some organizational structure, a clear leadership, and engage in illegal activities. Otherwise, the definition is rather general.[16] The cases are listed in the appendix to this chapter. The data have no claim to be representative.

LEGAL MARKETS

Workers in the new market economy have plenty of reasons to feel exploited and thus enter into disputes with their employers. For one, they might want to sue the companies for the appalling working conditions that they have to accept. In the four factories between Shenzhen and Dongguan that I visited, workers slept on bunks ten to twelve to a room in close proximity to unsanitary lavatories and were fed a basic meal (rice, a meat dish, and some soup), with the day starting at around 7:00 a.m. for a total of ten to twelve hours of work. The rooms were cold and had thick metal bars on the windows. A manager accompanying me explained that the bars were necessary to ensure against workers stealing production material. More generally, the security situation in factories in Dongguan is serious, he added, because workers "steal all the time and misuse factory equipment. For instance, the Nike shoes you can find in markets in Guangzhou are perfect replicas of the authentic shoes, because they are produced at night in the same factory! So they are pretty close to the real thing." According to him, factory management in Dongguan adopts a "ten percent ratio"—namely, it hires ten guards for every one hundred workers.[17]

Metal bars might prevent theft, but they also endanger residents in case of an emergency. Indeed, an instance that shocked China in 1993 was a fire in a Shenzhen factory that subcontracted work for a European toy maker. The flames claimed the lives of eighty workers, and a score of others were seriously burned and injured. (In a factory producing office furniture, I saw employees not wearing any protective equipment. Splinters of wood flew everywhere, and sometimes workers would look into the holes being drilled, putting their eyesight at risk.) Often employers simply failed to pay the promised wages, as in the case of a Mr. Zhang reported on Beijing Television in February 2007. Mr. Zhang had convinced an entire brigade of fellow villagers to accept work at a construction site in 2004, but when the time came to pay them, the management refused to shell out the salaries. The villagers followed procedures and filed a lawsuit to demand payment. The court issued an order in their favor, but when it was time to enforce the court order, the boss and other managers of the construction project disappeared. This is not an isolated instance; an official survey conducted in 2003 discovered that some 75 percent of migrant workers experience various forms of wage nonpayment.[18]

Prosecutors admit that legal avenues to settle disputes are wanting. Yunfeng Zhai, the deputy attorney general of the Qinhuai District (Nanjing) Procurator's Office, says:

> There are many drawbacks in settling commercial disputes through the courts. Firstly, it is expensive. If the creditor relies on the trial procedure to settle commercial disputes, he or she has to pay the litigation fee, enforcement fee, travel expenses, and counsel fee. In addition, the process is complicated and time-consuming. Secondly, trial procedure takes a long time. The first instance of an ordinary civil case takes about half a year, and the second instance about three months, excluding any postponement in the proceedings. Most creditors lack the patience to go through the whole trial procedure, especially if the value of the matter is not great. Thirdly, the enforcement of court orders is difficult. Even though the creditor wins the case, he or she cannot get the money back with simply a note from the court acknowledging the debt.[19]

The situation is no better in Guangdong. In an interview, Chief Justice Botao Lu of the Guangdong Provincial Higher People's Court acknowledged that the courts' inability to enforce decisions relating to business disputes in a timely fashion had reduced public confidence in the judicial system. Justice Lu stressed that "people are reluctant to go to court to settle disputes" because it is "time consuming and expensive," and it is difficult to "get the compensation back [even if] you win the case."[20]

Empirical studies conducted by Chinese scholars confirm that the civil court system is not well equipped to adjudicate cases competently, quickly, and effectively. Cases submitted to the courts have increased dramatically without an equivalent increase in resources, and are more complicated in nature than in the prereform era, while judges have for the most part a basic legal education. In addition, several structural features make it more difficult to reach decisions in Chinese courts than in other countries. One such feature is that the judge is supposed to not only adjudicate on the merits of the case but also collect evidence directly in appeal cases. Judges are not entirely independent of political pressure, especially from the local administration (a lawyer admitted that "whenever there is a business dispute and the case is being handled in court, we always try to find a high ranking government official to tell the court how to decide the case").[21] Finally, the enforcement of court decisions is particularly weak, and more so when the respondents are outside the territorial limit of the original court. More than two million court orders and decisions were officially recorded as "pending for enforcement" in 1998. In the 1990s, around 50 percent of the rulings in cases concerning economic disputes were enforced, but the situation was, according to a particular study, worse in lawsuits between banks and companies (banks won 95 percent of the lawsuits, yet only 15 percent of the rulings were enforced). Not surprisingly, people's confidence in the judicial system is low. A full-length study of courts in China by Qing-Yun Jiang describes the situation as a "judicial crisis."[22]

Often workers do not even sign official contracts and, operating in the informal economy, cannot turn to the courts. Estimates suggest that between two-thirds and three-quarters of all new employment in China is in the burgeoning informal economy that already incorporates eighty million people. The Department of Labor in Suizhou City in Hubei carried out random checks on 134 companies and found that not one had issued a contract. The *Jinan Daily* reported research conducted in the city according to which eight out of ten migrants did not even know what a labor contract was—and of the few who did know, most thought contracts were ineffective. The managers of labor-intensive industries frequently prefer a cheap and easy-to-dismiss workforce, bypassing trade union controls and saving on health provisions, while independent labor unions are still illegal in China. Legions of workers are therefore excluded from state-supplied forms of protection and legitimate avenues of dispute settlement.[23]

Let me take stock of the evidence presented so far: China is undergoing an economic boom; the state is unable to settle disputes swiftly and effectively; generally there is little trust in government or interpersonal trust; a vast sector of the population operates in the shadow economy, where by definition it cannot count on legal venues of dispute settlement; and foreign triads have been operating on the mainland. Does it follow that the latter are intercepting the demand for protection that the state is unable to offer? Rather than foreign mafiosi, members of the state apparatus featured prominently in the interviews that I conducted with businesspeople in the industrial heartland between Shenzhen and Dongguan. In order to interview the owner of a lightbulb factory, I took a bus that crossed the Dongguan industrial area—the same bus that takes workers to their places of employment and residence (the entire ride takes six hours). Factories tend to cluster around a number of cement constructions where workers can shop and find entertainment. On the way to the meeting, we passed Changping, a suburb outside Dongguan, a particularly poor district with high levels of unemployment, and a hub for drug dealing and cheap sex.

The factory owner is a middle-level businessman from Taiwan. He has been operating in the industrial wasteland of Dongguan since the early 1990s. "Until 2001 it was truly a Wild East," he says. "People were going around with guns for self-protection. I myself saw several bodies just left on the side of the streets. If one shot someone else, nobody would know. The situation has improved significantly these days, but security and protection are still a major concern and we factory owners are very sensitive to this issue." Protection of a higher order is also necessary. In order to operate, he continues, one has to develop a working relationship with a member of the state apparatus who will help in case of need. They will also tell you whom to hire. He had to take on a woman, who was well connected with the local administration and the military. After a few years, he decided to fire the lady. Since she was well connected, she was able to mobilize an army unit on her behalf. The unit surrounded the factory. The owner, however, had also formed his own links with the military. Thus, he could call on the help of another unit, which encircled the first unit. "The factory yard seemed a battle ground, with two armies facing each other and ready to fire," he laughed. Ultimately, both parties lost a lot of money because they had to pay off their respective military friends for this service. He concluded, "It is much better to solve matters in a nonconfrontational way, simply because it is cheaper." He was able to fire the woman, but had to compensate her more than he had wished to.[24]

In a similar case, an investor obtained a license to build a factory producing plastic in Dongguan. According to the terms of his license, he could import raw material without paying import duties, but he was not allowed to sell his products on the Chinese market, only to export them or sell them to foreign-owned companies. He negotiated the terms of the license with a set of local officials in return for upfront bribes and the promise to pay them a fraction of the profit he made by breaking the license agreement. In return, the officials ensured him protection against inspections. This arrangement gave rise to a typical situation of asymmetrical information, whereby the officials would not know if the businessperson was cheating on the deal. In order to monitor him, they forced him to hire a chief accountant and a manager. At regular intervals, the factory gets "inspected" by the officials. If they are not satisfied with the accounts, they detain either the owner or the accountants for breaking tax regulations (at some point, they suspected that the accountants were colluding with the entrepreneur and pocketing what was due to them).[25] The interlocked system between officials and entrepreneur went beyond a one-off corruption benefit (obtaining a license), and evolved into a long-term partnership.

As documented by several scholars, such arrangements are ubiquitous in the Middle Kingdom and are known as "protective umbrella" (*baohusan*): fragments of the state apparatus agree to protect businesspeople against the authorities and other competitors in exchange for regular payment.[26] These solutions differ from standard corruption, where one corrupter pays a corruptee for a specific service (say, obtaining a passport or license). They are more far reaching and involve a wider menu of protection services. Since any economic activity in China is subject to intrusive inspections and requires several permits, and independent courts are not effective in protecting the victims of officials' harassment, even entrepreneurs producing legal commodities, such as lightbulbs, can benefit from entering into such arrangements. The system of protective umbrellas has a striking parallel in the "roof system" that emerged after the transition to the market economy in the Soviet Union and Russia. Roof providers in Russia include the Federal Security Services, the Ministry of Internal Affairs, and other official organizations as well as criminal gangs.[27] Although the Chinese authorities in Beijing pride themselves on having followed a path into capitalism that is noticeably different from the Soviet Union's lawless collapse, ultimately a similar equilibrium has emerged. One might further speculate that the umbrella system ensures continued control over the economy by officials, albeit one that distorts incentives and produces significant waste, and that is occasionally punished by the center with exemplary show trials.[28] In both countries, a precarious balance between local incentives to develop protective umbrellas and the center's aspiration to remain in overall control is constantly negotiated.

Mobilizing one's umbrella is costly and hence regarded as a strategy of last resort. At times, one can just invoke it in the hope that it will be sufficient. One respondent explained to me that in a dispute he had about badly produced glass products, he made it clear that he could count on the services of a specific military umbrella. The name in itself was enough to have the supplier rework the product. Directly mobilizing the umbrella might also alert the protector to new business that the entrepreneur is keen to keep away from the usually greedy hands of the official. In addition, the same respondent suggested, a small-time businessperson might not be valuable enough for an umbrella to take them under their protection, and thus the entrepreneur might turn to one-off protection services.[29] In this context, purely private and unregistered debt collection and dispute resolution agencies have emerged, in which many of the employees have a criminal record. A conservative estimate puts the number of people employed as debt collectors by unregistered companies in China at more than one hundred thousand. Clients include ordinary people and migrant workers.[30]

The following story from the city of Nanjing is telling. In May 2006, Liu paid more than 150,000 yuan to Wang, the manager of a chemical company. Yet Wang did not deliver any chemical product to Liu, nor did he pay the money back. Liu demanded repayment several times, but in vain. Finally, Liu saw an advertisement for a debt collection company in the local newspaper. He signed a contract with the agency and agreed to pay a fee equivalent to 30 percent of the sum to be recovered. On the night of February 10, 2007, four collectors chased Wang's car and forced him out. Wang ran for his life, but was soon caught by his chasers and received a severe beating. He was forced to leave his car as collateral for the unpaid debt. As soon as he was free, Wang reported the case to the authorities, and the police detained four individuals. The investigation established that the top four debt collection agencies in the city were retrieving millions every year for their clients through the use of violence. A follow-up investigation by the Procurator's Office revealed that most employees of these firms had criminal records.[31]

Rather than regulating the industry, the government has taken steps to outlaw debt collection companies. In 1995, the Ministry of Public Security along with the Administrative Department for Industry and Commerce

A debt collection agency, Nanjing, China. The advertisement on the second floor reads "Professional debt recovery." Photo Credit: Zhejiang online.

issued a notification that forbade the establishment of debt-collecting companies by any institution or person. The notification ordered organs of the Administrative Department for Industry and Commerce to close down existing debt-collecting companies, and notify them to apply for a cancellation or change-of-business license. Any company that failed to abide by the notification would have its business license withdrawn by the department organs. This provision was confirmed by further legislation.[32] "Obviously, all debt-collecting companies have been made illegal by the government," concludes Hanshan Lei, the chief partner of Yihe Law Firm of Nanjing.[33] Professor Jiuhong Yuan of the Southeast University of China has perceptively suggested that this legislation increases immensely "the possibility that such companies will collude with mafia groups or develop into mafias."[34]

A professional debt collector, Nanjing, China. The man wears a vest with two Chinese characters, which read "Debt collecting." Photo Credit: South China Daily.

Have local criminal groups emerged as suppliers of services of dispute settlement and debt collection for legal entrepreneurs? Among the seventy-four cases I reviewed in depth, the majority of the gangs involved in dispute settlement and debt collection were also running casinos and/or prostitution rings.[35] For example, two former inmates running a gang for nine years (1991–2002) in Zunyi, Guizhou Province, were eventually found guilty of "running a sauna fitness club as a stronghold for gambling, prostitution and debt-collection, armed robbery, extortion, illegal detention of others, and bribing several police inspectors."[36] When a group is effective at collecting gambling debts, it has the resources to collect other debts as well. Two cases refer to companies that appear to have been legal firms gone underground

Mafia debt collection agency cartoon, China. The cartoon by Yao Wen depicts a debt-collecting company recruiting its staff. Big Brother asks the applicants, "Have you ever killed someone?" The advertisement on the wall reads "People who ever killed someone, who once were prisoners, and who are bold and aggressive enough would be desirable." Image Credit: Yao Wen.

(one was called "solving your problem"). In conclusion, these findings suggest that some legitimate debt collection firms have gone underground, and that the groups involved in gambling and prostitution are also branching out in offering services of debt collection.

I now return to the core preoccupation of this book—whether foreign triads have been able to supply services of dispute settlement and protection to entrepreneurs dealing in legal commodities in mainland China. I have not come across any such case during my field trip. Taiwanese triads are present on the mainland, as I have established above, but to the extent that they are involved in solving problems, they can go only as far as settling disputes among Taiwanese businesspeople. Ko-Lin Chin interviewed some Taiwanese gangsters in 2000 in Changan, a town near Shenzhen. These individuals were only helping Taiwanese investors settle disputes among themselves. One Bamboo brother based in Changan told Chin: "There are many disputes among Taiwanese businessmen and whenever they have conflicts, they like to seek help from us because they don't have much confidence in the Chinese legal system."[37] There is no indication that they have gone beyond the Taiwanese economic community and established themselves as independent suppliers of protection services. Clearly, as the number of Taiwanese businesspeople grows in China, it is possible that crime groups from that country will grow in importance.

Gambling

The booming gambling sector has generated a vast set of opportunities for loan sharks, and a demand for debt recovery and dispute settlement services. Since the beginning of Deng's policy to open the country to the market economy, more and more people have been traveling from several parts of China to gamble in Macau—from 1999 a special region of the People's Republic of China—and Guangdong. In 2005, Macau drew 10.5 million mainland Chinese visitors—a 147 percent increase on three years earlier. In a move aimed at undercutting competition, the Chinese government forced the Burmese to shut down more than eighty casinos along the border with southwestern China in 2005. Although the average table in Macau earns three times more than a comparable one in Las Vegas, the global financial crisis of 2008 did not spare the former Portuguese colony, bringing to a halt construction on nine multibillion-dollar casinos and hotels. When I visited in late 2009, steel and concrete skeletons covered swaths of the Cotai Strip, the new development to the south of the main Macau peninsula. Beijing also tightened visa regulations on mainland visitors in 2008. Yet since August 2009, the Chinese government has quietly relaxed the curbs, and gamblers from the mainland have increased significantly since 2008. Underground gambling dens also exist on the mainland. In May 2006, China Central Television, the major broadcasting television network in the country, reported that the number of underground casinos exceeded one hundred in the small county of Lianping in northern Guangdong Province. Gamblers from all over Guangdong and several adjacent provinces converged on the Lianping casinos to gamble day and night. In 2003 alone, the Guangdong police raided more than eighteen hundred underground lottery outlets and casinos in Guangdong.[38]

Gambling gives rise to loan sharking. According to official data, loan sharking accounts for the second-highest number of arrests after drug-related crimes in Macau. Kidnappings for the purpose of repayment of gambling debts increased from twenty-four cases in 2005 to forty-eight in 2006. Diamantino Santos, the coordinator of the Macau Security Bureau, explains that "95 percent of these cases in Macau are usually related to gambling-linked crimes, like loan sharking."[39] The 2006 figures also show a rise in illegal activities closely tied to the gaming industry, such as fraud, robbery, or abuse of confidence.[40]

The inducement of Chinese high rollers to VIP rooms in Macau and the loans they are given generates specific opportunities for strong-arm people to act as enforcers of gambling debts in China. I now turn to a detailed exposition of this system, with the aim of linking it to an as yet underexplored push factor for the transplantation of triads from Macau and Hong Kong to mainland China. VIP rooms are sections within a casino where high rollers stake their bets. They exist in all major gambling venues. For instance, in Las Vegas high rollers are known as "whales" and are actively pursued by casino promoters, who offer them inducements to patronize their casino (and only theirs). The VIP system in Macau, however, is somewhat peculiar.

A visit to the former Portuguese colony with the appropriate guide can help make sense of this system. I visited the Grand Lisboa, a giant, Fabergé egg-shaped casino sitting underneath a fifty-two-story hotel tower shaped as a soaring lotus flower that opened to the public in 2007 and caters mostly to mainland Chinese. The Grand Lisboa stands next to Casino Lisboa, built in the 1970s. The famed Macau multibillionaire Stanley Ho, who held the monopoly on gambling on the island from 1962 to 2002, owns both casinos. My guide and I quickly walked across the main hall where regular players spend their time (and money) at the "mass gaming tables," and entered a VIP room. Two heavily built bouncers dressed in tuxedos were standing in front of the door, ushering us through an additional metal detector, but there was no need to hand over eyeglass cases, bags, or keys. The decor was garish, with fake gilded columns, richly decorated canapés, and statuettes of ancient warriors. Plenty of waiters were on call to answer requests for drinks and food. We also saw a cage dispensing chips and, at one of the three tables, a croupier servicing a loud party of mainland Chinese who, to my guide, looked like the family of a wealthy official. The gambler was playing baccarat, the card game favored by James Bond (in *Casino Royale*, Bond and le Chiffre play a variant of baccarat called *chemin-de-fer*). To me, it was striking how superstitious he seemed to be, praying and hissing as the cards were dealt and uncovered. The women and the younger members of the party gathered around the older man, groaning and gasping at every deal. Hovering around was a peculiar majordomo, who made sure that the gambler had his drink and enough room to move. He also seemed busy substituting the chips that the player was winning with what to me looked like similar chips, of the same value but differently shaped.[41]

I was to receive an education on how the VIP rooms work in Macau from a hulking Chinese man based in Hong Kong. Mr. *Xin* is a "junket operator," offering free trips to mainland Chinese high rollers to Macau VIP rooms. Xin is attached to a room run by a "promoter," who rents it from the casino and puts down collateral to gain access to chips. Traditionally, junket operators were jobless individuals who would scout for gamblers from the cities in the vicinity of Macau and get paid a small fee by the casino. Macau's gambling world underwent a sea change when the island lost its status as a Portuguese territory in 1999. When the Chinese took over, they revoked Ho's concession, thereby opening the market to Western operators. Mainland residents soon became the main players. At this point, junket dealers went from being lowlifes trying to entice local players to a table to marketing agents of the casino on the mainland.[42] This was the case of the majordomo I had observed.

Xin had made deals with travel agencies in three different cities in Guangdong, offering free trips to Macau to high rollers. Ultimately, his business is to entice wealthy Chinese players to a VIP room similar to the one I had visited at the Grand Lisboa and to act as their lackey (by 2008, some 80 percent of the VIP players came from mainland China).[43] Once the players land in Macau, Xin accompanies them to the VIP room, where he lends them chips to play—in the region of five hundred thousand Hong Kong dollars (almost sixty thousand U.S. dollars). The high rollers thus do not need to carry a lot of cash and can bypass the laws regulating the export of money out of China. Moreover, the players can avoid declaring the source of their money (most likely they would be highly embarrassed if they had to). The chips that the junket operator lends—called "dead," "junket," or "clay" chips—cannot be redeemed by the players for cash in the main casino and have a market value that is slightly lower than the nominal value (in the region of 0.7–0.8, I was told). As the players receive chips from their wins, the junket operator replaces the redeemable chips with unredeemable ones, making a profit (notably, the junket operator profits from the game lasting a long time, rather than from either the gambler or the house winning). The junket operator also offers advice and possibly other services, such as introductions to a good sauna, massage, and prostitutes. When the game is finished, in theory the gambler might have won, thereby simply paying the debt back and offering a tip to their "friend." Most likely, the gambler loses, and thus the operator has to collect his debt. I was told that in most cases, the VIP players pay up. Occasionally they do not. If the junket operators cannot recover the debt, they face losing a considerable sum. Loans offered in the VIP rooms exist in limbo and cannot be legally enforced in mainland China.[44]

The VIP room system remains profitable for casinos, which can count on a wide-ranging network of marketing agents without running any risk. The revenues generated by VIP rooms are enormous. The average VIP room share of total gaming revenues for the period 2000–2007 is almost 70 percent, although the mass-market sector is becoming larger.[45] The casino management is a few steps removed from any violence related to eventual disputes. Junket operators face far greater risks, but can reap significant earnings. The system, however, opens up scope for extralegal services of debt collection. Such a situation creates a demand for muscle, and potentially a link between Macau-based triads and the mainland. Some debtors are allowed to return home to gather the money; others are imprisoned in Macau, from where they instruct relatives to pay.

Collecting gambling debts is a significant business for crime groups in mainland China. This particular activity also leads local groups to team up—while remaining separate—with foreign mafias in an effort to chase Chinese gamblers who fail to pay their dues while gambling in Macau. I have come across five such cases. For instance, the Foshan Water Room gang based in the city of Foshan, Guangdong, had teamed up with the Macau Sui Fong (Water Room) triad, the main Macau mafia group. The leader had copied the structure of the Water Room gang, appointing three underlings to manage three different aspects of the gang's activities. Most importantly, they assisted the Macau-based triad in tracking down the families of mainland gamblers who had failed to pay up for their losses in the Las Vegas of the East. They also expanded into loan sharking and betting for sports events. Eventually, they were brought to justice in 2000, after operating for five years (the Water Room triad has also forged ties with a group in Fujian for similar purposes).[46] Another Macau triad, the Great Ring Gang, had set up relations with a gang operating for six years in Guangzhou. As reported in an indictment, the gang "established action teams in the mainland to collect gambling debts."[47] An official at the Guangdong Department of Justice confirmed to me that Hong Kong triads have great influence in Guangzhou.[48]

A high official at Zhuhai Bureau of Justice, a city a few kilometers north of Macau in Guangdong Province, told me that

> there are four main [triads] groups in Macau, 14K, Water Gang, Great Ring Gang, and Wo Shing Yee. All the four main groups were discovered in Zhuhai. Their main businesses included collecting debts for Macau casinos, organizing prostitution, smuggling, kidnapping, manufacturing and selling counterfeit money and collecting protection fees. . . . [I]t was common that Macau mafias came to Zhuhai and other cities in Guangdong to recruit local members, or forge alliances with local gangs to commit crimes. This was a strategy to extend their territory of influence. For example, Wo Shing Yee of Macau established a gang in Jiangmen city [a city some one hundred kilometers northwest of Zhuhai] and provided financial support for the gang to conduct business in the mainland. But the gangsters were local thugs.[49]

The 14K triad (based in both Macau and Hong Kong) also wanted to ensure that it had an outpost on the mainland to track down gamblers who failed to honor their debts. As is often the case, prison provides valuable contacts for gangsters. Two members of the 14K, "Four-Eyed Xiong" Chen and his brother "Big Jie," had shared a cell with two Guangzhou criminals—Jinxin Jiang and Jijun Zeng. The latter eventually became the 14K contacts in the city. Jiang and Zeng would track down gamblers who had not paid their debts and had slipped back to the mainland. After the funds were recovered, they would be transferred by the Guangzhou outpost to the brothers in Hong Kong and Macau using a network of underground banks and legitimate businesses. For instance, on the afternoon of November 18, 1996, Big Jie, Jiang, and Zeng went to the China Grand Hotel in Guangzhou to demand the repayment of HK$2.6 million from a gambler who had borrowed money in a VIP room in Macau and failed to pay it back. Violence ensued, and one person was severely wounded. In another case, in November 1998, the general manager of the Yushun Company of Shanghai borrowed HK$300,000 from the 14K while at the gambling table of the New Century Casino in Macau. The Chen brothers demanded the repayment of this debt several times, but the manager did not return the money. In March 1999 they dispatched their team to Shanghai, where they ultimately killed the gambler's girlfriend.[50]

When Zeng was sentenced to death in 2001, the Chen brothers joined forces with another heavy, Guoqing Mai, who in turn worked with a local gang leader, Deliang Li. As the group grew in strength, it moved beyond collecting gambling debts and formed a debt collection agency, which recovered debts for local customers. Within a short period, the group made at least 7 million yuan in profit. An indictment against the group lists several cases of the violent recovery of ordinary business debts. For example, in February 2001 a customer offered to pay Mai and Li to recover 250,000 yuan from a man called Wu, who lived in the Liwan District in Guangzhou. The gang went to Wu's residence and took the man to the Jiahua Restaurant, in another part of town. They then moved the hostage several times to a variety of locations, mainly around the city airport. He was beaten and tortured. Once the gang was tipped off that the police were after them, they moved their hostage to a farm and were later arrested. Wu escaped alive. In a similar situation in December 2001, two Hong Kong businesspeople asked the gang to recover HK$6 million from a debtor, Kuang, from Guangzhou—offering a fee of 30 percent of the money to be recovered. Kuang, who was kidnapped and tortured at a secret location, finally agreed to pay 3.6 million yuan. Mai demanded the immediate payment of 1.5 million to a designated bank account as a condition for freeing the debtor. Mai stressed that the rest had to be paid within one month. Kuang and his brother eventually paid back the money, and Mai and Li got 900,000 yuan for their services. According to a twenty-four-page indictment issued by Guangzhou Procurator's Office, thirty people were tried in 2003 for twenty-four crimes.[51]

Taiwanese gang leaders interviewed by Ko-Lin Chin in Changan (an industrial town north of Shenzhen) confirm the picture that emerged above: that they settle gambling disputes among Taiwanese businesspeople only, for debts incurred in Taiwan. A Taiwanese brother who owns a restaurant in Changan had this to say:

> I helped [Mr. Hsieh, a businessman from Taiwan] take care of gambling debt of ten million yuan he owed another Taiwanese businessman. A group of brothers from Taiwan were coming over to Changan to settle it, possibly by taking over Mr. Hsieh's factory. Mr. Hsieh asked me for help, and I had the whole thing settled by having Mr. Hsieh pay the businessman NT$700,000. Mr. Hsieh initially said that he could come up with only NT$500,000, but the businessman and his people said no. So I asked Mr. Hsieh to come up with more, and he increased the amount to NT$700,000. That was a pretty good deal for him.[52]

The collection of gambling debts provides a link between Macau and Hong Kong triads and mainland Chinese gangs. The former team up with the latter in order to track down gamblers and their families who failed to pay their debts. It is still too early to say whether foreign triads will become entrenched on the mainland. This criminal activity remains in any case an important source of contacts, and has the potential to allow Hong Kong and Macau mafias to spread on the mainland. As for Taiwanese triads, they appear to be, at most, dealing with debts incurred by gamblers in Taiwan itself.

PROSTITUTION

The junket operator who educated me about his business was keen to let me know that he could provide overall care for any customer, including me if I wished. In particular, he would take me to "the best sauna in Macau." Without the need to insist much, he let me into his secret: the best place in town for prostitutes was the sauna at the Golden Dragon Hotel called "18," a place that I had read about before traveling to Macau, where it was rumored that Uzbek women are trafficked (no evidence was proved in court).[53] Located just off the main street that connects the Hong Kong ferry pier to the center of town, "18" is on the third floor of a glittering four-star hotel and can be reached via an elevator. A plastic-coated price list is placed on a freestanding lectern at the entrance. Ethnicity is a price discriminator: Taiwanese are the most expensive, and Uzbeks are the cheapest. One can also opt to have a sauna only or a standard Chinese massage. Payment is at the end. After perusing the "menu," the customer is whisked to a changing room to undress. He is then led to a large hall with a mammoth bathtub in the middle, and steam rooms and showers to the left. Half-naked girls appear on a balcony and start to dance, eventually undressing fully. Then a parade of some seventy women marches into the main hall, each with a number and a colored pin attached to their bathing costume. They slowly do the room, stopping in front of men draped in their bathrobes for a minute or two, and then move forward. A customer does not need to follow the parade. When he makes up his mind, the john informs the majordomo of his choice and is accompanied to a room, where he and his companion have sex. Men whose bodies are covered in elaborate tattoos are easily found at "18."[54]

While prostitution is legal in Macau, it is not in China. Following the Communist takeover in 1949, local governments were given the task of eliminating counter-revolutionary decadence. The first crackdown against brothels took place in the capital in 1949. Several others followed. During Mao's reign, prostitutes faced severe penalties and could be sent to labor camps for education. In 1958, the Chinese Communist Party announced that prostitution had been eradicated. Even the twenty-nine venereal disease research institutes were closed.[55]

Since the beginning of China's transition to the market economy in 1978, all forms of sex for cash have reemerged. Initially, the phenomenon was limited to the eastern, coastal cities, but since the 1990s it has spread across the country. Arrests of prostitutes, clients, and pimps have increased every year since 1982. Some suggest that the business employs ten million people, with an annual turnover of one trillion yuan. The bulk of the sex trade takes place in karaoke bars, hotels, saunas, beauty salons, and teahouses. A common euphemism for hostesses working in karaoke bars is "ladies of the three accompaniments." In theory, they accompany men by chatting, drinking, and dancing. In reality, they allow clients to fondle them and are willing to engage in sexual intercourse. "Dingdong ladies" are women who phone hotel guests offering sex, while "street girls" try their luck at the lowest level of this profession.[56]

Contrary to common misperceptions, Chinese law does not depart significantly from Western countries' provision in this sphere. The law distinguishes those who organize and induce others into prostitution from those who engage in the act by paying or receiving money (the clients and the workers). Statutes passed since 1991 have made the involvement of a third party, such as a pimp, a criminal offense, even punishable with death. Bar, sauna, and massage parlor owners all face the risk of long prison sentences if found guilty. Sex workers and their clients are mainly dealt with through administrative law, although they face arrest and heavy fines. Hostesses are the most vulnerable, since local authorities have several means at their disposal to harass and humiliate them. The Communist Party has issued specific disciplinary measures to expel members caught red-handed.[57] How do actors in this market, especially the owners of brothels, negotiate protection against police arrest? To whom do they turn to fend off rowdy customers and violent thugs?

After an interview in a factory outside Guangzhou, the owner showed us an upscale karaoke bar in a nearby town that he patronizes regularly. I asked if he knew whether the establishment has entered into a protective umbrella with anyone. According to the factory owner, the hotel was under the wing of police officers to whom it could turn if there was a serious dispute and who protect it against random police raids, while the hotel security guards fend off local thugs and unruly customers. He added that low-level establishments are at much greater risk from local thugs and other bar owners—who harass competitors and try to steal their workers—because they are located in red-light districts and dangerous neighborhoods. The police protectors would not offer help in these fights and would indeed expect them to be handled with discretion, so that attention is not drawn to the bar. Many officials justify their actions by arguing that karaoke bars promote the local economy as well as help businesspeople forge stronger bonds and strike deals.[58]

A Chinese scholar who worked in a karaoke bar for twenty months in Dalian between 1999 and 2002 confirms that officials—especially police officers—are regularly paid for protecting these establishments. One Public Security Bureau officer remarked to her: "Karaoke bars and hostesses are our source of livelihood. We basically cannot live without them."[59] As in the case of legitimate businesspeople who are forced to hire individuals suggested by their umbrella, police officers have devised a system to keep informed on the activities of the brothels: they maintain a group of "spy hostesses" who report on the club conditions as well as act as these officials' personal harem.[60]

The case of Chen Kai from Fujian has brought to the fore the reach of protective umbrellas. Chen Kai was sentenced to death in 2005 for organizing prostitution in Fuzhou. Before being arrested, he was the head of a conglomerate that included a hotel, a nightclub, three restaurants, a real estate development firm, and three saunas. Chen Kai had started as a street seller and then entered the electronic gambling industry. As his business interests grew and expanded into entertainment, he struck a deal with the city chief of police, who was known as the "Godfather of Fuzhou," and named the chief's son the vice president of his company. Whenever an investigation was initiated, the chief of police would block it. No less than fifty officials were eventually found guilty at the Chen Kai trial in 2003. They were, as the *China Daily* noted, the protective umbrella for Chen Kai operations.[61] People familiar with the case suggest that Chen was nothing but a brothel owner, and the violence used by him was limited to maintaining order within his premises and occasionally forcing waiters into providing sexual services for officials who took a fancy to them.[62] Protection was coming from his umbrella.

Among the seventy-four cases that I reviewed in depth, nine groups were found guilty of running brothels. None is on record as trying to monopolize the business. These cases seem to refer to instances of involvement in managing a brothel, rather than wide-ranging attempts to control the market. There is no evidence that foreign triads played a role in this business. In sum, it appears that fragments of the state, and in particular the very people who are supposed to fight prostitution, act as the industry's protectors and there is yet more evidence that these arrangements are localized in nature.

DRUG TRAFFICKING

Chinese drug traffickers benefit from proximity to a 150,000-square-mile patch of land in the Wa area of the northern Shan state of Burma, known to the world as the golden triangle. Burma is the second-largest opium-producing country in the world after Afghanistan. The methamphetamine production plants blamed for the "speed" epidemic in Thailand in the

1990s are also located here. After the country gained independence in 1948, the Communist Party of Burma controlled most of the area. In the same year as the Berlin wall collapsed and Eastern Europe was freed from Soviet influence, the leaders of the Wa ethnic group dissociated themselves from the Communist Party of Burma and signed a peace treaty with the government. Under the conditions of the treaty, the Wa army was allowed to remain in control of the territory and retain its arsenal, while the Burmese leadership could direct its attention to crushing the indigenous democratic movement. The Wa army—defined by the U.S. Department of Justice as "one of the largest heroin-producing and trafficking groups in the world"—continued its long-standing involvement in the cultivation, production, and distribution of drugs.[63] Here opium cultivation is legal and is a major source of tax revenue for the Wa leadership. Local farmers pay a compulsory tax in opium regardless of whether they grow the plant or not, thereby forcing them to either start cultivation or buy opium to pay the tax. Heroin and methamphetamine factories are illegal, although they operate under the informal protection of army officers.[64]

In the early 1990s, legitimate and illegitimate cross-border trade between Burma and China began to flourish. Many entrepreneurs from China shuttled between the Wa region and the newly established special economic zones in search of opportunities. With the arrival of the Chinese, heroin production grew. The presence of a developed chemical industry in China makes it relatively easy to obtain and import the precursor chemicals needed for narcotics production from China into Burma, and export the finished product from Burma back to China and then onward internationally. Methamphetamine production took off when the Thai authorities decided to crack down on this drug in their own country in the mid-1990s. Chinese entrepreneurs operating in China, Burma, and Thailand took advantage of the situation, and began to mass-produce methamphetamine in the Wa area to meet the enormous demand in Thailand.[65]

The heroin produced in the Wa region travels into China through the province of Yunnan, onward through Guangdong, Shenzhen, and Hong Kong, and finally reaches North America. As the cross-border trade of legal commodities between China and Burma started to swell in the 1980s, and continued to expand rapidly in the 1990s, drug trafficking along the border area also flourished. Significant seizures of heroin in Yunnan Province are on record since at least 1986. In the 1990s, there was a noticeable

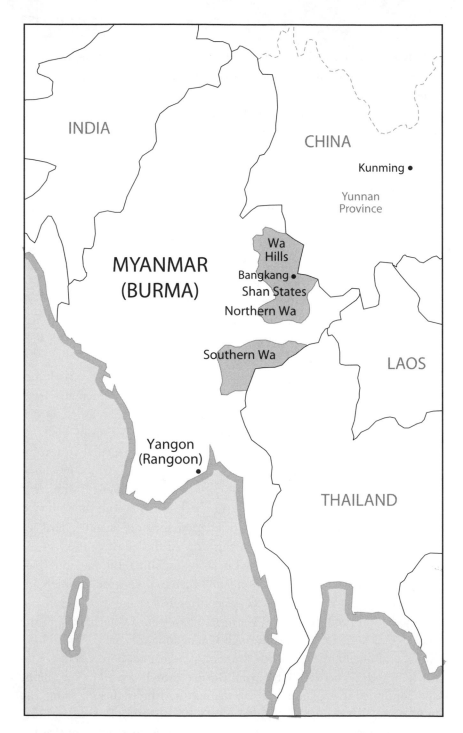

Figure 6.2 Map of the Wa area

increase in the number of detected cross-border drug trafficking cases. As reported by the U.S. Drug Enforcement Administration in 2002, "China's Yunnan province has become the primary transit point for Burmese heroin."[66] The drug then reaches Guangdong Province, the primary distribution point for both the domestic and international market. In 2002 only, the Guangdong police seized 1,618.72 kilograms of drugs and cracked down on 5,745 drug-related criminal activities. In describing the situation, an officer in charge of narcotics control stressed that "Guangdong has become the major channel and distributing center for drug smuggling activities."[67]

Once in Guangdong, the drug reaches the United States via Shenzhen and Hong Kong. In the late 1980s, a change in the export methods employed by the Chinese was detected. Instead of using drug couriers traveling to U.S. airports from Hong Kong and Bangkok, Chinese traffickers began to send large quantities of heroin (from fifty to one hundred pounds or more) to the seaports of Newark and Elizabeth, New Jersey, and Chicago, hidden in cargo containers shipped from Asian ports, such as Shenzhen and Hong Kong. The drugs were carefully stuffed into products such as furniture and frozen seafood. In one instance, drug traffickers stuffed heroin into five boxes of goldfish that were to be shipped to an aquarium in San Francisco. The trick was discovered, and led to the exposure of the activities of a drug-trafficking ring between mainland China, Hong Kong, and the United States.[68]

For such complex transshipping operations to be successful, several actors must be involved at various points of the trade and protection must be arranged. Are foreign triads the main suppliers of such service? There is no evidence that triads are directly involved in smuggling drugs or that they offer protection to the trade (the distinction is crucial). The traders responsible for the bulk of heroin imported from Burma through China into the United States are international businesspeople of Chinese origin who take advantage of their connections and legitimate commercial operations to carry out the transportation of drugs from the source countries. The major traffickers are entrepreneurs who have links with the communities to which the drug is exported.[69] Since the adoption of the open-door policy, Chinese investors—especially from the provinces of Yunnan and Sichuan—have visited the Wa area of Burma. Their presence has helped

the Wa leaders to develop the manufacturing of drugs. They also organize the trafficking of the product back to China, independently of any
connection with Hong Kong and Taiwanese triads. They use legitimate
transportation networks to reach Shenzhen and Hong Kong. Once there,
one would expect that Hong Kong triads might control the harbors. The
reality is, however, different. Hong Kong triads control low-level drug dealing in the city for local consumption, but they have never become the dominant players in the international trade. At every stage, successful traffickers
rely on officials to turn a blind eye, as several observers have suggested.[70]

Two members of the security branch of a Western multinational operating in Asia whom I interviewed in Hong Kong dismissed the idea that triads are prominent in any smuggling activities, of either humans or drugs. In
their extensive investigations of the matter (which include running informants and intercepting communications), they have come across only one
reference to a Taiwanese triad member who seemed somewhat connected,
although in a personal capacity rather than as a member of his mafia group.
In their opinion, the smuggling of illegal products out of China is overseen
by corrupt officials. "We know that during the recent Olympic Games, officials in Beijing phoned their opposite numbers in the provinces ordering
them to suspend shipments of illegal commodities. The order was meant to
last until the end of the Paralympics!"[71] They added that illegal trafficking is
greatly facilitated by the Container Security Initiative.

The Container Security Initiative allows U.S. Customs and Border Protection officials to inspect containers in foreign seaports before they are
loaded on board vessels destined for the United States. The inspections
take place with the support of local customs officials. In China, the ports
of Hong Kong, Shenzhen, and Shanghai are part of the initiative. Indeed,
Hong Kong and Shanghai are the largest ports in the world shipping goods
to the United States. In the immediate wake of the World Trade Center attack in 2001, U.S. customs developed this initiative to address "the threat
to border security and global trade posed by the potential for terrorist
use of a maritime container to deliver a weapon," as its Web site recites.
The containers deemed to pose a threat are examined at the port of origin
using "sophisticated technology" aimed at detecting nuclear and radiological material. Once they have passed the check, they can enter the United
States without further scrutiny.[72]

In effect, "local custom officials tell U.S. agents where to look and where not to look," one of my informants told me. They added, "It is like having the crooks telling the police what to do."[73] To put it differently, this source claims that local bureaucrats, who speak the language and know the American operative procedures, have worked out what kinds of goods would not be picked up by the U.S. technology. The surest way to ensure that cigarettes or drugs are smuggled into the United States is to have the containers inspected for nuclear and radiological material. Since the technology does not detect other commodities, the container is then given a clean bill of health and allowed to enter the United States without any further check.[74]

CONCLUSIONS

So far, China counts as another negative case in the general argument of this book. Members and bosses of foreign triads are present on the mainland, but have not yet emerged as a viable mafia supplying private protection. As in the case of Bardonecchia and Rome, mafiosi did not decide to migrate out of their own free will. Their presence in the new territory is the unintended consequence of police action in their country of origin. Once they found themselves on the mainland, they quickly realized that the new China offered many opportunities to invest some of their gangs' funds, but they have so far failed to establish themselves as viable protectors for legal entrepreneurs. Some conditions for their success were present: a language and ancestry in common with the locals (Taiwanese is similar to the dialect of southern Fujian; some Hong Kong triads members originated from Guangdong region); the presence of many new immigrants from other parts of China who were underemployed or out of work; and the presence of new and booming markets, including illegal markets such as gambling and prostitution (table 6.1). Such a situation should have generated a demand for criminal protection and offered opportunities for mafiosi, local or foreign. In reality, though, the outcome was different because a powerful protector was already on the ground: corrupt fragments of the state apparatus.

Remarkably, the jargon word for the activities of the latter is protective umbrella—a clear indication that what officials offer goes beyond simple, one-off corruption services and encompasses long-term arrangements to take care of (and profit from) private entrepreneurs. In the Russian case, some criminal gangs became powerful roofs for businesspeople, although official roofs played the biggest role in the market for informal, illegal private protection. The case of China indicates that few criminal groups have managed to take on the role of protective umbrellas. Instead, corrupt elements of the state apparatus, such as the military, police, and the local administration, act as the protectors of legitimate businesspeople (table 6.1), like the producer of lightbulbs that I encountered in Dongguan. As suggested in chapter 2, it would be an uphill struggle for an incoming mafia to dislodge an existing local criminal protector, especially one with the organs of state power at its disposal.

Since the opening of the economy, illegal markets have also boomed in China: gambling, prostitution, human smuggling (an issue that I have touched on only tangentially in this chapter), and drug trafficking. For the most part, it seems that even in illegal markets, fragments of the state apparatus offer protection. This is especially evident in the protection of prostitution. Gambling gives rise to loan sharking and a demand to recoup debts incurred at the tables in Macau by mainland Chinese. In such cases, Macau triads may team up with gangs on the mainland to trace the gamblers—or their families—and some of these gangs have then expanded their business into the collection of ordinary, business debts. If allowed to expand further, these gangs could develop into fully fledged mafia groups offering generalized protection services to whomever can pay. Since they enforce promises on behalf of foreign triads, in my view this represents a potential mechanism for long-distance cooperation and the transplantation of foreign triads to China. Yet there is no strong evidence that such transplantation has taken place. Quite to the contrary, it appears that local authorities have been quick to outlaw debt collection agencies and have arrested those tied to triads.

Have foreign triads been able to penetrate the lucrative drug trade? The short answer is, again, no. The heroin that leaves the Wa area of Burma is transported into China by low-level couriers organized by respectable businesspeople. When the drug reaches the ports of Shenzhen and Hong Kong, crucially placed custom officials exploit the system to sign off cargo bound for U.S. ports. The Container Security Initiative might have prevented the shipment of nuclear and bacteriologic weapons to U.S. soil,

TABLE 6.1
Factors Facilitating Mafia Transplantation, Bardonecchia, Verona, Budapest, Rome, New York City, Rosario, and Southern China

Factors facilitating mafia transplantation/cases	Bardonecchia	Verona	Budapest	Rome	New York City (1910–30)	Rosario (1910–30)	Shenzhen/ Guangzhou
Generalized migration	Yes	No	No	No	Yes	Yes	Yes
Mafiosi migration (willing/unwilling)	Yes (unwilling)	Yes (unwilling)	Yes (unwilling)	Yes (unwilling)	Yes (unwilling)	Yes (unwilling)	Yes (unwilling)
Supply of mafiosi	Yes	Yes	Yes	Yes	Yes	Yes	Yes
Local conditions							
Level of trust/civic engagement	High	High	Low	Low	Low	Low	Low
Presence of local illegal protectors	No	No	No	No	No	No	Yes
Size of locale	Small	Large	Large	Large	Large	Large	Large
New and/or booming markets*	Yes	Yes	Yes	No	Yes	Yes	Yes
Demand for mafia services	Yes	No	Yes	No	Yes	No	No
Transplantation	Yes	No	Yes	No	Yes	No	No

* The markets considered are construction (Bardonecchia and Rosario), drugs (Verona and China), property rights (Budapest and China), oil (Budapest), alcohol (New York City), gambling (New York City and China), and prostitution (China).

but has also ensured that cargoes checked in China enter directly into the United States without further inspection. It might prove a devil's pact.

This chapter has raised some questions that cannot be fully answered at this stage and would require a separate study. It is nevertheless worth spelling them out. Who is allowed to acquire a protective umbrella? On the basis of the respondents' suggestions, it appears that the protection industry is stratified. Small entrepreneurs are not large and profitable enough to be of interest, and therefore may be more likely to enlist the services of independent debt collection agencies when they enter into a dispute. Since the government has moved to outlaw legitimate debt collection agencies, it could in effect have pushed low-level businesspeople into the hands of now-criminalized and unregistered agencies.

A second issue that I have touched on is the relationship between the center and periphery. To what extent can Beijing dictate to the provinces what to do in terms of illegal activities? There are several instances in which it appears that the center retains a degree of control. When the latter decides to arrest gang leaders protected by officials, it bypasses the local police and simply descends on the city to round up the suspects. In order to avoid embarrassment during high-profile events such as the Olympic Games or the sixtieth-anniversary celebrations for the People's Republic of China, Beijing appears to have been able to tell the periphery to stop smuggling operations, and enforce more strictly antiprostitution and drug consumption rules, as I learned in the disco in Shenzhen in late September 2009. And yet the periphery can also "bribe" the center. In order to obtain the go-ahead and funding for major public works, local cadres can entice national-level officials. Once the project is approved, local officials have plenty of opportunities to handpick the construction company and extract bribes, as documented by Xueliang Ding.[75] This system produces what the Chinese call "doufu-zha structures"—deeply flawed constructions that put lives at risk.

As Timothy Garton Ash has remarked recently, China might well be the defining geopolitical story of our time.[76] Yet observers routinely fail to connect the macropicture with microlevel processes. A recent report from the McKinsey Global Institute points out that China underconsumes and overinvests, mostly in building projects. The stimulus plan that China enacted in 2009 focused almost entirely on building infrastructure and public works, while other countries have also passed tax breaks and improved social safety nets.[77] Only by recognizing the massive opportunities for kickbacks that construction projects open up for officials in both the center and periphery, can one make full sense of macroeconomic decisions. The equilibrium between central government and cadres in the provinces appears precarious, and deserves a full study of its own. To the extent that criminal gangs in the periphery overpower local power holders, they could become the interlocutor of the center, and China might well develop pockets where mafias are entrenched, like in southern Italy, certain parts of Latin America, and the former Soviet Union.

APPENDIX

TABLE A6.1

Summary Information on Seventy-four "Organizations with an Underworld Nature," China, 1992–2009

Name of gang	Length of activity in years	Start date	Location (region)	Size	Background leadership*	Main charges
1. Anda LU Brothers	16	1992	Heilongjiang	54	3	Kidnapping, loan-sharking, raping, gambling, prostitution, corruption, frauds
2. Black Leopard	1	1995	Sichuan	N/A	N/A	Robbery, protection racket, contract killing
3. Blue Clothes squad	7	2000	Liaoning	N/A	3	Debt collection and dispute settlement in real estate
4. Bo TIAN's gang	6	1995	Jilin	N/A	1	Kidnapping, extortion, monopolization of coal sector
5. Broadsword	1	N/A	Shanghai	N/A	N/A	Robbery, debt collection, extortion, monopolization of entertainment sector, drug trafficking
6. Caiping XIE's gang	5	2004	Chongqing	18	1	Loan-sharking, gambling, dispute settlement
7. Central China overlord	1	1994	Henan	N/A	1	Raping, hooliganism, attempts to control transport sector
8. Changli He's gang	1	N/A	Henan	N/A	1	Corruption

TABLE A6.1 (*cont.*)

Name of gang	Length of activity in years	Start date	Location (region)	Size	Background leadership*	Main charges
9. Chongqing Mingliang CHEN's gang	8	2001	Chongqing	47	N/A	Kidnapping, extortion, prostitution, drug trafficking
10. Deliang LI and Guoqing MAI's gang	6	1996	Guangdong	N/A	4	Kidnapping, robbery, collection of gambling debts, extortion, protection rackets, blackmailing
11. Deping JIANG's gang	5	1997	Jiangsu	20	3	Monopolization of excavation sector
12. Fang Guangcheng's gang	9	1996	Beijing	36	1	Extortion, monopolization of construction
13. Foshan Water Gang	5	1995	Guangdong	N/A	3	Collection of gambling debts, arms dealing, loan-sharking, gambling
14. Great Ring (or Big Circle Boys)	4	1994	Macao	N/A	2	Kidnapping, robbery
15. Guanglong ZHOU's gang	6	1995	Guangdong	N/A	1	Protection racket, monopolization of transportation and taxi industry
16. Guizhen MA's gang	14	1995	Jilin	10	N/A	Loan-sharking, extortion, gambling, corruption
17. Guojian LI's gang	1	2007	Hubei	7	4	Monopolization of fruit and vegetable market
18. Handan Lifa LIN's gang	5	2003	Hebei	24	N/A	Extortion in construction
19. Hong YANG's gang	3	2004	Hubei	N/A	3	Debt collection, collection of gambling debts, extortion, gambling
20. Hongyong ZHANG's gang	4	2005	Hebei	90	2	Tax evasion, theft of raw materials
21. HU Brothers	9	1996	Beijing	34	N/A	Kidnapping, arms dealing, illegal sand excavation, illegal detention, corruption

Table A6.1 (*cont.*)

Name of gang	Length of activity in years	Start date	Location (region)	Size	Background leadership*	Main charges
22. Huaibei mafia	16	1993	Anhui	N/A	N/A	Debt collection, loan-sharking, protection racket, gambling, control of coal sector
23. Jianshe LI's gang	8	1994	Hebei	40	1	Kidnapping, debt collection, extortion, controlling officials, dispute settlement, illegal detention
24. Jinwen XIONG's gang	8	1992	Yunnan	N/A	3	Kidnapping, extortion, rape, gambling, illegal activities in mining, illegal detention
25. Kai ZHAO's gang	9	2000	Jilin	10	N/A	Monopolization of gas sector, dispute settlement
26. LI Brothers	3	1997	Gansu	54	1	Robbery, protection racket, gambling
27. Lifeng TANG's gang	1	1998	Henan	N/A	4	Debt collection, protection racket, control of elections, gambling
28. Luoma group		N/A	Sichuan	N/A	N/A	Monopolization of entertainment and car repair business
29. MA and DING's gang	9	1992	Gansu	60	N/A	Robbery, extortion, protection rackets, gambling, monopolization of entertainment
30. Mun FENG's gang	8	1993	Chongqing	110	3	Extortion, monopolization of real estate and construction, control of officials, dispute settlement, corruption
31. Mingran ZHU's gang	2	1999	Xinjiang Uigur	N/A	4	Extortion, monopolization of fruit and vegetable market
32. Nanyang Yugang BAI's gang	5	2004	Henan	27	N/A	Extortion, monopolization of excavation and mining
33. Nine Brothers	N/A	N/A	Guangdong	N/A	N/A	Protection racket, gambling, usury
34. Pengfei SONG's gang	15	1993	Liaoning	95	5	Monopolization of transportation

TABLE A6.1 (*cont.*)

Name of gang	Length of activity in years	Start date	Location (region)	Size	Background leadership*	Main charges
35. Pingyuan mafia	12	1980	Yunnan	N/A	1	Arms dealing, protection racket, drugs, control of officials, mining, and stolen cars
36. Qiaosi criminal syndicate	7	1990	Heilongjiang	N/A	2	Extortion, rape, monopolization of entertainment and construction
37. Renhao ZHENG's gang	3	1998	Heilongjiang	N/A	3	Kidnapping, extortion at fruit and vegetable market
38. Shaoxi ZOU's gang	15	1994	Guizhou	N/A		Arms dealing, gambling, prostitution
39. Shengli LI-ANG's gang	14	N/A	Henan	143	3	Debt collection, monopolization of entertainment, construction, and transportation, dispute settlement
40. Shiwei REN's gang	13	1995	Liaoning	43		Hooliganism
41. Shounan ZHOU and Xu DING's gang	9	1991	Guizhou	N/A	3	Robbery, debt collection, collection of gambling debts, extortion, gambling, prostitution, illegal detention, corruption
42. Sicong XIA's gang	N/A	N/A	Hubei	21	1	Monopolization of construction
43. Sister Nine's gang	6	1996	Sichuan	N/A	3	Kidnapping, debt collection, protection racket, gambling, prostitution, drugs, illegal detention
44. Solving Your Problems gang	3	N/A	Hunan	N/A	3	Robbery, extortion, protection racket, dispute settlement, illegal detention
45. Songyu HU's gang	2	2006	Gansu	53	N/A	Robbery, protection racket, entertainment, illegal detention
46. Tao HUANG's gang	5	1997	Jiangxi	N/A	4	Kidnapping, robbery, extortion of taxi drivers, protection racket, gambling

TABLE A6.1 (*cont.*)

Name of gang	Length of activity in years	Start date	Location (region)	Size	Background leadership*	Main charges
47. Thirteen Protectors	5	1997	Yunnan	N/A	N/A	Debt collection, arms dealing, extortion, protection racket, gambling, monopolization of transportation
48. Tianqing YANG's gang	4	2005	Chongqing	9	3	Debt collection, loan-sharking, extortion
49. TU Brothers	3	1998	Guizhou	N/A	3	Debt collection, protection racket in entertainment and prostitution
50. Underworld 110	1	2005	Hunan	13	N/A	Debt collection, extortion
51. Wanchun HAO's gang	8	2008	Liaoning	24	N/A	Extortion, frauds
52. Wei ZHANG's gang	6	1995	Zhejiang	N/A	3	Bid rigging, real estate, corruption, stolen cars, frauds
53. Weiguo ZHENG's gang	3	1998	Shaanxi	N/A	1	Protection racket, bid rigging, monopolization of excavation
54. West gang	6	1993	Guangxi	N/A	2	Debt collection, loan-sharking, gambling
55. White Dragon	N/A	N/A	Guizhou	16	N/A	Robbery, transportation
56. Wolf	6	N/A	Shanxi	49	3	Robbery, arms dealing, extortion, rape, gambling, usury
57. Xiangji ZHUANG's gang	4	1996	Hunan	N/A	3	Monopolization of construction sector
58. Xiangu DU's gang	4	1997	Heilongjiang	N/A	4	Robbery
59. Xianliang FU's gang	2	1999	Sichuan	N/A	3	Collection of gambling debts, loan-sharking, gambling, transportation, usury
60. Xiaoming LIANG criminal syndicate	4	1994	Jilin	N/A	2	Kidnapping, robbery, gambling, prostitution

TABLE A6.1 (*cont.*)

Name of gang	Length of activity in years	Start date	Location (region)	Size	Background leadership*	Main charges
61. Xu's criminal syndicate	2	1992	Zhejiang	N/A	3	Robbery, arms dealing, extortion, rape, monopolization of transportation, drug trafficking, dispute settlement
62. Yali YU's gang	11	1998	Jilin	13	N/A	Corruption, frauds, tax evasion
63. Yang and Xie's gang	4	N/A	Fujian	N/A	N/A	Robbery
64. Yangjiang mafia	15	N/A	Guangdong	N/A	4	Protection racket, monopolization of entertainment, transportation, gasoline, and construction materials
65. Yanhong BAI's gang	15	1993	Sichuan	8	N/A	Gambling, drug trafficking, controlling officials
66. Ye Ba Er gang	19	1990	Guizhou	23	3	Gambling, prostitution, dispute settlement, illegal detention, illegal logging
67. Yibing CHEN's gang	3	1998	Beijing	N/A	1	Protection racket of transportation and retail
68. Yong LIU's gang	5	1995	Liaoning	N/A	1	Monopolization of entertainment, supermarkets, real estate, sale of cigarettes, and construction
69. Yongfeng WEI's gang	5	2002	Shaanxi	18	N/A	Kidnapping, robbery, debt collection, extortion, protection rackets, gambling, monopolization of waste disposal and gambling, illegal detention
70. Yu ZHOU's gang	4	2002	Hubei	40	N/A	Prostitution, entertainment
71. Zhenhuang DU's gang (or White Pig)	8	2000	Fujian	N/A	N/A	Extortion, gambling, dispute settlement

TABLE A6.1 (*cont.*)

Name of gang	Length of activity in years	Start date	Location (region)	Size	Background leadership*	Main charges
72. ZHU family	12	1989	Jiangxi	N/A	1	Kidnapping, debt collection, loan-sharking, corruption, gambling, extortion in transportation, mining, fruit and vegetable market, gasoline, waste disposal
73. ZI family	4	1997	Heilongjiang	N/A	3	Arms dealing, prostitution, monopolization of entertainment and real estate, stolen cars, illegal logging
74. Ziqiang ZHANG and Jihuan YE's gang	6	1990	Guangdong	N/A	3	Kidnapping, arms dealing, robbery

* Key to "background of leadership": 1 — official/politician/relative of; 2 = police officer; 3 = ex-prisoner/criminal; 4 = businessperson; 5 = migrant worker.
Sources: He 2003; Zhang 2006; Li and Ke 2006; Kang Kang 1998; selected official press reports.
Note: The cases listed in table A6.1 come under the Chinese definition of mafia group ("organizations with an underworld nature"), but do not all display the features of a mafia group as defined in this book. Clearly, this list does not claim to be representative. The cases were deemed important by the sources listed above.

SEVEN

Mafia Origins, Transplantation, and the Paradoxes of Democracy

Boris Sergeev, the Solntsevskaya associate operating in Rome, was a flitter, laying his eggs in many nests. Born in Moscow, he lived in Vienna and Paris. His police file lists several aliases. He was a polygamist and forger. Unconfirmed sources claim that he had worked for the KGB in the 1980s. When negotiating with Islamist fighters to smuggle Chechen oil to countries under the UN embargo, he grew a beard. For reasons as yet unknown, he surfaced in Rome in the early 1990s. When the Solntsevskaya boss arrived in the Italian capital a year or two later, Sergeev offered to help: he registered some of Yakovlev's companies at his address, arranged invitations to Austria for the boss's lieutenant (a fugitive from justice), supplied false German passports, and allowed the crew to use his bank accounts for the transit of vast sums of money. Around April 1996, however, the two grew apart. Yakovlev suspected Sergeev of embezzling money entrusted to him.

Sergeev had been accused of embezzlement before. A few years earlier, he had taken funds from a Russian businessman, *Nikita Morozov*, but never invested or returned them. As one might expect, Morozov was no ordinary businessman. When he died in 1994, he was a partner in two Russian companies based in Vienna and controlled by Ivan'kov, who had escaped to the United States in 1992. Together with two other Russians connected to the Solntsevskaya, Morozov came to the attention of the U.S. authorities when he threatened a drug trafficker based in Antwerp who had started cooperating with U.S. intelligence. The three Russians were trying to obtain a share in the trafficker's legitimate shipping company. Sergeev had a talent for upsetting powerful people.

When Morozov's son, *Akim*, and his wife, *Ekaterina*, showed up in Rome in June 1996 asking for the money, Sergeev and his wife welcomed them with open arms. After a lavish lunch at their house, they pulled a gun on the couple. According to Ekaterina, a young and attractive blond, they first beat them and then Sergeev tried to rape her. In the ensuing bedlam, Sergeev's wife was holding the pistol. The couple managed to escape after a struggle by climbing over the garden fence. The railing was not high; to this day Sergeev's abode is the same two-story, white, detached house with a small pool in the garden, an estate agent told me. Ekaterina and Akim stopped a police car on the busy main street of the tourist town on the Lazio coast and reported Sergeev. The attack on the Morozovs had momentous consequences. Sergeev was arrested for assault, and the house was searched for over three days by local and special units. On the first day, the police found twenty-two caliber-nine cartridges, several Russian and Polish passports, a gun holster, and a piece of paper listing all Russian criminal groups, including the name of the person in charge and the banks they used. On the second day, they retrieved a gun from the water tank behind the toilet—a rather rudimentary way to hide a weapon. On the third day, Italian authorities found more documents, mainly related to arms sales.

During the summer of 1996 Sergeev was hard at work on his last scam: the sale of cheap Bulgarian meat in Russia. Through political contacts within the European Union, he obtained a certificate stating that his product was from high-quality Italian livestock and intended for humanitarian aid to Russia. The certification allowed him to avoid paying duties in Europe. Once in Russia, the meat would have been sold at market price. To pull off this scam worth twenty million U.S. dollars, he needed capital and official support on the Russian side too. He thought that he had secured the backing of a Moscow brigada. This was the reason for his last trip to his native city in 1996 described in the introduction of this book. Although there is no final word on who ordered and carried out Sergeev's murder at the Tverskaya hotel in September, it is plausible that the Solntsevskaya had grown tired of him and decided to end his career. Some ventured the theory that the hit was carried out with the blessing of officials involved in illegal oil deals in Chechnya. Yakovlev, the boss in Rome, received a call informing him of Sergeev's death at 17.52 Italian time, just one minute after Sergeev's wife got the news. He remarked, "What, did they kill him? I am not surprised; he has stolen money from half of Russia."[1]

Seen from a distance, international organized crime appears as a monolithic and self-assured Global Corp. Inc. The Solntsevskaya sends a boss to Rome, where he sets up an outpost, and quickly penetrates the upper echelons of national and international finance. Waiting for him is an infrastructure that includes local fixers and a fellow Russian with international contacts that range, according to newspaper reports, from top Moscow apparatchiki to Swiss financiers linked to the Democratic Party in the United States.

Such a picture is not entirely inaccurate, but the complications of the story have been erased. The Solntsevskaya is not a single organization but rather an alliance of independent brigades. The "envoy" to Rome was running for his life after his mentor had been murdered in Moscow. The local help consisted of two people operating a travel agency. The Russian fixer was not a full-time member of the organization but instead a freelance con artist with apparently constrained intellectual capacity and certainly limited credibility, whose plans often floundered and backfired.

The first step for observers of international organized crime is to draw some basic distinctions. Sergeev was part of the "service industry" of organized crime. Although some might be tempted to portray him as a global criminal mastermind floating in hyperspace, a present-day Moriarty, he and other unsavory characters that fill popular accounts of this phenomenon are not independent variables; they are hired to carry out work for states, secret services, legitimate corporations, or mafia groups. When they lose the trust of their paymasters, they are removed and leave no trace.

Mafias do not flit. Rather than being liquid entities, they are firmly entrenched in the territory that they govern. One surprising finding of this study is that most mafiosi do not migrate away from their territory of their own volition (the surprise is of course directly proportional to the belief that mafias migrate easily). They are not the CEOs of a global corporation exploring rationally the best mix of tax breaks, law enforcement, and climatic conditions. In the cases covered here, mafiosi move to new territories in order to escape state prosecution, mafia wars, and internal disputes, or because they are ordered by the state to move away. The recent transplantation of gangs from Southern California to El Salvador and Guatemala is another case of less-than-willing migration. The first wave of migration of Central American youths to Southern California was due to civil wars and military conflict in Central America in the 1980s. Once in the United States, some individuals joined Latino gangs. In the early 1990s, the U.S. government forced more than 150,000 Central Americans to return to their home countries in a three-year period. Some of them brought their criminal expertise with them, taking over and transforming local bands. By the mid-1990s, one could find "clones" of Los Angeles gangs—such as Mara Salvatrucha and the 18th gang in San Salvador, and the White Fence and Latin Kings in Guatemala. Contrary to what was suggested by the media and some scholars, though, the members of Latino gangs in California had not sought to expand their franchise and drug distribution network through relocation to Central America. They had been forced there by state policies.[2]

Mafiosi are stationary because the service they provide is inherently local. They ensure selective access to resources in a given territory. In order to do so, they build long-term relationships with the place in which they operate as well as with the people, officeholders, and police. Rather than with a CEO, a more apt comparison is with a politician—say, a British Member of Parliament or U.S. Senator. Candidates who have built their power base in a given constituency do not simply pack up and try their luck in the French or Italian political system, even if the salaries and allowances are larger. They would not have enough local knowledge and therefore cannot hope to get things done because they do not have connections to local power holders. As a rule, political (and criminal) reputations are local and are the product of costly investments. To start afresh somewhere else is expensive. As Tocqueville wrote in *Democracy in America*, "The happy and the powerful do not go into exile." Rather, "poverty and misfortune" make them move.

Only under a special set of circumstances do mafias reproduce themselves in new areas. This book has tried to untangle the factors that account for mafia migration and successful transplantation. In so doing, it has challenged some widespread conceptions regarding migration. Generalized population migration on its own cannot explain the mob's successful and long-term transplantation in a new territory. The migration of individuals with specific mafia skills surely increases the risk of mafias becoming entrenched, yet this "variable" is not sufficient for a mafia to become deep-rooted in a new territory.

The findings of this book also qualify the effect of globalization on organized crime. I found no instances in which mafiosi opened outposts abroad in order to obtain resources such as labor and specialized equipment, or where mafiosi rationally decided to start a protection racket in a faraway land—what I called market-seeking motivations. To the extent that globalization has increased labor mobility, mafias have even less reason to open branches abroad to look for recruits. If mafias seek specialized technical equipment, such as arms, globalization could increase the number of international locations from which they obtain these resources, but it also reduces the motivation to own resources abroad. In the mid-1990s, for instance, Russian bosses occasionally traveled to Germany to buy arms. Rather than establishing an outpost in that country, they simply bought arms on the open market. Thus, globalization affects how crime is committed in a given country, instead of making mobsters want to migrate abroad.

Mafias do reinvest the proceeds of their crimes in different markets. A specific function that a mafioso can carry out abroad is to monitor investments for their group back home. The case of Yakovlev partly fits this picture. Although he ended up in Rome because he was fleeing death threats in Moscow, while abroad he kept himself busy investing the funds of his own brigada in the Italian economy. He also had won the trust of other Russian criminal groups and was managing some of their funds as well. Other cases are on record. Anthony Spilotro oversaw the Chicago outfit's investments in Las Vegas in the 1970s, although he did not do a particularly good job. Pippo Calò, the boss of the Porta Nuova Sicilian mafia family, moved to Rome at the start of the 1970s to monitor its investments in real estate and banking. The presence of the Neapolitan Camorra in the Scottish city of Aberdeen also reflected mafia attempts to launder money and invest in the local legal economy.[3] In these cases, the initial motivation for the mafias' presence was not to establish control over a specific sector of the economy.

Why would a mafia send an envoy abroad rather than just monitor its investments from a distance? Mafia investments are informal and often in cash; no recourse to the legal system exists in the event of a dispute. Moreover, money laundering and investments in the legal economy can involve several hundred one-shot transactions between business associates of the criminal group and legitimate firms in foreign and inhospitable countries. Those tasked with undertaking these decisions enjoy a significant amount of discretion and are difficult to monitor. Investments can go wrong, and the bosses back home cannot easily verify claims and reports. This situation generates specific incentives for mafiosi to go abroad so as to monitor directly transactions with legitimate entrepreneurs. The boss might well be tempted to go himself, since he cannot trust agents fully. On the other hand, if he leaves his territory for a long time, he weakens his position back home. Bosses thus face a dilemma to which there is no optimal solution. While one should not underestimate the danger of criminal groups making such inroads into the legitimate economy, this strategy and its impact differ from territorial penetration. For the latter to succeed, several local conditions must also be in place—most notably a demand for private protection.

Origins and Transplantations

Can our conclusions on transplantation form the basis of a broader theory of mafia emergence and transplantation? Scholars have already explored in considerable depth the reasons why mafias emerged in their territories of origin. Contrary to the view prominent until the early 1990s that these organizations were the product of social and economic backwardness and chaos, recent studies have shown that mafias emerge in societies that are undergoing a sudden and late transition to the market economy, lack a legal structure that reliably protects property rights or settles business disputes, and have a supply of people trained in violence who become unemployed at this specific juncture.[4]

For instance, the origin of the Sicilian mafia is best explained as a perverse response to a late and rapid transition to the market economy in the early nineteenth century, in the presence of a state that failed to clearly define and protect the newly granted property rights, and a supply of individuals trained in the use of violence who became suddenly unemployed. The armed guards (*campieri*) formerly at the service of the feudal lords were now out of work. In addition, the Bourbon army had disbanded after the unification of Italy and its soldiers were in search of a purpose. At this point in history, some members of the violent classes turned to banditry, while others started to offer their services to more than one aristocratic family. The lethal combination of a demand for the protection of property and property rights, the presence of a threat from banditry and disputes with other owners, and a supply of disbanded soldiers and unemployed field guards ready to offer private protection gave rise to the Sicilian mafia in the early to mid-nineteenth century.[5]

This perspective—what could be called the "property rights theory of mafia emergence"—can be applied to other cases, such as Japan and post–Soviet Russia, to explain how mafias might emerge in times of rapid but flawed transitions to the market economy. Japan made a rapid transition from an agrarian, feudal society to a modern, industrialized economy in the Meiji period, which is traditionally dated from 1868 to 1911. During the Meiji period, the country saw the end of feudalism, the spread of property ownership (mainly in land), the enactment of legal reforms—including land reform (1873–76), a written constitution (1889), and a French-style civil code (1898)—and a process of centralization of government. As a consequence of the spread of property ownership, disputes increased, both between individuals and the state (mainly over the levels of taxation) and between individual owners. The state, however, failed to provide mechanisms for dispute resolution that were quick and efficient. At the same time, the transition to the market produced a crisis for the large and economically useless warrior class. A supply of people trained in violence started to offer services of dispute resolution and protection outside the scope of the state, giving rise to the modern yakuza.[6]

As I have argued elsewhere, Russia underwent a similar process. From 1986 onward, the country witnessed a rapid spread of property rights that was not matched by the establishment of adequate formal enforcement mechanisms by the state. This generated a demand for nonstate sources of protection. Such a demand coincided with the presence of individuals who had acquired violent skills and found themselves unemployed. In the Russian case, these individuals were former Red Army soldiers, Afghan veterans, unemployed sportsmen, and ex-prisoners. The Russian mafia emerged at this historical juncture, and many groups adopted similar norms and rituals.[7]

The property rights theory of mafia emergence remains the most convincing perspective on the origins of mafias. Yet it has also proved to be a special case. Not all mafias have developed during times of transition to the market as in Sicily and Japan in the nineteenth century and Russia at the end of the twentieth. Mafias may well emerge within functioning market economies, and for reasons other than to ensure the protection of property rights. A sudden boom in a local market that is not governed by the state can lead to a demand for criminal protection, even in countries where property rights are clearly defined, trust is high, and courts work relatively well at settling legitimate disputes among market actors. The presence of a supply of people trained in violence and capable of offering such protection might lead to the emergence of a mafia or the transplantation of a foreign group. Endogenous mafia emergence or transplantation, however, are not a mechanical product of sudden changes in the economy. Authorities or market operators can take actions to govern the transformation, thereby preventing the rise of a demand for mafia protection.

DEMOCRATIC PARADOXES

A key insight of the perspective outlined above is that the Sicilian, Japanese, and Russian mafias all emerged at times when the market and the political process were both undergoing a process of democratization. Can democracy also provide the means to fight mafias effectively? Chinese authorities battle organized crime and corruption by routinely arresting criminals, and then meting out harsh sentences. As I was writing these lines in early January 2010, seven corrupt officials and criminals were executed in Hebei Province for a variety of crimes. But the structural conditions that give rise to opportunities for graft have not been tackled. Random and personalized "justice" is dispensed from the center, and businesspeople are vulnerable to the changes in fortune of their official protectors. The stability much valued by Beijing rulers in fact betrays uncertainty and deep insecurity for market players.[8]

One might then conclude that the solution is to transit to a fully democratic system of government as quickly as possible. Democracies can fight mafias effectively, yet they also generate their own paradoxes. First, the development of democratic institutions offers a major opportunity for organized crime by creating a market for a commodity that is not meant to be traded: votes. Mafias can help politicians ensure that a section of the electorate is rewarded for selling their votes to the highest bidder. Politicians can return the favor in the way they dispense the resources under their control, such as public contracts, tips on police investigations, passports, and travel documents, to name a few. The defiant antimafia campaigner and mayor of Bardonecchia, Mario Corino, could not defeat his political opponents when they commanded the support of the few hundred voters controlled by the Calabrese boss Rocco Lo Presti. When constituencies are small, it is easier for an organized minority to control a significant amount of voters and thereby dominate the democratic process. As constituencies grow in size, it becomes ceteris paribus more difficult to control and organize a sufficient number of voters to suppress widespread discontent.[9] Indeed, when Lo Presti tried to get an associate elected to the Piedmont Regional Assembly, he failed. He did not muster enough votes.

William Jay Gaynor, now a relatively forgotten figure of U.S. politics, is also the product of democracy—more specifically, of a reform that enlarged the constituency that elected the mayor of New York and an electorate disgusted by pervasive graft. In 1897, some forty municipal entities were "consolidated" under the single mantle of Greater New York, so that several thousand votes were needed to win the election.[10] Public opinion aided by preachers and the independent media mobilized in support of a change in government. Mayor Gaynor was thus able to reform the city administration, enforce key measures to protect trade unions, and bring an end to the official corruption that protected brothels and gambling dens ("protective umbrella"). As a consequence of his reforms, many city employees were fired, and one was so outraged that he shot the mayor in the throat early in his first term. Gaynor would eventually die because of this wound.

The political legacy of Mayor Gaynor is paradoxical, however. By dismantling the system of protective umbrellas, he opened the way for the Italian American mafia to evolve from petty criminals to a fully formed structure of governance. After his reforms, individuals trained in violence replaced the protective umbrellas. Mobsters now organized the saloons, brothels, and gambling establishments. A well-meaning reform thus had a crucial unintended effect. Likewise, I would expect that a sudden transition to democracy in China might well create a bonanza for mafias.

The media in a democracy can be a powerful tool to fight organized crime. Public opinion leaders at the time of Mayor Gaynor included the Reverend Charles H. Parkhurst of the Madison Square Presbyterian Church. His powerful sermons and personal forays in the vice district of New York City—Satan's Circle—helped galvanize the anticorruption movement. The

press was mostly supportive as well. Joseph Pulitzer's *New York World*
and its fierce competitor, William Randolph Hearst's *New York Morning
Journal*, both campaigned against corruption, in conjunction with two
other influential local papers, the *Herald* and the *New York Times*. Quite
crucially, Hearst commissioned Stephen Crane (the author in 1895 of the
Civil War novel *The Red Badge of Courage*) to write a series of pieces on
police corruption and brutality in Satan's Circle. Yet both the *World* and
the *Journal* also had a possibly pernicious influence. In order to fight its
war against the *Journal*, the *World*, through its reporter Herbert B. Swope,
led a relentless campaign against a New York Police Department captain,
Charles Backer, who was ultimately unjustly accused of murdering the operator of a gambling den and sentenced to die in the electric chair.[11] The
fact that prosecutors in the case were also running for office further high-
lights the paradoxes of democracy. For his part, Hearst—the inspiration for
the lead character in Orson Welles's film *Citizen Kane*—used his paper to
campaign ferociously against Gaynor—possibly because he stood against
him in the election of 1909 and lost. Although the relationship between
the media and the fight against the mafia is a complex one, and cannot be
explored here, the former follows a logic of its own, which does not always
coincide with the latter.

Gaynor's reforms led indirectly to the entrenchment of the Italian
American mafia in some key illegal markets, such as prostitution and gambling. The very same Progressive movement that was behind the clean up
of City Hall and the New York Police Department was also responsible for
passing, a few years later, the Volsted Act and the policy that has come to
be known as Prohibition (Hearst was a major supporter of the war against
marijuana that led to its prohibition in 1937 in the United States). The
New York families were now best placed to reap the benefits of the largest
illegal market at the time. As a result of Prohibition, they became a force
in New York City and arguably U.S. history.

One might then simply suggest that authorities should pursue the mafia
in illegal markets as well, as vigorously as possible. But another paradox
presents itself. In markets for illegal commodities, mafias restrict competition, and ensure a degree of order and predictability. In this instance, the
public (at least notionally) should welcome inefficient firms organized in
cartels, and not want the cheap and efficient delivery of, say, drugs, prostitution, and the like. The fight against the mafias in illegal markets might

then have the effect of making available more products that people generally do not want on the streets. The ability of Cosa Nostra to control the
docks of New York City, for example, gave it the possibility to organize
the traffic of heroin into the United States. The mafia became the primary
supplier of the product across the country for a period. Still, the fact that
heroin was going through the New York docks also limited the amount of
heroin entering the country. The organization had an incentive to restrict
the supply and increase the price, with the end result being a lower quantity
available. When Cosa Nostra failed to maintain control of the New York
heroin market in the 1970s, by contrast, the city was flooded. The crack
epidemic of the 1980s is a postmafia phenomenon.

A further consequence of the fight against the mafia is the displacement
effect that I have highlighted in the chapters above. Effective repression of
the mafia in one country can simply displace the problem. To use the language of this book, police repression is a most important factor in pushing
the supply to other countries. While such measures might go some way to
reducing the problem at home, they show a perverse effect of policing. As
no country can afford to ignore the entrenchment of the mafia in another
land, displacing the problem might just serve to postpone facing up to it.

Subsidies and administrative regulations can foster mafia involvement
in frauds and racketeering. A case in point are the subsidies from the Organization for Economic Cooperation and Development and the European
Union for the production of crops. Such subsidies have been hijacked by
organized crime in many parts of southern Italy. Instead of protecting hard-
hit farmers and the countryside, they have generated further exploitation
and crime. In order to save on labor costs and rather than work the land
themselves, landowners in Calabria employ cheap illegal workers from the
Maghreb and sub-Saharan Africa. Workers come in the winter to harvest
oranges and clementines for a pittance (the going daily wage is twenty-five
euros). The living conditions are dreadful, and immigrants are routinely
harassed. When I visited this part of Italy in March 2010, I was taken to
a disused factory lacking any sanitation or toilets where immigrants camp
out. Racketeers extract five euros from each worker a day. When vast sectors of the population exist beyond the reach of state institutions, as is the
case with large communities of illegal migrants, a demand for extralegal
services of dispute settlement and governance can emerge among the mi-

grants as well as the entrepreneurs who exploit them. Legitimate structures should prevent the emergence of such pockets of poverty and lawlessness. By ensuring this, they also help prevent mafia emergence.

In recent years, the European Union has curbed some such subsidies, forcing Italian farmers to compete against Spanish and Latin American producers of oranges and orange juice. While previously the ʻNdrangheta had helped landowners control and exploit illegal immigrant workers, it could not protect farmers against global competition—in this case, competition against Brazilian and Spanish products. As I have shown in this book, mafias are able to protect local markets, but they find it next to impossible to protect export markets. Thus, a clear policy implication is that more global competition would weaken this criminal organization. Yet deregulation and global competition must be introduced with a grain of salt. In January 2010, riots between immigrants and locals broke out in the town of Rosarno, the epicenter of the labor racket and a ʻNdrangheta stronghold. The root cause of the violence was the lack of work. Farmers, who could not squeeze the workers' salaries any further and had failed to modernize, decided to leave the fruit to rot in the fields and just rely on the lump-sum subsidy that the European Union still pays to owners of a field. In a heated social climate, a minor scuffle between a black immigrant and the owner of a car led to large-scale riots. Social tension was the unexpected outcome of a measure intended—among other things—to curb the role of organized crime.

How can we make sense of the paradox that reforms aimed at introducing democracy, reducing corruption, and opening up markets can give rise to a demand for mafia services? Or that riots break out when the mafia is weakened? Observers and policymakers routinely fail to recognize that mafias can serve powerful and entrenched interests in a democracy. In markets for legal commodities, mafias offer, in a nutshell, a form of protectionism against cutthroat competition. Market insiders might prefer this protection to competition that would force them to make painful changes. Elected politicians sometimes find it easier to enlist the services of thugs than to compete fairly with their opponents. Those who pay the price are ordinary people who have to cope with inflated prices and lousy representatives.[12] In illegal markets, mafias bring some order to the trade and can reduce uncertainty. It is not surprising, then, that police forces and some politicians are tempted to come to terms with organized crime in illegal markets; it makes their work easier (the occasional bribe surely helps).

This book is not a list of specific recipes to fight the mafia. It simply suggests that a demand for mafia services originates in the economy, and that state action can foster or hinder such a demand. The best way to fight the presence of a mafia is to drain the demand for its services. It is not enough to reform the public administration or liberalize markets, or let booms go unchecked. Liberalization should be accompanied by effective measures aimed at preventing the formation of cartels in local markets and easing the effect of liberalization on the local workforce to avoid social tension. Liberalization requires more, not less, state intervention in the economy. Opening markets to competition requires state structures strong enough to ensure that market actors are free to sell in a territory. The prohibition and criminalization of certain substances, such as alcohol and drugs, should not be undertaken lightly, as they will generate a demand for forms of governance in illegal markets.

The political climate at the end of the twentieth century and in this decade has promoted the erosion of state monopolies over policing and security, and citizens are encouraged by governments to become "responsible" for the provision of their own protection. Rather than civic associations devoted to the defense of rights, mafias and mafia-like groups are well placed to exploit such a protection deficit. Already in many developing countries—whose local economies revolve around agricultural goods sold at markets, where the demand for the protection of property, goods, trading spots, and transportation routes is high—communities rely on alternatives to state security, such as informal organized security groups, religious police, and ethnic militias, some of which are effective. Although it might be early to speak of full-fledged mafias, groups such as the Bakassi Boys in Nigeria—youths armed with machetes, guns, and charms who engage in anticrime vigilante activities in the Igbo area, and often are accused of illegal activities and human rights abuses—have the potential to turn into mafias.[13]

Once the demand for mafia services has been sapped, it is also necessary to neutralize the threat posed by the supply. The utmost determination on the part of authorities is a central ingredient of any fight against the mafia. Effective policing makes life difficult for bosses, increases mistrust among the rank and file, and helps to dislodge deeply entrenched criminal groups. And ultimately any fight against criminal organizations set on using violence on the population cannot get started without the actions of a few dedicated campaigners who risk their lives to bring about a better world. This book is dedicated to them.

INTRODUCTION

1. Shelley 2006, 43.

2. Williams 2001, 71; see also Shelley 1999.

3. Castells 2000, 201.

4. Shelley, Picarelli, and Corpora 2003, 145; see also Veltri and Laudati 2009, 198; CPA 2008.

5. Castells 2000, 168; Barak 2001; Shelley 2006. See also *Newsweek* special report on the "Global Mafia," December 31, 1993.

6. Albrow 1996; Bauman 1998; Beck 1999. For perceptive studies of the connection between globalization, security, and crime, see Nelken 2003; Loader and Walker 2007; Zedner 2009.

7. Reuter 1985, 21–22, 31; Gambetta 1993, 249–51.

8. Gambetta 1993; Chu 2000; Varese 2001; Frye 2002; Hill 2003; Chin 2003, 54–58. See also Dixit 2004.

9. For instance, the pure extortion of film crews has been recorded in Palermo, Hong Kong, and Moscow (see, respectively, Gambetta 2009, 255–56; Chu 2000, 71; *Independent*, November 2, 1995). The shooting of movies is particularly susceptible to extortion because crews work on tight schedules and cannot afford even the smallest delay in production; as they also tend to be from outside, they have no long-term connection with local men of honor (see Gambetta 2009, 256). In some cases, film crews have entered into partnerships with "location agents" who have ensured a safe production schedule, presumably because they enjoy long-term connections with the local mafiosi.

10. Extortion is often confused with other phenomena, such as the imposition of a tribute and overcharging for a service. Failing to appreciate that protection is subject to economies of scale generates the first confusion. If a group has the resources to protect client X and scare that person's enemies away, the same group must have all the qualities it takes to protect other people as well. This leads protectors to impose their protection on others. Just as states impose their protection on their subjects, so do mafias, although it does not follow that the service provided is bogus. Failing to appreciate that protection is also a natural monopoly leads to the second confusion. Since protectors are monopolists, they will charge a monopoly price and obtain a monopoly profit. Just as states charge more for their protection services than it costs to produce them, so do mafias. For a broader discussion of the economics of protection, see Lane 1958.

11. For parallels between state action and mafia behavior, see Tilly 1985.

12. For instances of services supplied by the mafia, see Bell [1953] 1988, 131; Block 1983, 43; Chu 2000, 43–76, 153–54; Gambetta 1993, 93–94, 171–79, 190–92, 197; Sabetti 1984, 90–91; Varese 2001, 69–72, 110–13, 115–17, 119; *New York Times*, August 29, 1999. For discussions of cartel agreement enforcement, see Landesco [1929] 1968; Reuter 1987; Gambetta 1993, 195–225; Gambetta and Reuter 1995. Nonetheless, extortion and protection are closely related in practice. What constitutes extortion and the consequent possible financial ruin for one victim of the mafia may be genuine protection for another. This is exemplified by a story narrated by Catania-boss-turned-state-witness Tonino Calderone. In the mid-1950s he placed a bomb in the chimney of the offices of the Rendo construction company, the main competitors of the Costanzos, who were then protected by his family. "The goal," he writes, "was to do the Costanzo brothers a favour." After the bomb was placed, "the usual phone call asking for money was made," although Calderone had no intention of supplying any genuine service (Arlacchi 1993, 53). What were extortionary demands on the Rendo amounted to protection against competition for the Costanzos. Joe Bonanno (with Lalli 1983, 79) put it best: "What is seen as extortion from the outsider is viewed as self-protection by the insider." From a dynamic perspective, external factors might turn protection into extortion. For instance, the shorter the group's time horizon, the more likely it will harass customers with purely extortionary demands. The view that extortion is the defining feature of the mafia might be a consequence of selection bias in the evidence that filters out from the underworld: extortion is more likely to require the use of violence. In turn, violent conflicts leave behind more evidence and are more easily reported (Gambetta 1993). For a discussion of these themes, see Gambetta 1993 and Varese 2010.

13. A word often used in Italian is colonization (see Massari 2001, 15). Mark Galeotti (2000, 38) calls it "hard" penetration.

CHAPTER 2: MAFIA TRANSPLANTATION

1. On the data for Russia, see *Itar-TASS*, July 21, 1998; for the `Ndrangheta, see chapter 3.

2. Reuter 1985, 21.

3. Gambetta 1993, 249, 251.

4. Chu 2000, 130; see also Finckenauer and Chin 2006, 23.

5. Hill 2002, 53; see also 2004, 112.

6. Ibid., 111; 2005, 1. For a perceptive study that downplays the presence of the Russian mafia in the Netherlands, see Weenink and van der Laan 2007. The prosecutors Paolo Giovagnoli and Morena Plazzi (R5 and R6) have concluded that a much-hyped case of alleged Russian mafia presence in Rimini amounted to financial improprieties (PRB 2007). See also *New York Times*, September 28, 1999; *La Repubblica*, August 24, 2008.

7. Reuter 1985, 21–22.

8. Ibid., 21–22nn53–54, 21–22n56, 33; Gambetta 1993, 249–51.

9. Arlacchi 1993, 28; Gambetta 1993, 251, 314; see also MA 1937.

10. Sciarrone 1998, 155–212. See, also, Massari 1998.

11. Chin 2003, 200. In this book, I will use the expression "Taiwanese triads," but organized crime groups in Taiwan are normally called *jiaotou*.

12. Linter 2004, 93.

13. He 2003, 201–3.

14. Hill 2004, 111–12, see also 2002, 55.

15. See, for example, Bovenkerk 2001; Waldinger 1995; Williams 1995.

16. See, for example, CRP 1983, 54, 68–69; CPA 1994, 854. TT 1990, 32 (quoted in Sciarrone 1998, 123) makes a rather crude link between migration and crime.

17. Gambetta 1993, 251. Monica Massari (2001, 29) mentions the settlement of significant immigrant communities from southern Italy as a factor in explaining the entrenchment of mafia groups in northern Italy.

18. Kefauver 1951.

19. Massari 2001, 12; Veltri and Laudati 2009, 198; see also TT 1990, 32 (quoted in Sciarrone 1998, 123), claiming that the soggiorno obbligato of Calabresi in the Canavese valleys is partly responsible (along with Calabrian migration) for the increase in crime.

20. Quoted in Massari 2001, 12.

21. For other examples, see, e.g., Sciarrone 1998, 248; Massari 2001, 10–11.

22. Finckenauer and Waring 1998, 112–13; see also Grant 1996. Claire Sterling (1995, 5; see also ibid., 1) instead inflates Ivan'kov's role in the United States, and assumes that he was tasked by the Solntsevskaya to turn "an assortment of

unruly and loosely articulated Russian gangs on American soil into a modern, nation-wide crime corporation," as (she assumes) Lucky Luciano did with the Italian American Mafia.

23. Hill 2004, 112.

24. Glonti and Lobjanidze 2004, 32, 37–38; Kukhianidze 2009, 220.

25. Kukhianidze 2009, 228–29.

26. Chin 2003, 193. Similarly, Dawood Ibrahim, the leader of the Mumbai-based crime group D-Company, was forced to move his operations to Dubai because of continued police crackdowns (Weinstein 2008, 28).

27. Campana 2010.

28. A typology first advanced by John Dunning (1993), and subsequently modified and expanded by Srilata Zaheer and Shalini Manrakhan (2001), focused on "resource-seeking," "market-seeking," and "efficiency-seeking" motivations. See also Dunning 1998, 2000.

29. Zaheer and Manrakhan 2001, 670.

30. Gambetta 1993. In one case, Sicilian mafiosi were forced to replace a Turkish-language translator because he had misconstrued a drug dealer's words, leading the parties involved to believe erroneously that a large debt had already been settled. A Swiss man was urgently brought in to sort out the dangerous misunderstanding (Gambetta 1993, 66).

31. For an instance where a mafia family was not so careful, see US 1988; Pistone and Woodley 1989; Pistone with Brant 2007.

32. Sifakis 1999, 397–98; Raab 2005, 205–6, 703; Pistone and Woodley 1989; Pistone with Brant 2007. A capo (also *caporegime* or captain) in a mafia family is a full member who is in charge of several "soldiers," and reports to the underboss and the boss (Davis 1993; Maas 1997; Raab 2005).

33. CAF 1989; Paoli 1995. In 2007, Calò was acquitted of this murder (*BBC News*, June 6, 2007).

34. Coleman 1990, 302.

35. Putnam 1993, 97, 149. The reason that he offers invokes the distant medieval past, and in particular the republican tradition of the city-states in the North and the Norman centralized, autocratic rule in the South: "Social patterns plainly traceable from early medieval Italy to today turn out to be decisive in explaining why, on the verge of the twenty-first century, some communities are better able than others to manage collective life and sustain effective institutions" (Putnam 1993, 121). An alternative view is that trust can be depleted by intentional strategies and is rather fragile, even in territories where it has flourished for centuries. See Pagden 1987; Doria [1709–10] 1973.

36. Rose-Ackerman 1998, 2001a, 2001b. See also Portes 1998; Farrell 2009.

37. Saviano 2007, 51; Varese 2009, 263.

38. Quoted in Pileggi 1987, 60–61.

39. Quoted in Chin 2003, 197.

40. See Sciarrone 1998, 252, 287.

41. Reuter 1995, 92.

42. Quoted in *Il Corriere della Sera*, July 1, 1998. Similarly, Japanese director Fukasaku Kinji said: "They [the yakuza] liked those movies because it made them look good. It was good for their image" (quoted in Desjardinis 2005, 25). For relevant discussions, see Gambetta 1993, 127–55; Varese 2006b; Gambetta 2009, 251–74.

43. On the possibility principle, see Mahoney and Goertz 2004. On the logic of the comparative method more generally, see the restatement in King, Keohane, and Verba 1994. As a substantive example of such research strategy, see the groundbreaking study by Stathis Kalyvas (2006), in particular his focus on two cases that are similar as far as many variables are concerned, except for one crucial outcome: the level of violence during the civil war in Greece in the 1940s. Papers with a similar design include Posner 2004; Miguel 2004; Varese 2006a.

CHAPTER 3: THE 'NDRANGHETA IN PIEDMONT AND VENETO

1. Quoted in Veltri and Laudati 2009, 148; Sergi 1991, 61.

2. Falcone with Padovani 1993, 109.

3. Ciconte 1992, 5–20; Paoli 2003, 37; Montalto [1940] 1973; *Il Corriere della Sera* February 10, 1978. Court sentences and police reports point to the existence of the 'Ndrangheta since the 1870s.

4. CPA 2000, 94; see also CPA 1993a, 700; 2000, 92, 97.

5. Sciarrone 2008, 77. Among the many references on 'ndrina, see Ciconte 1992, 20; 1996, 17. Cosca or family are also used. For the origins of the word, see Martino 1988.

6. PRC 1998, quoted in CPA 2000, 95. According to former member Francesco Fonti, "Almost all male inhabitants belong to the 'Ndrangheta" in San Luca (quoted in Paoli 2003, 29). On Fonti, see Ciconte 1998, 45–48, 202–28; TT 1996. For evidence of the continuing relevence of the Sanctuary of Our Lady of Polsi, see the investigation reported in *Repubblica* July 14, 2010.

7. Quoted in Paoli 2003, 59.

8. CPA 2000, 94–95. Some evidence on the ability of the crimine to rein in local 'ndrine does exist. In one case, the annual meeting deprived the locale of Sant'Eufemia d'Aspromonte of its mafia status because it proved unable to prevent the mourning of a police officer killed in the line of duty, and some 'ndranghesti even attended the funeral (CPA 2000, 94). The Apalachin meeting of the Italian American mafia took place on November 14, 1957, in Apalachin, New York. Some one hundred crime bosses attended. On the many sources for this event, see, for example, Raab 2005.

9. CPA 2000, 96. Letizia Paoli (2003, 32) writes that "though enjoying a high degree of operational independence, these units are considered by their own members and their Calabrian correspondents as belonging for all intents and purposes to the `Ndrangheta."

10. CPA 2000, 98. In the northern Irish conflict 3,700 people were killed between 1969 and 1998, which amounts to 128 deaths per year. The average death in the 1986–91 period in Calabria was 136. Since 1991, violence between different groups has declined considerably (DIA 2002, 85).

11. See CPA 1993a, 704–5; 2000, 98; Paoli 2003, 59. For the earliest evidence, see Ciconte 1992, 118–27.

12. CPA 1993a, 705. The `Ndrangheta is also present in the Calabrian provinces Catanzaro and Cosenza. Paoli (2003, 30) reports that there are eighty-six groups in the same province.

13. CPA 2000, 24, 37; 1993, 702. The prefect of Catanzaro, Francesco Stranges, notes that the sum of money regularly demanded from entrepreneurs by the `Ndrangheta is often small. "The mafiosi, since they are not very greedy, practice extortion at an acceptable level, hence it is difficult to find individuals willing to testify in these cases" (quoted in ibid., 37). Mafiosi themselves have expressed concern with high rates of extortion. In one instance, the head of the mafia family of San Luca, which is considered the repository of "certified" values and rules of this mafia, expressed concern at the excessive demands that the head of the Locri family was imposing on the latter's victims. He was overheard saying: "Do you know why I came here [to meet you]? Totò, be careful—when the human race, the people go against you, you will lose what you have achieved in thirty years! You just lose it! When you destroy the shop of one guy, burn the car of another, the people will rebel!" (quoted in ibid., 38). On the resurgence of severe violence in Reggio Calabria, see *Il Sole 24 Ore*, August 26, 2001.

14. CPA 1993a, 702, 709; 2000, 25–27, 35; Mangano 2010, 33–44.

15. *Deutsche Welle*, August 17, 2007; CPA 2008; Forgione 2009.

16. Quoted in CPA 2000, 92.

17. Paoli 2003, 31. Similarly, Antonio Zagari, also a former member, states that "from their birth . . . the sons of Calabrian men of honour are, by right, considered *giovani d'onore*" (quoted in Paoli 2003, 232).

18. Quoted in CPA 1993b, 700.

19. Ibid., 700–701; Falcone with Padovani 1993, 109; Arlacchi 1983, 157. Usually, members of a ruling blood family rise to the post of boss, although political or military merit plays a role in upward mobility within each unit. Also, the *locali* have developed a complex system of ranks that does not always coincide with kin relationships. See Paoli 2003, 50.

20. CPA 1993a, 700–701; 2000, 13, 101–2.

21. See Allum 2001, 332–33; 2006. Unlike the 'Ndrangheta, Camorra groups have no notion of being part of the same entity, although some of them are grouped in cartels (for example, the Alleanza di Secondigliano and the Clan dei Casalesi). Recently, the number of Camorra members who have turned state's witness (pentiti) has risen significantly, when bosses started to turn state witnesses. Such a move has prompted many other family members to turn, surely a strategic and collective decision. For the relevant, more recent data, see CPA 2008, 24. I am grateful to Paolo Campana for a discussion on this point.

22. CPA 2000, 102; see also 1993a, 701.

23. See Ciconte 1996, 160–98; 1998; CPA 2000, 13, 15, 17; Paoli 2003, 32; Veltri and Laudati 2009, 150; Forgione 2009. For Canada and Australia, see Minuti and Nicaso 1994.

24. Quoted in CPA 1993a, 703; see also Massari 2001, 15.

25. For instance, a member tried to buy a bank in Saint Petersburg (CPA 2000, 112). The push to export criminal proceeding is partly due to the fact that Italian authorities are quite successful at confiscating properties and businesses bought by the mafia *in loco* (ibid., 59–60).

26. Information on the town comes from Molino 1996; http://www .bardonecchiasci.it/; TT 1996, 59. The resident populations of Bardonecchia and Cuorgnè were—in 1961 and 1971, respectively—2,667 and 3,081 (Bardonecchia) and 8,211 and 9,334 (Cuorgnè). See ISTAT 1971.

27. The Civic Community Index is based on four indicators: preference voting, referendum turnout, newspaper readership, and the scarcity of sports and cultural associations. Data were collected in the 1970s and 1980s (Putnam 1993, 96–97). The variables that form the historical index are the strength of mass parties, the incidence of cooperatives, membership in mutual aid societies, electoral turnout, and local associations founded before 1860 (ibid., 149–50).

28. CRP 1983, 70–71; ASC-CT 2001, table 1. Overall, in the 1950s and 1960s some four million people migrated from southern to northern Italy. See Bonaguidi 1985; Sonnino 1995.

29. See Gratteri and Nicaso 2006, 185–88; Veltri and Laudati 2009, 206–30; Carlucci and Caruso 2009.

30. CPA 1976, 279–80, 289; Sciarrone 1998, 255–56; Massari 2001, 13. Of the forty-eight individuals who resettled in Turin Province during the period 1970–82 due to soggiorno obbligato, Public Prosecutor Sebastiano Sorbello points out that "none appears to be a significant mafia boss" (quoted in CRP 1983, 55). This judgment possibly indicates that although these criminals were not prominent bosses when they arrived, they became prominent under new conditions, so transplantation could be seen as a ladder for upward mobility.

31. The data refer to legally obtained construction licenses.

32. CRP 1983, 26.

33. In 1994 alone, the city council collected five billion lira in residential dwelling taxes. Similar increases occurred in the nearby Canavese Valley (Sciarrone 1998, 264; *La Luna Nuova*, November 7, 1995).

34. Sciarrone 1998, 257.

35. B5.

36. Quoted in TT 2002, 19–20.

37. B1.

38. CPA 1976, 279; B2; B3.

39. Quoted in TT 1996, 30.

40. CRP 1983, 24. See also CPA 1976, 280; Sciarrone 1998, 257; Massari 2001, 7.

41. CRP 1983, 25.

42. Sciarrone 1998, 273.

43. CRP 1983, 27, 48; *La Stampa*, November 14, 1995.

44. TT 2002, 21. The witness is Francesco Fonti, a high-profile state witness. Bardonecchia's chief inspector (B2) told me that he had no evidence of any motive other than extortion.

45. The murder of another Calabrese took place in Cuorgnè in August 1978 (CRP 1983, 27).

46. One of the most important state witnesses, Francesco Fonti, testified to this effect (see TT 1996, 8).

47. Quoted in ibid., 9. For other instances, reaching well into the 1990s, see ibid., 32; 2002, 27. Lo Presti himself stated in a phone call that "we are at the source of everything here, do you understand?" (quoted in ibid., 32).

48. PT 1995, 15–17; TT 1996, 15–17; *La Stampa*, October 5, 1994; October 26, 1995; November 14, 1995; November 23, 1998; September 19, 2002; October 31, 2002; Caselli 2003a, 2, 4; *La Stampa*, January 24, 2009; *Cronaca Qui*, January 27, 2009; http://www.sosimpresa.it/news.php?id=7922; Ciccarello 2009. See also Saccomanno 2005, 120–55. Interestingly, the name of Lo Presti has been pirated by lesser criminals banking on the reputation of the "real thing." A *Lucio* Lo Presti, also from southern Italy (although Messina, not Reggio Calabria) tried to collect a million lira from a shopkeeper (*La Stampa*, November 9, 2001).

49. Quoted in TT 2002, 19–20; see also ibid., 24.

50. Sciarrone 1998, 260. Stefano Caselli (2003a) gives a different date (1971) for Mazzaferro's move to Bardonecchia. See also Ciconte 1992, 302.

51. Caselli 2003a. Mazzaferro belongs to the reputed Mazzaferro crime family and acted as the representative of the `Ndrangheta to the provincial commission

of the Sicilian mafia. He was arrested again in 1993 and found guilty of drug trafficking.

52. Sciarrone 1998, 271.

53. PT 1995, 3. An investigation established that Lo Presti directly chose the subcontractors in the Campo Smith development (TT 1996, 28–29). For several instances, see *La Stampa*, November 14, 1995.

54. Quoted in PT 1995, 14.

55. Quoted in TT 1996, 10; 2002, 23 (emphasis added).

56. PT 1995, 15. Lo Presti was never convicted, due to an amnesty. See also CPA 1976, 10.

57. CRP 1983, 26; *La Stampa*, November 14, 1995.

58. CRP 1983, 27, 48.

59. Ibid., 51, 61.

60. *La Stampa*, October 24, 1995.

61. Ibid., October 15, 1995; B2.

62. For instance, Mario Mezzani Mezzacuva, who was running a construction company with offices in Calabria and Cuorgnè, and was a reputed member of the 'Ndranghera, was killed in Calabria in 1985. He had been present at the annual gathering in 1969 at the Sanctuary of Our Lady of Polsi that was raided by police. Two individuals were first wounded and then burned alive in 1996 (*La Stampa*, July 16, 1996). The same article includes a list of unsolved murders in the period 1991–96. On July 14, 1998, two construction workers from Calabria who had previous convictions were murdered in Santa Lucia di Cuorgnè (see CRP 1983, 27; *Il Corriere della Sera*, July 15, 1998).

63. TT 1996, 18–19; *La Luna Nuova*, September 12, 1995; *La Stampa*, November 15, 1995; February 6, 1996; January 17, 2001; October 31, 2002; Caselli 2003a, 3.

64. Caselli 2003a, 4; see also TT 1996, 24. The sentence in 2002 against Lo Presti stresses that the "trial has proved the presence of *omertà* and submission in Bardonecchia and Val Susa" (quoted in Caselli 2003a, 4).

65. PT 1995, 8; TT 1996, 26; *La Stampa*, October 5, 1994; Caselli 2003a, 4.

66. *La Stampa*, October 6, 1996.

67. See ibid., April 29, 1995; September 7, 1995.

68. CRP 1983, 25; *La Stampa*, November 14, 1995. The same level of fear among construction workers was observed in the 1990s by trade unionists interviewed in *La Stampa* (May 3, 1995), and episodes of intimidation continue to be recorded (see, for example, ibid., November 16, 1995).

69. Sciarrone 1998, 257.

70. Direzione Centrale per i Servizi Antidroga, available at http://www .vivoscuola.it/us/geometri-pozzo-trento/droghe/2F/ecstasy/ECSTASY.PDF;

http://www.exodus.it/sostanze/ ecstasy/belpaese.htm. For more instances of drugs dealing, see TT 1996, 9–10; 2002, 25. Arms sold illegally in Val Susa were found in the possession of members of the `Ndrangheta in Calabria (see *La Stampa*, June 7, 1996; June 8, 1996; *La Luna Nuova*, May 1, 1998).

71. *La Luna Nuova*, April 17, 1998.

72. TT 2002, 142–43; B2. There were 414 new residents from 1961 to 1971.

73. PT 1995, 8, 18–19; *La Stampa*, April 30, 1995; November 14, 1995; December 8, 1995.

74. Quoted in TT 1996, 40. See also *La Stampa*, November 15, 1995.

75. Quoted in *La Repubblica* (Turin), October 6, 1994; see also TT 1996, 41; TT 2002, 43; *La Stampa*, April 29, 1995.

76. *La Luna Nuova*, October 7, 1994, quoted in Sciarrone 1998, 268; see also TT 1996, 41.

77. PT 1995; PR 1995; MI 1995; TT 1996, 28; Caselli 2003b; Laudi 2003. Additional information is in *La Stampa*, October 6, 1994; October 25, 1995; November 17, 1995; October 5, 1996.

78. PT 1995, 5; TT 1996, 61–62; see also press reports in *Il Corriere della Sera*, March 16, 1995; April 29, 1995; June 5, 1995; *La Stampa*, April 29, 1995; June 27, 1995; Caselli 2003a, 2. For discussions of law 221/91 utilized to disband city councils due to mafia influence, see Gullotti 2003; Maresco and Serpone 2005; Mete 2007. It should be noted that this legislation has come under criticism since it does not apply to administrative post holders. It only revokes the elected officials and calls for new elections within a relatively short period of time. Up to 1995, this procedure had been used for city councils in Calabria (fourteen), Campania (thirty-six), Sicilia (twenty-four), Apulia (seven), and Basilicata (one).

79. Data on the composition of the local administration are taken from *La Stampa*, November 19, 1996; November 20, 1996; October 20, 1996; December 4, 1996; May 15, 2001; June 6, 2001; *La Luna Nuova*, May 15, 2001. For earlier instances of intimidation against elected opposition officials opposed to development projects, see TT 1996, 27. Within Cuorgnè, Giovanni Iaria has a position similar to that of Lo Presti in Bardonecchia. One significant difference is the distinguished political career that he managed to achieve, rising rapidly through the ranks of the Italian Socialist Party to become the deputy leader of Turin Province in 1988 and being elected to a number of offices in the city council. See *La Stampa*, November 15, 1994; Sciarrone 1998, 264, 255, 276–77.

80. TT 2002, 29; see also ibid., 33.

81. Quoted in *La Stampa*, October 5, 1994; see also *La Luna Nuova*, October 7, 1994.

82. Quoted in *La Stampa*, April 29, 1995; February 4, 1994.

83. *La Repubblica* (Turin), quoted in Sciarrone 1998, 271.

84. *La Stampa*, January 19, 2001.

85. B1.

86. *La Luna Nuova*, February 5, 2010.

87. Quoted in *La Stampa*, April 30, 1995.

88. On the march, see ibid., October 5, 1994; October 9, 1994; April 30, 1995. In 1982, a priest accepted thirty million liras from Lo Presti, promising him that he would influence the outcome of a trial, although he failed to deliver. Ibid., December 30, 1994; July 12, 1996.

89. PSB 1995. Naturally, the reason for such lack of enthusiasm for the Lega's rally might be due to the local population's aversion to this political party. Yet in the European elections of June 12, 1994, the Lega obtained 11.13 percent of the valid votes and was the second party after Forza Italia (47.17 percent). Data available at http://elezionistorico.interno.it/index.php.

90. *La Stampa*, April 30, 1995.

91. Data from http://elezionistorico.interno.it/index.php.

92. See TT 1996, 10, 12; 1997, 13. One Aldo Bertolotto testifies that he traveled back to Palmi to undergo the "formal entry ritual" (TT 1996, 10).

93. Data contained in a 1995 report by the Direzione Investigativa Antimafia (DIA, Antimafia Directorate). See an extensive summary of the 1995 DIA report in *La Stampa*, August 6, 1995.

94. B3; *La Stampa*, November 16, 1995; November 21, 1995; December 2, 1995; Caselli 2003a, 4.

95. B4.

96. *La Stampa*, April 29, 1993; April 4, 1995.

97. B2; TT 2002, 33.

98. Putnam 1993, 97. In fact, both regions obtain the same high score on the Civic Community Index. Veneto achieves the same (high) score in the historical index on civic traditions, 1860–1920 (ibid., 150). The indicators mentioned in the text refer to the period 1980–85. See *Il Mondo*, August 29, 1983; Arlacchi and Lewis 1990, 22–23; Ruggiero and Vass 1992, 282.

99. Brugoli 1985; Gaburro 1985.

100. Arlacchi and Lewis 1990, 33.

101. CV 2001.

102. In 1971, the Veneto region's agriculture sector employed 30 percent of the number it employed at the time of the 1951 census (Anastasia and Tattara 2003; Gaburro 1985, 74). As shown by Anna Maria Birindelli (2004, 240), positive and significant "medium range inter-provincial mobility" affected Verona as well as Vicenza, Treviso, and Padua in the 1960s and 1970s, while other provinces in the Veneto region, most notably Venice and Rovigo, lost population. The

unemployment rate was between 4 and 6 percent from the early 1960s to the late 1970s (Anastasia and Tattara 2003).

103. FPCI 1981, 13.

104. *L'Arena di Verona*, February 23, 1974.

105. Generally, on the Veronese neofascists in this period, see FPCI 1981, 30–32. On the Rosa dei Venti investigation, see the several articles that appeared in *L'Arena di Verona* in 1974, especially January 3, 1974 and March 28, 1974. For the investigation into Veronesi linked to the Brescia bombing, see, for example, ibid., June 7, 1974; June 11, 1974; June 20, 1974.

106. FPCI 1981, 11. This number is around ten thousand, according to AFV 1983.

107. *L'Arena di Verona*, April 28, 1974; May 15, 1974; June 13, 1974; July 28, 1974; Pedrini 1979, 5; FPCI 1981, 21–3.

108. Arlacchi and Lewis 1990, 51, 73; V4; see also TV 1987; Fogliata, Carrarini, and Mazzoccoli 1987, 25, 27–28.

109. FPCI 1981, 11, 29.

110. V1. The Interporto Web page is available at http://www.quadranteeuropa.it/en/interporto_en.php.

111. AFV 1983, 67; Facchini 1982, 12; V4.

112. *L'Arena di Verona*, February 17, 1974; *La Repubblica*, February 4, 1988; Arlacchi and Lewis 1990, 15, 59–60, 66.

113. *La Repubblica*, November 4, 1988; Arlacchi and Lewis 1990, 46, 51, 53–54.

114. V3; V4; *L'Arena di Verona*, March 23, 2008.

115. FPCI 1981, 34; *L'Arena di Verona*, January 13, 1974.

116. FPCI 1981, 34–35, 49; *L'Arena di Verona*, June 14, 1974.

117. *L'Arena di Verona*, January 18, 1974; April 1, 1974; May 24, 1974; FPCI 1981, 28; Arlacchi and Lewis 1990, 68.

118. FPCI 1981, 50; V1.

119. CD 1986, 46278; V4.

120. FPCI 1981, 27; Facchini 1982, 13; AFV 1983, 70–71.

121. *L'Arena di Verona*, February 12, 1974; FPCI 1981, 32–35.

122. FPCI 1981, 32–35, 28.

123. *L'Unità*, July 9, 1982; Facchini 1982, 14; AFV 1983, 59–62; V1; V2.

124. CD 1980, 21784; V1; V2; *L'Arena di Verona*, March 23, 2008.

125. *La Repubblica*, February 21, 1980; March 10, 1981; April 22, 1981; *Verona Fedele*, November 30, 1980; FPCI 1981, 14, 86–89; AFV 1983; V1; V2.

126. AFV 1983, 87.

127. Ibid., 78–84, 94–95.

128. FPCI 1981, 73–75.

129. See, for example, *L'Arena di Verona*, February 23, 1974; March 29, 1974.

130. FPCI 1981, 60; *Paese Sera*, March 14, 1981.

131. CD 1980, 21784–85; FPCI 1981, 60; AFV 1983, 15–16, 46, 60; *L'Arena di Verona*, March 22, 1981; *Il Nuovo Veronese*, May 29, 1982; V1.

132. FPCI 1981, 16.

133. Arlacchi and Lewis 1990, 69.

134. *La Repubblica*, February 4, 1988; V3.

135. *L'Arena di Verona*, March 23, 2008.

136. For other examples, see Reuter 1995, 91–92.

137. See remarks by ibid., 1985, 31.

CHAPTER 4: THE RUSSIAN MAFIA IN ROME AND BUDAPEST

1. Glenny 2008, 79.

2. "He was arrested twice again—once for racketeering, another time for the murder of a casino owner—but was not convicted" (*New York Times*, January 10, 1999). Glenny (2008, 78–79) puts his arrest at 1986.

3. *Moscow Times*, February 22, 2000. On the Solntsevskaya, see also Modestov 1996; Maksimov 1997; Finckenauer and Waring 1998, 110–14; Galeotti 2000; Varese 2001; Karyshev 2001; Glenny 2008, 78–82, 86–89.

4. *Komsomol'skaya Pravda*, December 4, 1998, cited in Varese 2001, 173–74.

5. On Elson in New York, see Friedman 2000, 19–20. On Ivan'kov, see Finckenauer and Waring 1998, 112–13; Grant 1996.

6. See Kochan 2005, 21–36. The Italian investigation into these bank transfers did not lead to any conviction (PRB 2008).

7. Although hard to believe, such an occurrence is not that rare. In 1969 Lefty Rosenthal, the central character of Martin Scorsese's film *Casino*, was able to throw out an indictment because the attorney general had failed to personally sign the wiretap orders (Pileggi 1996, 13).

8. In short, refugees were not allowed to apply for a visa to the United States in Moscow, so they would leave the USSR with an Israeli visa and then stop in Rome, where they applied for refugee status to enter the United States.

9. During the 1970s some 370,000 people, mostly Soviet Jews, were allowed to leave the USSR (Mynz 1995) .

10. In 1989, more than seven thousand Russians were in Ladispoli and Rome awaiting visas to the United States. Overall, seventy-one thousand Russian Jews applied for refugee status to enter the United States that year. A vivid memoir of this migration to the United States is contained in a book evoking everyday life in Rome in 1989 by Anatoly Rozenblat, *Hello America!*

11. Friedman 2000, 15.

12. *Paese Sera*, February 24, 1977.

13. Friedman 2000, 14.

14. R7; American Jewish Year Book 1991, 128–29; Skolnik 2006, 2:62; Rozenblat 2006.

15. The population in Rome (city) was 2,775,250 in 1991 and 2,663,182 in 2001. In 1995, twenty individuals were recorded as having been born in a former Soviet republic, constituting 0.13 percent of the total population and 5.08 percent of the foreign population of the town. These percentages rose to 0.25 and 8.39, respectively, in 1997, when the group was arrested.

16. SCO 1997a, 16–17.

17. SCO 1997b, 31.

18. Ibid., 31.

19. SCO 1997a, 21, 187; SCO 1997b, 36.

20. SCO 1997a, 47–75.

21. Ibid., 191; 1997c, 31.

22. CPA 1997, 18–19.

23. SCO 1997a, 180; 1997c, 37; CPA 1997, 20.

24. SCO 1997a, 81–96.

25. A third Italian, also married to a Russian woman (*Olga Ferrari*), was *Marco Ferrari*, a petty criminal who both consumed and sold drugs, and was a resident of Margherita Laziale. He became a partner in a company set up in Italy by the group and worked mainly in the area of fictitious marriages.

26. Becucci 2006.

27. SCO 1997a, 93, 120; CPA 1997, 19.

28. SCO 1997a, 85.

29. Ibid., 83; SCO 1997b, 65.

30. For example, one such deal was worth US$300 million (SCO 1997b, 98; see also CPA 1997, 21).

31. SCO 1997b, 110.

32. SCO 1997a, 132, 163–64; SCO 1997c, 40–41.

33. SCO 1997a, 120, 89, 51–52.

34. Ibid., 101.

35. Ibid., 244, 188. On protection as a natural monopoly, see Lane 1958; Nozick 1974.

36. SCO 1997a, 97–102.

37. SCO 1997c, 40.

38. SCO 1997a, 204.

39. Ibid., 24–26, 163–64; CPA 1997, 19. At first, Yakovlev was hesitant about killing Vlasik. In a conversation with Yakovlev, Sidelnikov (one of Yakov's deputies) said he wanted Vlasik killed right away, but Yakovlev demurred: "No, better

talk to him, tell him that he should think twice before deciding to cut loose from his own friends." Sidelnikov agreed. Yakovlev had also planned to kidnap and torture Rostovtsev's secretary (SCO 1997a, 26).

40. See, respectively, ibid., 99, 53.

41. Ibid., 77; see also CPA 1997, 19–20.

42. SCO 1997a, 20.

43. R1.

44. Varese 2006c.

45. R1; R2; R3.

46. Friedman 2000, 240–41. Mikhailov reportedly owns a luxury hotel in Budapest. See Maksimov 1997, 329.

47. *Washington Post*, December 21, 1998; see also Wright 1997, 70.

48. Kwist 1991; *Washington Post*, December 21, 1998; Wright 1997, 70; Guy 1997, 83.

49. Information in this paragraph comes from Urbán 1997, 240; Csáki and Karsai 2001, 5, 66; Sárközy 1993, 243; Kornai 1996.

50. Data from Központi Statisztikai Hivatal (Central Statistics Office), available at http://portal.ksh.hu/pls/ksh/docs/eng/xstadat/xstadat_annual/tabl3_01_01ie .html; http://portal.ksh.hu/pls/ksh/docs/hun/xstadat/xstadat_eves/tabl3 01 08i .html.

51. Urbán 1997, 243. For pointed criticisms of the early privatization plans and a blueprint for postsocialist transition in Eastern Europe, see Kornai 1990. For a general assessment of the economic transition and political transformation in Hungary, see Kornai 1996; Rose-Ackerman 2007.

52. Csáki and Karsai 2001, 69.

53. Ibid., 71, 72.

54. Ibid., 71; see also Wright 1997, 74.

55. Csáki and Karsai 2001, 71.

56. Ibid., 71; see also Wright 1997, 69.

57. Csáki and Karsai 2001, 72. Alan Wright (1997, 71) claims that in 1992, Hungary was the third-largest money launderer in Europe, and official statistics up to the end of 1996 record no conviction or completed proceedings for money laundering.

58. Csáki and Karsai 2001, 72.

59. Pap 2001; see also Mawby and Wright 2001.

60. The 31 percent estimate is by Mária Lackó (1997) and is based on electric energy consumption in the year 1994. See also Tóth 1997–98; http://rru.www .worldbank.org. According to *Budapest Week* (February 23–29, 1995, quoted in Wright 1997, 74), between 20 and 40 percent of Hungary's half-million unemployed are estimated to be involved in the shadow economy.

61. Mink 1997, 78–79.

62. Furthermore, the international trade embargo against Yugoslavia offered extraordinary profits for smugglers in the southern and eastern cities of the country, such as Miskolc, Kecskemét, and Kiskörös (Mink 1997).

63. Firearms and explosives have also been easily available since the transition to the market. See Wright 1997, 72; especially Nagy 2000.

64. "The Billion Dollar Don," *BBC1 Panorama*, December 6, 1999.

65. See also Wright 1997, 72.

66. *Hetek*, August 1999; *Russian Business Monitor*, September 1, 1999; *Times* (London), August 20, 1999; *RFE/RL Organized Crime and Terrorism Watch*, January 16, 2003; March 13, 2003; *Jane's Intelligence Digest*, January 31, 2003; *St. Petersburg Times*, February 28, 2003; Kupchinsky 2009. Mogilevich bought 95 percent of the Army Co-op through Arigon Ltd. A rare but significant confirmation of the fact that Mogilevich used Solntsevskaya funds for his investments comes from a phone conversation intercepted by the Austrian police and reported in the Italian file on Yakovlev. The conversation, between Averin and Mogilevich, took place in April 1994. The former reminds the latter that he has to return money that he obtained from the group's common fund. The money involved was US$5 million (SCO 1997a, 79). Most notoriously, Mogilevich injected US$30 million from Arigon Ltd. into YBM Magnex International, which merged with Magnex 2000 (Friedman 2000, 249–51).

67. *Moscow Times*, February 22, 2000.

68. Silber and Little 1996, 102–3; Glenny 1996, 103. In any case and for the purpose of this discussion, it is still a well-meaning policy (intended to help an ally at war) that led to the unintended consequence described above.

69. Mink 1997; *CTK Czech News Agency*, November 8, 1999.

70. "The Billion Dollar Don," *BBC1 Panorama*, December 6, 1999.

71. *CTK Czech News Agency*, November 8, 1999; *Index* (Budapest), June 9, 2000.

72. *Hungarian News Agency (MTI)*, September 17, 1998.

73. *Moscow Times*, February 22, 2000.

74. *Hungarian News Agency (MTI)*, November 19, 1998.

75. Clodo created a bomb-making facility in Budapest, where bombs later used in the wave of attacks on criminals and businesspeople in the period 1996–98 were produced (*Duna Satellite TV* [BBC Monitoring], November 6, 2000; December 29, 2001).

76. *Heti Világgazdaság*, November 11, 2000. Steigura was also active in the oil market in Budapest (*Világgazdaság*, November 22, 2000).

77. *Hungarian News Agency (MTI)*, November 5, 2003. Mogilevich was arrested in Russia on January 24, 2008 and released a year later (*Moscow Times*, April 7, 2008; *RIA Novosti* July 27, 2009).

78. Available at http://nbh.gov.hu/english/bmenu7.htm.

79. Spaventa 1999.

80. R1.

81. Gambetta 1993, 104.

Chapter 5: Lessons from the Past

1. Gentile [1963] 1993. There is some dispute on the exact year of Gentile's birth. The year 1884 is claimed somewhere, but 1885 is the year that Gentile himself gave, and it is backed by his Federal Narcotics Bureau file and naturalization records (Critchley, personal communication, January 26, 2009 and December 19, 2009).

2. Extracts from the report are in Farrell 1997, 29–30. See also Hess [1973] 1998, 151; Gambetta 1988, 161; 1993, 97.

3. Franchetti [1876] 1993; Gambetta and Reuter 1995, 121–22. The English press favorably reviewed Franchetti's book at the time. See, for example, *Pall Mall Gazette*, February 26, 1877; March 12, 1877; *Birmingham Daily Post*, February 15, 1894; *Times* (London), April 8, 1891. On the official, inconclusive inquiry that preceded Franchetti's trip, see the discussion in *Pall Mall Gazette*, February 26, 1877. Newspaper reports on the existence of such a "vast organization of the dangerous classes" (*New York Times*, September 24, 1874) had been published in London, Manchester, and New York as early as 1874. See, for example, *Times* (London), September 22, 1874; October 7, 1874; October 15, 1874; October 24, 1874; June 9, 1875; June 21, 1875. Consistent with Franchetti's findings is a piece titled "The Sicilian Maffia" published in the *New York Times* on September 24, 1874: the mafia "comprehends noblemen, judges, lawyers, merchants, agriculturists, every grade of life in short." The author perceptively links the mafia's origin to a lack of trust in the government and absentee landlords who rely on daily laborers and live in cities, feeling no connection to the land or their employees.

4. The 1886 book is Alongi [1886] 1977; see also Lupo 1996, 33. On the *Sangiorgi* report, see Lupo 1988, 466–67; 1996, 117; Paoli 2003, 35; Dickie 2007, 100. Defendants for whose trial the report had been written got light sentences and walked free.

5. Baily 1999, 25; see also Eckerson 1966; Goldin 1994, 238; compare to Raab 2005, 24. Immigration into the United States came to a virtual halt in 1929, when the United States introduced stricter immigration quotas.

6. Klein 1983, 311; Baily 1983, 296; 1999, 61; Lankevich 2002, 119, 122. Data on Italian migration to the United States and Argentina are in Baily 1999, 26, 47. For a discussion of why most Italians preferred the United States over Argentina, see Baily 1999, 56.

7. On Lupo, see Critchley 2009, 47. See also the cases of Giovanni Pecoraro and Joseph Palermo, who were both wanted for murder in Palermo (Critchley 2009, 67, 69). On Masseria's arrival, see Nash 1993, 278; Repetto 2004, 105; Cohen 1998, 58. David Critchley (2009) disputes that he was facing a murder charge. The report of the Immigration Commission discusses three Italian police certificates stating that the individuals are considered "mafiosi" by all in their villages of origin (IC 1911, 282). Oddly, Albini (1971, 168), who discusses these data, does not take them to suggest that mafiosi had arrived in the United States.

8. The *Brooklyn Eagle* reported on March 16, 1875 that a letter sent to the Brooklyn police in 1866 alleged that the Deodati executioners were indeed hired in Sicily, and intended to go to Mexico or Canada immediately after committing the deed. The "murder in the woods" was widely reported at the time. See, for example, *Brooklyn Eagle*, June 3, 1865; June 9, 1865; June 10, 1865; June 13, 1865; June 14, 1865; June 16, 1865; June 17, 1865; November 1, 1865; see also Critchley 2009, 38–39. For additional instances, see, for example, Hess [1973] 1998, 163–64; Lupo 1996, 144. Of course, cases of mafiosi running in the other direction are also on record—namely, persons condemned by the U.S. mafia escaping back to Sicily. See Gentile [1963] 1993, 70–71; Arlacchi 1993, 26.

9. Bonanno with Lalli 1983, 52. See also Lupo 1996, 180. For instance, Mori arrested 450 people from the town of Gangi, 300 of whom were accused of harboring mafiosi. A U.S. anthropologist who was doing fieldwork in Milocca, a town of some 2,500 inhabitants, recounts how the people were rounded up and forced to walk, together with their animals, to the village of Mussomeli, where more than 100 were eventually jailed (Gower Chapman 1971, 7–8). Mori was also instrumental in the reduction of licenses to carry guns in Palermo Province—from 25,459 in 1922 to 11,570 in 1923 and 6,224 in 1928 (according data in Mori 1933, 224). Murders dropped from 268 in 1925 to 77 in 1926; see also Hess [1973] 1998, 182–83. This suggests that Mori's campaign was having an effect. Yet other evidence indicates that the mafia was still able to determine who was to undertake construction work in Palermo (MA 1937); see also Mori's reflections (1933, 151–229).

10. Melchiorre Allegra (b. 1881), a doctor practicing in Palermo who had joined the mafia in 1916, declared that in the 1924 elections, mafiosi had planned to support both the democratic and fascist party lists. In the end, they simply sold their votes to the highest bidder. Allegra himself stood for election, with the support of Salvatore Maranzano, who at the time was still in Italy (MA 1937). See also Lupo 1996, 171; Lupo 2008, 44; Critchley 2009, 144; Gambetta 1993, 293fn20.

11. Arlacchi 1993, 41.

12. When Melchiorre Allegra joined the organization in 1916 in Palermo, he was told by his mentors that the "sect, according to them, had powerful ramifications, not just in Sicily, but also in Tunis, the Americas and in some other centres

of the continent such as, for instance, Marseilles" (MA 1937). Calderone's discussion of the Tunis family is in Arlacchi (1992, 15). Bonanno (with Lalli 1983, 55) had an uncle living in Tunis, although he might not have been in the mafia. For other evidence of Italian criminals passing through Tunis, see IC 1911, 284–85. Tunisia—a French protectorate—was, along with the United States and Argentina, a destination of significant Italian migration, mainly from Sicily and Sardinia, at the end of the nineteenth century. At the beginning of the twentieth century, more than a hundred thousand Italians resided in Tunisia (Alberti Russell 1977, 34–37), mostly living in Tunis. In those years, Sicilians made up 72.5 percent of the community's population (Bonura 1929, 59). Buscetta's reference to his boss's escape to France is in Arlacchi 1996, 99.

13. Bonanno with Lalli 1983, 52. One prominent mafioso that reached the United States in this period was Salvatore Maranzano. He arrived in 1925, at age forty-three, and was soon to become the leader of the Schiro (later Bonanno) family in New York.

14. Chandler 1976, 57–58. Compare to Critchley 2009, 208.

15. Lankevich 2002, 112.

16. I am drawing here on ibid., especially 112, 117, 123.

17. Ibid., 124.

18. Turner 1909, 119; see also the influential investigation, *How the Other Half Lives*, by Jacob Riis ([1890] 1970).

19. Cited in Turner 1909, 120.

20. Lankevich 2002, 127, 130; Dash 2007.

21. Nelli 1976, 115; Dash 2007, 33–34; Turner 1909, 117, 119; Czitrom 1991; Lardner and Reppetto 2000, 96–97; Lankevich 2002, 117–18; see also Nelli 1976, 112. The Tammany Hall leader mentioned in the text is Richard Croker: see Dash 2007, 35–6, 367–8.

22. Thomas 1969, 254; Dash 2007, 40, 49; Lardner and Reppetto 2000, 104; Lankevich 2002, 129; see also Anbinder 2001, 228.

23. Cited in Dash 2007, 47, 49. For the information in this paragraph, see especially Thomas 1969, 256, 260–61; Dash 2007, 39, 47, 58; Turner 1909, 119–34; Lankevich 2002, 140; see also Fogleson, Carrarini, and Mazzoccoli 1977, 3; Lardner and Reppetto 2000, 95, 97; Anbinder 2001, 228. Each time a police officer arrived in a post, all the brothels, gambling dens, and dubious saloons that operated in their district were forced to pay an "initiation fee," in the region of $500 each. Similar payments were expected whenever an illegal business changed owner or a gambler or madam expanded into a new building. It cost $500 to reopen a brothel or gaming house after a raid (Dash 2007, 65).

24. *New York Times*, February 9, 1900; Dash 2007, 80.

25. This paragraph is based on Dash 2007, 77–80, 383–84.

26. Quoted in Thomas 1969, 261.

27. This paragraph draws on *New York Times*, May 24, 1911; Thomas 1969, 256–57, 261; Lankevich 2002, 141, 147–49; Dash 2007, 94, 117; see also Thomas 1967; Lardner and Reppetto 2000, 102–7. On the 1910s wave of strikes in New York City, see Lankevich 2002, 149; Drehle 2003. Gaynor also established the rule that vacant positions on the police force should be filled by choosing candidates from the top of the civil service eligible list, in strict numerical order.

28. Quoted in Thomas 1969, 411.

29. Ibid., 261–62, 264; Dash 2007, 119.

30. Dash 2007, 120.

31. Ibid., 335; Critchley 2009, 72. It should be noted that other aspects of the criminal justice system were not reformed. For instance, appointments to magistrate's courts continued to be "rewards for party service and favors in return were expected and received" (Block 1983, 33).

32. Quoted in *New York Times*, October 22, 1888.

33. For evidence on early Italian involvement in counterfeiting, see Critchley 2009, 38–39. The Messina gang exposed in 1865 is mentioned in *New York Times*, June 3, 1865; *Brooklyn Eagle*, June 9, 1865; June 10, 1865; June 13, 1865; June 14, 1865; June 17, 1865. On Morello and Lupo, see Asbury [1928] 1998, 248–49; Nelli 1976, 124; Dash 2009. Lupo was also known as Ignazio Saietta (Asbury 1950, 229). Morello was arrested in 1900 for counterfeiting and eventually slain during the Castellammare War in August 1930. On the mafia oath, see FBI 1963, cited in Critchley 2009, 255n95.

34. *New York Times*, October 31, 1909.

35. See *New York Times*, October 14, 1908; October 31, 1909; Asbury [1928] 1998, 248; Selvaggi 1978, 25; Critchley 2009, 101–3. The Terranova brothers had been linked to horse stealing.

36. Raab 2005, 19; Nelli 1976, 69–100; Pitkin and Cordasco 1977; Critchley 2009, 20–35. A reference to the Black Hand appeared for the first time in the U.S. press in 1903, according to Humbert Nelli (1976, 75–76); see also Pitkin and Cordasco 1977, 15–16. Robert Lombardo (2004) concludes that the Black Hand in Chicago was first reported in 1904 and had disappeared by 1920. By 1915, the Black Hand brand had vanished in New York City (Critchley 2009, 33). For a discussion of criminal brands that are pirated, see Smith and Varese 2001; Gambetta 1993.

37. On the 1910s' wave of strikes in New York City, see Lankevich 2002, 149; Drehle 2003. On early mafia involvement in labor disputes, see, for example, *New York Times*, October 12, 1913; Critchley 2009, 23. On Paul Kelly, see Nelli 1976, 109. Other data come from Critchley 2009, 77, 147–48, 151. More gen-

erally on the role of the mafia in various markets in New York City, see Jacobs, Friel, and Raddick 1999.

38. See Merz 1932; Behr 1997, 82–86; Kerr 1985. Finland enacted similar legislation, leading to the prohibition of alcohol from 1919 to 1928 (Wuorinen 1932). Immigrant communities more likely thought of Prohibition as the product of bigotry and racist sentiments directed against them (Lerner 2007, 3; Bonanno with Lalli 1983, 64). Beer drinking was of course part of life for German American immigrants, "prohibition's first victims" (Behr 1997, 69–71). On enforcement of the legislation, see Wickersham Commission 1931; Sawyer 1932; Asbury 1950, 220; Bonanno with Lalli 1983, 65; Merz 1932, 130–57.

39. On estimates of the market size, see Sinclair 1962, 222; see also Raab 2005, 25.

40. Asbury 1950, 216–64; Carse 1961, 17; Sinclair 1962, 197.

41. New York Times, February 4, 1923; Moray 1929, 82–95, 125–30, 179–88; Asbury 1950, 241–64; Carse 1961, 61–81; Sinclair 1962, 198. Liquor was also coming from the West Indies, in particular the Bahamas, Mexico, and Cuba (Asbury 1950, 242; Carse 1961, 17).

42. Asbury 1950, 251.

43. Moray 1929, 211, which adds: "Several raids have been carried out, actually by one of the partners in a rum-runner. One boat about five miles east of us was raided not long ago" (ibid.).

44. Asbury 1950, 250–51; Moray 1929, xiii, 210; Cohen 1998, 53–54; see also Carse 1961, 62.

45. Ashbury 1950, 251.

46. See Cohen 1998, 54–55.

47. See several reports in New York Times, October 13, 1920; October 14, 1920; October 15, 1920; October 16, 1920; October 17, 1920; November 14, 1920; November 20, 1920; February 11, 1921; March 22, 1921; March 30, 1921; February 24, 1922; March 21, 1922; May 9, 1922; August 29, 1922; September 17, 1922; November 4, 1922; December 31, 1922). Elizabeth Street, to the left of Bowery and in the heart of the curb exchange area, housed the core of the New York City Sicilian community (Gabaccia 1984). A report in the New York Times (August 29, 1922) contains the list and quotes the prices.

48. New York Times, October 13, 1920.

49. Ibid.

50. Ibid., March 21, 1921 ("four barrels and six gallons").

51. Ibid., August 29, 1922; see also ibid., October 13, 1920.

52. Ibid., October 13, 1920.

53. Ibid., August 29, 1922; see also November 20, 1920; November 4, 1922.

54. Ibid., April 15, 1913; October 17, 1920; February 11, 1921; February 24, 1922; April 9, 1922; May 9, 1922; Bonanno with Lalli 1983, 85; Critchley 2009, 154–57.

55. Critchley 2009, 155.

56. Asbury 1950, 263; Sinclair 1962, 199; Cohen 1998, 54–55; Critchley 2009, 142–43. See also Repetto 2004, 110. The "Big Seven" was a short-lived cartel of smugglers active along the Atlantic coast bringing in Canadian liquor. There were originally seven groups (hence the Big Seven), but their number grew to about a dozen. The purpose of the Big Seven was to stabilize the price of imported booze. Established in October 1932, the cartel handled some eight thousand cases of rum monthly. But despite its powerful membership, the cartel broke up in spring 1933 (Prohibition ended on December 5, 1933). *New York Times*, April 1, 1939; April 2, 1939; April 11, 1939; Critchley 2009, 142.

57. Bonanno with Lalli 1983, 70, 75; Critchley 2009, 144, 146; see also MA 1937; Lupo 2008, 84. His warehouses stretched across Dutchess County, New York, where Maranzano bought a house. In March 1929, Rocco Germano, one of Maranzano's associates, fired on a liquor truck traveling on Main Street in Poughkeepsie. The truck's driver and friend abandoned the vehicle, which had been stolen in the Bronx. Detectives concluded that the men in the truck had failed to hand over what they owed to Maranzano. A five-thousand-gallon plant was uncovered as a result of the investigation. In the first decade of the twentieth century, New York was the brewing center of the nation (Lankevich 2002, 146), making it easier to continue the production underground.

58. *New York Times*, September 29, 1929, quoted in Lerner 2007, 1.

59. Landesco 1932; Bonanno with Lalli 1983, 85, 93, 126; Sinclair 1962, 221, 223, 230. This does not imply that the Italian mafia was accepting non-Italians after 1931, nor that a unified structure emerged.

60. Bonanno with Lalli 1983, 76. Buscetta, in his testimony to Italian authorities, recalls that "it used to be possible for a man of honor who migrated to the United States to become immediately, by virtue of his position, a member of the American Cosa Nostra" (quoted in Gambetta 1993, 118; see also Arlacchi 1996, 62).

61. As evidence of such letters of reference, see Flynn 1919, 207; see also Buscetta's testimony in Arlacchi 1996, 62. On Gentile's mafia membership, see Critchley 2009, 93, 269n206; Gentile [1963] 1993.

62. I am grateful to David Critchley for his advice. See also Maas 1997, 46.

63. Quoted in MA 1937.

64. Arlacchi 1996, 62, 52; Gambetta 1993, 117–18. Calderone also makes it clear that the two organizations were independent in the postwar period (Arlacchi 1993, 78; see also Critchley 2009, 196, 187; Cressey 1969, 46). A conversa-

tion recorded in Montreal in 1974 between Paul Violi, most likely a Bonanno man and the head of the Montreal family, and a Sicilian who had plans to set himself up in Canada, demonstrates that the Sicilian and North American mafias were two fully separate and independent entities. Violi makes it clear that if a mafioso were to move to Canada, he would be put on a five-year probation, during which he would be assessed "so that everyone can figure out what he is like" (quoted in OSPA Stajano 1992, 59; see also 60). According to Calderone, Violi was instead a member of the Gambino family operating in Canada (Gambetta 1993, 296n41). Yet the Sicilians were not that accurately informed about the membership of the U.S. families (David Critchley, personal communication, December 19, 2009).

65. Critchley 2009, 91; see also Maas [1968] 2003. Relevant examples are George Barone, Sammy the Bull Gravano, and John Gotti. Still, some mainland Italians like Genovese and Anastasia had been admitted into the New York City mafia during the 1920s, before the Castellammare War. Buscetta claims that even Jews and Irish had been admitted at the height of the Castellammare War — a move that was kept secret for several years (Arlacchi 1996, 164). Generally, criminal groups try to increase their ranks in times of war (see, for example, the case of British street gangs in Yearwood and Hayes 2000, 16; Densley 2009, 6).

66. See, for example, Lupsha 1986, 44; Gambetta 1993, 252.

67. Nelli 1976, 122.

68. Carrasco 1886; Baily 1983, 1999; Gallo 1983; Devoto 1993.

69. Klein 1983, 311; Baily 1983, 296; 1999, 61; Rosoli 1978.

70. Cacopardo and Moreno 1985; Frid de Silberstein 1994.

71. Johns 1991, 491–92; Frid de Silberstein 1993, 133; Gallo 1983; Lanciotti 2004.

72. Carina Frid de Silberstein, personal communication, January 31, 2010.

73. Information presented in this section comes from Frid de Silberstein 1992; 1993, 130, 141–43; 1994; Johns 1994. Chiavari and Lavagna in Liguria were the hub of the first wave of Italian migration to Rosario. The city is famous in Italy for the heartbreaking story of a Genovese child who had gone in search of his mother all the way to Rosario, narrated in De Amicis's *Il Libro Cuore* ([1886] 2001). The city is also the birthplace of Ernesto "Che" Guevara (Anderson 1997, 3–9).

74. Frid de Silberstein 1994, 509, 512; personal communication, January 31, 2010. Frid de Silberstein's estimate is based on the number of Agrigentani that are mentioned in marriage records between 1900 and 1905 in six districts of the city (N = 234 in this period). After applying a coefficient of 4 (a rather conservative one to estimate the average family unit), we get a figure of 936. This figure most likely still underrepresents the total number of Agrigentani who immigrated to Rosario in the first decade of the twentieth century since it is based on civil

marriages only for those five years (ibid., personal communication, January 31, 2010; see also Mormino and Pozzetta 1998).

75. Aguirre 2000, 74, 191; Rossi 2003, 148. Although Rosario was referred to as the Chicago Argentina, the origin of such a name refers to the workers who were killed during a strike in Chicago in 1886. Other historians suggest that the Chicago Argentina refers to the leading position of Rosario as a grain market and grain port (still nowadays, Chicago's Grain Stock Exchange does not close its daily blackboard prices until Rosario's prices are delivered). It was soon used to refer to its criminal reputation (Rossi 2003, 171; Aguirre 2006). Mafia activities were also reported in Andean provinces (San Juan) and to the north of Argentina (La Rioja, Salta, and Santiago del Estero). The Catanesi mentioned in the text were from Regalbuto, Mineo, and San Filippo. Cuffaro is also the last name of a Raffadali mafia boss in the 1970s, Giuseppe Cuffaro.

76. For the press dubbing Galiffi a local Al Capone, see, for example, "Como en Chicago, Contra Al Capone," *Crítica*, October 9, 1932; February 27, 1933. Data on his life are in Caimari 2007, 19; Aguirre 2000, 173–215; Rossi 2003, 149.

77. MHPR 1938a. Samburgo confessed in 1938 before the Comisario de Investigaciones Teodoro Alemán while he was imprisoned at the Penitenciaría Nacional in Buenos Aires.

78. New arrivals pushed out of Sicily by Mussolini included Romeo Capuani, Felipe Campeoni, Santos Gerardo, and Juan D'Angelo. Data on Marrone's life and criminal activities are in MHPR 1938a, folio 122; 1938b, folio 198. The Spanish version of the mafia titles recorded in the judicial documents are "Jefes, sub-jefes, jefes de grupo, consejeros."

79. Alvarez 1943, 14, quoted in Johns 1991, 491. This paragraph draws on Johns 1991, 490–91. See also Gallo 1976, 5–23.

80. Johns 1991, 499.

81. Ibid., 495–46, 498, 507; Gallo 1970; 1983, 166–67. Data on large Italian land properties are also in Frid de Silberstein 1993, 139 (for example, Castagnigno and Pignasco, seventeen thousand hectares). As for manufacturing, the Refinería Argentina, employing eight hundred workers between 1894 and 1920, was the main producer of refined sugar and alcohol in the country (ibid., 152).

82. The words by Ricardo Caballero are quoted in Karush 1999, 597–58. See Gallo 1983; Johns 1991, 494; Thompson 1984; Hasbrouck 1935.

83. Palacio 2004.

84. Johns 1991, 500; Lanciotti 2004. More than a fourth of the population lived in tenements.

85. Lanciotti 2009, 229, 231–32, 189. By 1913, the construction market started to contract.

86. Although I have data for the value of each projects (with some gaps), it should be noted that the owners had an incentive to underreport the cost of the work for tax purposes.

87. Pendino worked in construction between the early 1880s to at least 1910. Frid de Silberstein 1991, 182–90; Aguirre 2000, 47–49.

88. The level of violence was lower in Rosario, although instances are on record. In the local newspaper *El Municipio*, eight reports of robbery of construction machinery and tools are mentioned between August 1909 and July 1910.

89. In Rosario, the number of firms obtaining permits between 1905 and 1909 stood at 172, while in Bardonecchia, in the boom periods 1965–69 and 1970–74, the equivalent figures were 42 and 49, respectively.

90. On the rural folk, see Johns 1991, 501. As documented by Norma Lanciotti (2009, 156–57), a significant number of real estate investors were themselves landowners (22.54 percent in the 1885–95 period and 15.85 percent in the 1896–1914 period of the total investors identified [N = 213]).

91. The defendant was a Carlos Cacciato. MHPR 1939. In another court file, Pendino is described by a defendant as a man "who was respected among his countrymen due to the fact that he always tried to help them" (MHPR 1938b, folio 97).

92. Frid de Silberstein 1991, 182–90; Aguirre 2000, 159. For the 1899 police document, see PR 1899; Revista Órgano Oficial de la Policía del Rosario (Rosario: Imprenta La Minerva, 1924). The shopkeeper mentioned in the text was Vicente Puteti (Aguirre 2000, 86). Puteti was the owner of a small grocery store along the *pampa gringa* (agricultural countryside) that performed a distinctive social function. Such stores provided credit to tenants (*arrendatarios*); they became a key source of information for both tenants and landowners since they usually gathered information on potential work qualifications, knowledge of techniques of agriculture, and capital of the prospective arrendatarios.

93. The victim was Dr. Enzo Bordhabere.

94. Frid 1993; Malamud 1997. The Liga del Sur's political platform included the reform of the electoral system in Argentina. It also supported the extension of citizenship to immigrants. See Gandolfo 1991.

95. Aguirre 2000, 88–89. Other victims of the Mano Negra were Jose Castiglione and Mariano Giangrecco. The Catanese gang was composed of Gaetano Pergola, José Perola, and José Costanzo, all born in Galliano (ibid., 89–91). The gang had attacked, among others, Martiré and Castiglione. Contrary to what Nelli (1969, 379) claims, Argentina did experience the phenomenon of the Black Hand.

96. Aguirre 2000, 122.

97. Aguirre 2000, 296; Caimari 2007, 5. In the 1910s, see the case of a boy, Juan Vicente Parisi, the son of a coal merchant, who was snatched from his parents

in 1915. In 1916, the group led by José Cuffaro successfully organized the kidnapping of Antonio Moressi, a carriage driver (other cases took place throughout 1916). In the 1930s, see the cases of F. Andueza (1931) and the son of the trader Julio Nannini (1932). The kidnapping of a respected Jewish doctor, Jaime Favelukes (1932), and that of another professional, Marcelo Martin (1933), shocked the nation. On the Favelukes's kidnapping, see, for example, *El Mundo*, October 8, 1932; October 13, 1932; *La Nación*, October 7, 1932; *Crítica*, October 7, 1932; October 11, 1932. See also Aguirre 2004.

98. A third movie on the case was produced in 1972, titled *La maffia* (Leopoldo Torre Nilsson) (Caimari 2007, 1, 29; Blanco Pazos and Clemente 2004, 12). The Senate approved the new framework for the Criminal Code in 1933. The death penalty had been abolished in 1922. On rumors regarding the case, see *Crítica*, October 19, 1932; December 14, 1932; December 29, 1932. On the funeral, see *La Nación*, February 24, 1933; Caimari 2007, 6–8. On the kidnappers, see Aguirre 2000, 360; Rossi 2003, 149.

99. *Time Magazine*, May 29, 1944; Zinni 1975, 161–80; Goris 1999; Aguirre 2000, 382–402; Rossi 2003, 147, 150–51. Despite the significant role of Italian crime in Rosario, Italians did not control some of the key criminal markets. For instance, prostitution and the trafficking of women from Eastern Europe was controlled by the Zwi Migdal gang, staffed by Polish criminals of Jewish origin (brothels in Buenos Aires also utilized women trafficked from Eastern Europe and were controlled by "Jewish" criminals). In the aftermath of a trial that decimated the Zwi Migdal in 1931, however, Italians extended their reach to some local brothels. Guy 1991; Rossi 2003, 171.

CHAPTER 6: THE FUTURE OF THE MAFIAS?

1. By China, I am referring to mainland China. For the purpose of this chapter, I also use the name "Burma" to refer to the state now officially called the Union of Myanmar. For data on foreign investments in China, see Hsing 1998, 3, 8, 21.

2. Chin 2003, 203; Ngai 2005, 38–39; Goldman 2006, 413.

3. Information in this paragraph comes from Druijven 1993, 151; Hsing 1998, 3, 4, 8, 15, 19–21, 25; Li 1996, 12; Boardman 2005; Bosworth and Collins 2008. The registered economic growth rate for Shenzhen and Zhuhai during 1978–84 averaged 9.5 percent annually. Approximately 75 percent of manufacturing workers had been laid off within less than ten years. In 1985 alone, the armed forces were reduced by over one million individuals. The personnel of the national army went from 4.238 million in 1987 to 3.199 million in 1990. The 1.039 million demobilized soldiers during the first round of disarmament represented 24.5 percent of the army's original strength. The second round of cuts in the strength of

the army started in 1997, when some 700,000 soldiers were made redundant from 1997 to 2003. Most of the redundant soldiers were posted in the northeast (Information Office of the State Council 2005; Zheng 2005; Chan 2002).

4. Tuñón 2006, 5, 6, 8; Hsing 1998, 9; Deshingkar 2006, 8; Zheng 2009, 5; Chang 2008, 12; Jian and Zhang 2005; Wang 2006, 186; see also Wu and Treiman 2004; Mallee 1995. Two hundred million is a 2006 estimate. Internal migration was made possible by the reform of the *hukou* system of internal registration. A clear discussion of definitional problems of the terms "migrant workers" and "agricultural workers" is in Wang 2006. In Beijing and Shanghai, migrants make up a quarter of the population (*Nanfang Daily*, January 11, 2003). Guangdong is one of migrant workers' primary choices, accommodating 35 percent of the total migrant workers in China in 2003. The influx of migrant workers altered the demographic composition of Guangdong. The province officially became the most populous in China in January 2005, with a population totaling 110 million, of which 72 percent were registered permanent residents and 28 percent were migrants from other provinces (*China Daily*, January 29, 2005). Shenzhen has been transformed into "a city of migrants," where 82.1 percent of the total population is composed of people from other provinces (Liu 2004). "In 1995, the number of recorded criminal cases in Guangdong accounted for 10 percent of the national total, whilst the recorded major and serious cases represented 16.7 percent" (Chong and Pu 1997, 252). Official statistics indicated that more than 60 percent of the crimes were committed by nonpermanent local residents, which caused an economic loss of 3.36 billion yuan. The situation was echoed in the statistics revealed by the Ministry of Public Security regarding the crimes in Guangzhou and Shenzhen. In 1994, the crimes committed by the migrant population represented 69.2 percent of the total in Guangzhou; the figure was 97 percent in Shenzhen (Feng 2001, 127). See also People's Government of Guangdong 2006.

5. C10; see also Hershatter 1997, 338; *Telegraph*, August 27, 2000; Ngai 2005, 180; *Sunday Times*, October 22, 2006.

6. He 2002, 353–54.

7. He 2002, 137.

8. Ibid., 136; *Yangcheng Evening Paper*, April 20, 2000; He 2003, 30, 256–57; Liu, Zhao, and Su 2005; Chu 2000, 131. The ransom was for 1.038 billion yuan (US$1.300 million). The Zhazhi ritual is a triad ceremony for the promotion of members. A Blue Lantern is medium-level rank in a triad society, the equivalent of a gang leader, while a Red Pole is the equivalent of an Area Boss (Chu 2000, 28). "The Shenzhen Public Security Bureau arrested over 300 members that were newly recruited by these triads. Liao Tiansong, head of Hong Kong 'Victory' issued a directive to his new members in Shenzhen, stating, 'Stand your ground in Shenzhen, keep growing and wait for the chance to do big things'" (He 2002, 353).

9. Chin 2003, 169.

10. He 2002, 137.

11. Chin 2003, 6–7, 168–72, 202–3, 205, 223; He 2002, 137. As a Taiwanese investor put it, "We speak the same language and enjoy the same food!" (Hsing 1998, 3). Bamboo United was created in 1956 and remains to this day the biggest mafia group in Taiwan (estimates put the membership at ten thousand). In the 1960s, the gang was restructured into five branches. Over the next twenty years the branches grew in number. By 1983, eighteen branches (*tangs*) had been established. As a testament to the international reach of the group, in 1982 an overseas branch (Chao Tang) was formally opened in Hong Kong, the only one outside Taiwan, although some members are said to operate in the United States, the Philippines, and Japan (Chin 2003, 33–34).

12. Chin 2003, 171–72, 202–3; He 2002; Chu 2000, 132; *Washington Post*, December 31, 2000. Some also went to Cambodia.

13. C8; He 2002, 139–40; Chu 2000, 132; Chin 2003, 202, 204; see also Kong 2004. On the 14K triad group, see Morgan 1960, 79–88; Chu 2000.

14. Morgan 1960; Chin and Godson 2006, 7.

15. He 2003; Zhang 2006; Li and Ke 2006; Kang Kang 1998.

16. He 2003, 116–17.

17. C5.

18. Ngai 2005, 1; see also Jiang and Fu 2006; "The Seventh Day," Channel 7, Beijing Television, February 4, 2007 available at at http://www.btv.org/btvweb/sh/2007-02/06/content_153538.htm. For details of the 2003 survey, see *Far Eastern Economic Review* January 22, 2004. Ching Kwan Lee (2007, 110), the author of a groundbreaking ethnography of labor disputes in China's Sunbelt, has concluded that the violation of labor rights and entitlements is "endemic." It is still too early to assess the effects of the introduction of the new Labor Contract Law on January 1, 2008 (available at http://www.bjreview.com.cn/document/txt/2007-10/16/content_80896.htm). On the low quality and unevenness of intellectual property rights enforcement in China, see the important study by Martin Dimitrov (2009).

19. Quoted in *Jiancha Daily*, May 16, 2007.

20. Quoted in Zheng and Xia 2006.

21. Quote from Chin and Godson 2006, 24–25. In a survey of 288 judges published in 1998, none regarded the jurisdiction of courts as completely independent, while 124 of them (43.1 percent) believed that judicial independence had not been achieved in China (Jiang 2004, 5).

22. For data mentioned in this paragraph, see Jiang 2004, 6–7, 9–11, 23–26; 2006, 200. Jiang (2004, 7n32) notes that "the quota [of decisions enforced by courts] could even be lower in reality as some pending cases were considered to be

settled due to long delay." He adds: "In several interviews, lawyers even reported that only around 20% of the judgments can be successfully enforced, and it is believed that the average rate of successful enforcement in all the courts is supposed to be 25–30%" (ibid., 36). In a poll conducted by the China Commercial Press just before the assembly of the People's Congress in December 2002, 91 percent of the respondents said that they were not confident in the judiciary and were pessimistic about "access to justice" (ibid., 1). Another distinctive feature of the court system in China that delays decisions is the presence of a "trial committee" that oversees each judge's decision (ibid., 8).

23. Tuñón 2006, 10–11; *Jinan Daily*, March 10, 2005; *CSR Asia Weekly* 1 (week 11): 10; Druijven 1993, 148; Pan 2008.

24. C10.

25. C7.

26. Chin and Godson 2006; Tian 2001, cited in Chin and Godson 2006, 6; see also Glenny 2008, 364.

27. Varese 2001, 59–72.

28. Forward-looking officials channel bribes to their children living abroad (Glenny 2008)

29. C11.

30. *Jiancha Daily*, May 16, 2007, available at http://www.jcrb.com/200706/ca608419.htm. On the accumulation of bad debts in the banking system, see Shih 2004.

31. Yuan and the other three debt collectors were convicted for using extortion and violence to recover debts (*Jiancha Daily*, May 16, 2007).

32. In 2000, the Ministry of Public Security along with the Administrative Department for Industry and Commerce proscribed by formal decree the operation of debt-collection companies, and forbade the establishment of such companies by any institution or person. In 2002, the Trademark Office of the Administrative Department for Industry and Commerce adjusted the scope of trademark registration. The department lifted restrictions on "detective companies" and "private bodyguards," but still strictly forbade the operation of debt-collection companies (ibid.).

33. Quoted in ibid.

34. Quoted in ibid.

35. Respectively, six out of ten and twelve out of fifteen cases. Seven of the ten cases listed as dispute settlement are also involved in debt collection, so there is significant overlap between the two categories.

36. He 2003, 133–37.

37. Quoted in Chin 2003, 206–7.

38. *New York Times*, March 25, 2007; Bruck 2008, 45; *Xinhua*, March 28, 2005; *Weekly Standard*, May 7–8, 2005; *CCTV Online*, May 12, 2006; *China*

Daily, June 17, 2004. Since Chinese nationals need a special permit to travel to Macau, this increase reflects a deliberate policy on the part of the government as well as an increase in the number of wealthy Chinese (Bruck 2008, 45). The *Standard* (October 2, 2009) reports that Guangdong residents may now apply for a visa every month, rather than every two or three months, as in the past.

39. Quoted in http://a2zmacau.com/macau-casino/combating-crime-in-macau/.

40. See Lo 2005; *South China Morning Post*, December 20, 2000. The official data cited in the text refer to 2004, available at http://www.pj.gov.mo/1024/pj_en/magazine_en.htm. There were 917 illicit activities related to gaming in 2006—only 4 more cases than in 2005. Of these, 164 cases involved loan sharking (4 more than in 2005) and 79 cases involved gambling chips theft (3 more than the previous year).

41. For an insider's account of how high rollers are lured on to the tables in casinos in Las Vegas, see Castleman 2009.

42. C6; SCBC 2003a, 2003b; Wang and Eadington 2008, 241; Siu and Eadington 2009; Godinho 2006; Leong 2002. A recent development is the creation of consortia of VIP room contractors and junket operators with the aim of increasing bargaining powers vis-à-vis the casinos. See https://rp1.tss.db.com/dbdr/publication/PressRel/4602_NOV112007100351PM.pdf; *Business Wire*, January 14, 2009; Wang and Eadington 2008, 251. The western casinos are the Las Vegas Sands, Wynn Resorts, PBL Melco, Galaxy, and MGM.

43. Wang and Eadington 2008, 250.

44. C6. The business of lending money to high rollers is known as the *dupma* business (SCBC 2003a). A case at the center of the Supreme Court of British Columbia involves a Guangzhou resident who failed to repay his debt and was pursued by the creditors. In some cases, lenders have "accounts" at more than one casino (SCBC 2003b). Law 5/2004 allows for operators to collect the debt in Macau courts, although, write Wuyi Wang and William Eadington (2008, 249), these debts are "neither legal nor illegal," and suggest that extralegal efforts to recover the debts are the most common. Jorge Godinho (2006) points out that after the passing of the 2004 law, it is not possible to enforce gaming debts arising in Macau in mainland China.

45. This average is based on data in Wang and Eadington 2008, 256.

46. He 2003, 31–35; Li and Ke 2006, 51.

47. He 2003, 81–85.

48. C2.

49. C1.

50. Ibid.; *China News Website*, April 9, 2003; He 2003, 82–85.

51. C1; *China News Website*, April 9, 2003; He 2003, 82–85. Gambling venues exist also across China, and local crime groups make sure debts are honored. For instance, Mr. Lifeng Tang ran a gang in Ruzhou, Henan Province, whose members had to wear black suits and were paid a monthly wage. This gang controlled the gambling and entertainment sector of the city, collected debts, and even extended its influence over the election of town elders. The members were arrested in 1999, after only one year of operation.

52. Quoted in Chin 2003, 207.

53. See http://mitchmoxley.ca/index.php?option=com_content&view=article& id=9.

54. C6. I also draw upon a video posted on YouTube titled "18 dance and parade."

55. Hershatter 1997, 304; Jeffreys 2004, 96; Zheng 2007, 125.

56. Hershatter 1997, 331, 333–34, table 2; Jeffreys 2004, 97, 168–69; Gil et al. 1994; Zheng 2007, 126; 2009, 3–4, 55, 66; C12. The one trillion yuan estimate refers to 1999. Gail Hershatter (1997) points out that prostitution never completely disappeared.

57. See article 358, Criminal Code of the People's Republic of China, 1998, see also discussion in Jeffreys 2004, 138–49; Zheng 2009, 69; compare to Jeffreys 2004, 151, 157. The lower bound for convicted offenders is five years in prison. Death sentences are usually imposed when some other aggravating factors are present, such as bribery and the use of violence. See, for example, the case of Fengxiang Zhang (*Beijing Fazhi Ribao*, August 26, 2003). Criminal charges would be brought against customers or workers who knowingly transmit sexual diseases or engaged in sex with minors (Jeffreys 2004, 168–69; Zheng 2007, 133).

58. C12.

59. Quoted in Zheng 2007, 132.

60. Ibid., 132; 2009, 70, 71.

61. *China Daily*, January 23, 2005; see also Chin and Godson 2006, 13–17.

62. Chin and Godson 2006, 17.

63. USDJ 2005. It should be noted that other groups in Burma are involved in the drug business in addition to the Wa. They include the Kokang, Mengla, Kachin, and Shan (Beyrer et al. 2000, 77; Chin 2009, 101, 234).

64. Chin 2009, 1, 3, 9, 75; *Bangkok Times*, December 21, 2003; Swanström 2006, 122. This section is greatly indebted to Ko-lin Chin's remarkable ethnography (2009) of the drug trade in the golden triangle. For estimates of heroin production, see Chin 2009, 8, 9, 86. Burmese poppy cultivation accounts for 90 percent of all southeast Asian opium production (USDS 1998). For various estimates of opium-producing countries, see Chin 1990, 147; Chu 2000, 109; Beyrer

et al. 2000, 76; Zhang and Chin 2003, 473. Some authors link the suppression of the popular uprising in 1988 in Burma to the rise of poppy cultivation (Beyrer et al. 2000, 77, 82).

65. Chin 2009, 4, 9, 44, 83, 89; Swanström 2006, 128.

66. USDJ 2002, 5.

67. Quoted in *Xinhua News Agency*, August 3, 2004. Data in this paragraph are in Beyrer et al. 2000, 78–79; Chin 2009, 112, 117; Chu 2000, 187; Swanström 2006, 122; *People's Daily*, June 27, 2002; *China Daily*, June 27, 2002. See also Yunnan Provincial Department of Commerce 2005; the *China Daily* (March 31, 2005) describes a family-run drug smuggling ring operating "in the corridor that runs from Myanmar to Yunnan to Harbin." Hong Kong is the hub for other illegal traffics, such as cigarettes and endangered species. See, for example, Sharma 2003–4, 1–2.

68. Chin 2009, 121; Chu 2000, 187.

69. Chin 2009, 229–30. For similar conclusions, see also Chao Tzang 1993; Milson 2005, both cited in Chin 2009.

70. Chu 2000, 109–14; 2002.

71. C9.

72. See also the discussion of this initiative in Glenny 2008, 389–90.

73. C9.

74. In a recent case, the Italian police proved that the `Ndrangheta had reached an agreement with Chinese smugglers to ensure safe passage through the Gioia Tauro harbor, another port part of the Container Security Initiative (*La Repubblica*, December 22, 2009).

75. Ding 2001; see also *Le Monde*, December 30, 2009.

76. *Times Literary Supplement*, November 27, 2009.

77. See http://www.mckinsey.com/mgi/publications/unleashing_chinese_consumer/index.asp; see also *New Yorker*, December 7, 2009.

Chapter 7: Mafia Origins, Transplantation, and the Paradoxes of Democracy

1. SCO 1997c, 2.

2. Cruz 2010; Arana 2005. Hard state repression helped further shape and strengthen gangs' identities. A large percentage of gang members who came from different areas of El Salvador were held in detention centers organized according to their gang affiliation. Such a policy helped members to meet and coordinate across the country.

3. RCC 2000, 38. More generally on the Camorra in Aberdeen, see Saviano 2007, 259–81; Campana 2010.

4. On the early 1990s viewpoint, see, for example, Hess [1973] 1998; compare to Ruggiero and Vass 1992. A notable exception is the classic inquiry by Leopoldo Franchetti ([1876] 1993).

5. Gambetta 1993; Bandiera 2003.

6. Milhaupt and West 2000; Varese 2003. On disputes over land in the Meiji period, see Brown 1993.

7. Varese 1994, 2001.

8. I am grateful to C3 and C4, both officials in the Hebei Province, for their insights into cases of official corruption and their punishments.

9. The ceteris paribus condition here is crucial. Obviously, in the presence of widespread violence, vote rigging, and electoral fraud, even large constituencies are not safe from manipulation.

10. I refer here to the so-called consolidation movement. Gaynor obtained 250,678 votes (43 percent of the total cast), while his Republican opponent, Otto Bannard, got 177,662 (30 percent). The third candidate, media tycoon William R. Hearst, received 153,843 votes (27 percent). See Thomas 1969, 192; Cerillo 2000; Lankevich 2002, 134, 148.

11. A fictionalized account of the gambler's murder is described by Meyer Wolfsheim in *The Great Gatsby* by F. Scott Fitzgerald ([1925] 1998). I take Becker's innocence from Cohen 2006 and Dash 2007.

12. A parallel exists with protectionist measures in the developing world. For a discussion of how to lift people out of poverty in the developing world, see Collier 2008.

13. Baker 2004.

PRIMARY SOURCES

ARCHIVES

Argentina

Dirección de Obras Particulares (DOP). Archivo de Obras Particulares, Municipalidad de Rosario.

Museo Histórico Provincial de Rosario (MHPR). Archivo de Tribunales Provinciales de Rosario.

China

Criminal Case Files, Supreme People's Court, Beijing.

Municipal Archives, Beijing. Available at http://www.bjma.gov.cn/index.ycs.

Provincial Archives, Guangdong Province. Available at http://www.da.gd.gov.cn/webwww/index.aspx.

Italy

Archivio, Tribunale di Bologna.

Archivio, Tribunale di Roma.

Archivio, Tribunale di Torino.

Archivio, Tribunale di Verona.

Ufficio Licenze Edilizie, Comune di Bardonecchia.

United States

Ellis Island Archive. Available at http://www.ellisisland.org/.

INTERVIEWS

B1 Francesco Avato, mayor of Bardonecchia, May 14, 2007.

B2 Chief inspector, Italian police, Bardonecchia, March 15, 2007.

B3   Maurizio Laudi, deputy district attorney, Turin, May 14, 2007.

B4   Francesco Saccomanno, deputy chief inspector, crime unit, police headquarters, Turin, May 28, 2007.

B5   Giorgio Bortoluzzi, opposition politician, City Council, Bardonecchia, May 17, 2010.

C1   Ministry of Justice official in Zhuhai, Guangdong, June 28, 2008.

C2   Official in Guangdong Department of Justice, Guangzhou, June 28, 2008.

C3   High-ranking prison official, Hebei Province, January 19, 2009.

C4   Official in the mayor's office, Shahe City, Hebei Province, January 20, 2009.

C5   Entrepreneur, Dongguan, September 27, 2009.

C6   Mr. Xin, casino junket operator, Hong Kong, October 3, 2009.

C7   Entrepreneur, Dongguan, October 1, 2009.

C8   Chu Kong, professor, University of Hong Kong, September 23, 2009.

C9   Private security agents, Hong Kong, September 22, 2009.

C10 Taiwanese entrepreneur, Dongguan, September 28, 2009.

C11 Entrepreneur, Shenzhen, September 26, 2009.

C12 Entrepreneur, Guangzhou, September 30, 2009.

R1   Aurelio Galasso, prosecutor, Rome, May 17, 2007.

R2   Police officer in charge of the Yakovev investigation, Rome, May 16, 2007.

R3   Luigi De Ficchy, prosecutor, Rome, May 16, 2007.

R5   Paolo Giovagnoli, prosecutor, Bologna, September 11, 2007.

R6   Morena Plazzi, prosecutor, Bologna, September 11, 2007.

R7   Pier Paolo Mudu, migration expert, Rome, October 18, 2006.

V1   Dino Facchini, former secretary of the Communist Party of Italy, city of Verona, Verona, September 7, 2007.

V2   Guido Papalia, district attorney, Verona, September 13, 2007.

V3   Former chief inspector, Italian police, Verona, September 13, 2007.

V4   Crime reporter, *L'Arena di Verona*, Verona, April 15, 2005.

NEWSPAPERS AND PERIODICALS

Argentina

La Crítica, Italia del Popolo, El Mundo, El Municipio, La Nación, Tribuna, La voz del Albañil (1920).

China

Beijing Fazhi Ribao, China Construction Daily, China Daily, China News Weekly, Globe Biweekly, Heilongjiang Daily, Jiancha Daily, Jinan Daily, Legal Daily, Nanfang Daily, People's Daily, Procuratorial Daily, South China Morning Post, South China Weekend, Xinhua News Agency, Yangcheng Evening Paper.

Hungary
  Hetek, Heti Világgazdaság, Hungarian News Agency (MTI), Index (Budapest),
  Népszava.
Italy
  *Il Corriere della Sera, Il Nuovo Veronese, Il Sole 24 Ore, L'Arena di Verona, L'Unità,
  La Luna Nuova, La Sentinella del Canavese, La Repubblica, La Stampa, Paese
  Sera, Verona Fedele.*
Russia
  *ITAR-TASS, Komsomol'skaya Pravda, Moscow Times, Russian Business Monitor,
  St. Petersburg Times.*

United Kingdom
  Birmingham Daily Post, Pall Mall Gazette, Times.

United States
  Brooklyn Daily Eagle (1841–1902), *New York Times* (1851–2002), *North American Review* (1821–1940), *Time Magazine, Washington Post.*

OFFICIAL DOCUMENTS

AFV (Associazione Famiglie Veronesi) 1983. Problema droga. Segnalazione
  articoli—Interviste pubblicate dalla stampa sull'associazione—Proposte e
  iniziative. Verona.
ASC-CT (Annuario Statistico Cittadino—Comune di Torino). 2001. Popolazione. Turin.
CAF (Corte d'assise di Firenze). 1989. Sentenza della Corte d'Assise di Firenze
  per la strage sul "Rapido 904." February 25. Available at http://www
  .fisicamente.net/BandaMaglianaCalogliaffariestremadestra).pdf.
CD (Camera dei Deputati). 1980. Atti Parlamentari. December 18, 1980 Session.
———. 1986. Atti Parlamentari. October 8, 1986 Session.
———. 2000. Conoscere le Mafie, Costruire la legalità. Dossier di documen-
  tazione. Available at http://www.camera.it/_bicamerali/antimafia/sportello/
  dossier/frdossier.htm.
CPA (Commissione Parlamentare Anti-Mafia). 1976. Relazione conclusiva. 6th
  Legislature, doc. 23, no. 2. Rome: Camera dei Deputati.
———. 1993a. Relazione sulla Camorra approvata il 21 Dicembre 1993. 11th
  Legislature. Rome: Camera dei Deputati, 1994.
———. 1993b. Relazione sulla situazione della criminalità in Calabria. Nota Inte-
  grativa del senatore Massimo Brutti, doc. 23, no. 8. 11th Legislature (March
  9, 1993–February 18, 1994), 700–721. Rome: Camera dei Deputati, 1995.

CPA (Commissione Parlamentare Anti-Mafia). 1994. Relazione sulle risultanze dell'attività del gruppo di lavoro incaricato di svolgere accertamenti su insediamenti e infiltrazioni di soggetti ed organizzazioni di tipo mafioso in aree non tradizionali, doc. 23, no. 11. 11th Legislature (March 9, 1993–February 18, 1994). Rome: Camera dei Deputati, 1995.

———. 1997. Audizione del Direttore del Servizio Centrale Operativo della Polizia di Stato, Alessandro Pansa. 13th Legislature, Disegni di Leggi e Relazioni, Documenti. Rome, April 7.

———. 2000. Relazione sullo stato della lotta alla criminalità organizzata in Calabria. 30th Legislature, doc. 23, no. 42. Rome: Camera dei Deputati.

———. 2008. Relazione annuale della Commissione parlamentare d'inchiesta sul fenomeno della criminalità organizzata mafiosa o similare: 'Ndrangheta. Relatore On. Francesco Forgione. 15th Legislature. Rome: Camera dei Deputati. Available at http://www.casadellalegalita.org/doc/ndrangheta.pdf.

CRP (Consiglio Regionale del Piemonte). 1983. Atti del Convegno: mafia e grande criminalità. Una questione nazionale. Turin, November 25–26.

CV (Comune di Verona–Ufficio Statistiche). 2001. Annuario Statistico. Comune di Verona. Available at http://www.comune.verona.it/Internet/Statistica.nsf/.

De Gennaro, Giuseppe. 1997. Statement, U.S. Congressional Committee on International Relations (01/X). Washington, DC. Available at http://pubs.marshallcenter.org/732/lesson5/1924.html.

DIA (Direzione Investigativa Antimafia). 2002. Analisi descrittiva attività svolta e risultati conseguiti. Second semester. Vol. 2. Rome.

FBI (Federal Bureau of Investigation). 1963. *La Causa Nostra*. New York office, January 31.

FPCI (Federazione Partito Comunista). 1981. Droga e Nuova Criminalità. Libro Bianco della Federazione Veronese del Partito Comunista Italiano. Prefazione di Giovanni Berlinguer. San Giovanni Lupatoto: Bortolazzi-Stei.

IC (Immigration Commission). 1911. Reports of the Immigration Commission: Immigration and crime. 61st Cong., 3d sess., doc. no. 750.

ISTAT (Istituto Centrale di Statistica). 1951. Censimento generale della popolazione: November 4, 1951. Rome: Istituto Centrale di Statistica, 1954–58.

———. 1961. Censimento generale della popolazione: October 15, 1961. Rome: Istituto Centrale di Statistica, 1963–70.

———. 1971. Censimento generale della popolazione: October 24, 1971. Rome: Istituto Centrale di Statistica, 1973–77.

———. 1981. Censimento generale della popolazione: October 25, 1981. Rome: Istituto Centrale di Statistica, 1982–89.

MA (Melchiorre Allegra). 1937. Testimony of Melchiorre Allegra given to the police in Castelvetrano, 1937, published in *L'Ora*, January 22–25, 1962.

MHPR (Museo Histórico Provincial de Rosario). 1938a. Juzgado de Instrucción N° 2 de Rosario. Copia de Expediente no. 19653. Butera Luis y otros. Por homicidio de F. Marrone. Testimonio de Simón Samburgo. Archivo de Tribunales Provinciales de Rosario. March 3.

———. 1938b. Juzgado del Crimen. 2ª Nominación. Legajo 17, 1938. Indagación Homicidio de Cayetano Pendino, Esteban Curabà, Luis Dainotto.

———. 1939. Juzgado del Crimen 1ª Nominación. Expediente sin número. "Blas Bonsignore, Felipe Scilabra, Santiago Buè, Salvador Mongiovi, Vicente Ipolito, Leonardo Costanzo, Juan Logiacomo, Diego Ulino, Luis Montana y Carlos Cacciato, por homicidio y asociación ilícita," Archivo de Tribunales Provinciales de Rosario.

MI (Ministro dell'Interno). 1995. Relazione al Presidente della Repubblica. April 27.

OSPA Stajano. 1992. Mafia: L'atto d'accusa dei giudici di Palermo compiled by Corrado Stajano (contains sections from Ordinanza per la Corte d'assise di Palermo contro Abbate Giovanni + 706, Palermo 1985, vol 40), Rome: Editori Riuniti.

PR (Policía del Rosario). 1899. Memoria. Archivo de Tribunales Provinciales de Rosario.

PR (Presidente della Repubblica) 1995. Decreto di Scioglimento del Consiglio Comunale di Bardonecchia (Turin). May 2.

PRB (Procura di Bologna). 2007. Richiesta di Archiviazione per Rizner Boris ed altri. N. 54431/99 ruolo generale notizie di reato. July 7.

PRC (Procura di Reggio Calabria). 1998. Richiesta di rinvio a giudizio a carico di Matacena Amedeo Gennaro, no. 42/97 ruolo generale notizie di reato. April 21.

PSB (Polizia di Stato, Commissariato di Bardonecchia). 1995. Relazione sulla situazione venutasi a creare a Bardonecchia. June 27.

PT (Prefettura di Torino). 1995. Relazione riepilogativa degli accertamenti espletati durante l'accesso eseguito preso il Comune di Bardonecchia. March 8.

RCC (Regione Carabinieri Campania). 2000. Informativa m. 471/53. Associazione per delinquere di stampo mafioso, omicidi, estorsioni ed altro. Naples.

SCBC (Supreme Court of British Columbia). 2003a. HMQ against See Chun Lee and Chuk Fong Tao. Vancouver, July 3.

———. 2003b. HMQ against See Chun Lee and Chuk Fong Tao. Vancouver, July 24.

SCO (Servizio Centrale Operativo). 1997a. Rapporto operativo [Yakovlev] et alii. Vol. 1. Rome: Polizia di Stato.

———. 1997b. Rapporto operativo [Yakovlev] et alii. Vol. 2. Rome: Polizia di Stato.

———. 1997c. Rapporto operativo [Yakovlev] et alii. Vol. 3. Rome: Polizia di Stato.

TT (Tribunale di Torino). 1990. Procedimento n. 5/89 mis. prev. nei confronti di Iaria G.—De Stefano L.F.—Lombardo G. Procura della Repubblica.

———. 1996. Decreto nella procedura a carico di Rocco Lo Presti e Paolo Spallita. Turin: Sezione Misure di Prevenzione.

———. 1997. Decreto nei confronti di Rocco Arcuri. Turin: Sezione Misure di Prevenzione.

———. 2002. Sentenza nei confronti di Lo Presti Rocco e Arcuri Rocco. October 15.

TV (Tribunale di Verona). 1987. Procedimento penale contro Andreoli Armando + 83. Verona.

US (U.S. Senate Permanent Subcommittee on Investigations of the Committee on Governmental Affairs). 1988. Testimony of Joseph D. Pistone, former special agent, Federal Bureau of Investigation. Text available at http://www.americanMafia.com/Pistone_Testimony.html.

USDJ (U.S. Department of Justice). 2002. Burma: Country brief. *Drug Intelligence Brief* (May).

———. 2005. Press release: Eight leaders of southeast Asia's largest narcotics trafficking organization indicted by a federal grand jury in Brooklyn, New York, U.S. Attorney's Office, Eastern District of New York, January 24.

USDS (U.S. Department of State). 1998. International narcotics control strategy report, March 1998. Washington, DC: U.S. Department of State.

Wickersham Commission. 1931. Enforcement of the Prohibition laws: Official records of the National Commission on Law Observance and Enforcement pertaining to its investigation of the facts as to the enforcement, the benefits, and the abuses under the Prohibition laws, both before and since the adoption of the Eighteenth Amendment to the Constitution. Washington, DC: U.S. Government. Printing Office.

SECONDARY SOURCES

Aguirre, Osvaldo. 2000. *Historias de la mafia en la Argentina*. Buenos Aires: Aguilar.

———. 2004. Secuestros extorsivos en la Argentina. *Todo es Historia* (September): 6–20.

————. 2006. *La Chicago Argentina: Crímenes, mafia y prostitución en Rosario*. Rosario: Fundación Ross.

Alberti Russell, Janice. 1977. *The Italian community in Tunisia, 1861–1961: A viable minority*. New York: Columbia University Press.

Albrow, Martin. 1996. *The global age: State and society beyond modernity*. Cambridge: Polity.

Allum, Felia. 2001. Becoming a *Camorrista*: Criminal culture and life choices in Naples. *Journal of Modern Italian Studies* 6 (3): 324–47.

————. 2006. *Camorristi, politicians, and businessmen: The transformation of organized crime in post-war Naples*. Leeds: Maney Publishing.

Alongi, Giuseppe. [1886] 1977. *La Maffia*. Palermo: Sellerio.

Alvarez, Juan. 1943. *Historia de Rosario (1689–1939)*. Buenos Aires: Imprenta López.

American Jewish Year Book. 1991. *Review of the Year*. New York: American Jewish Committee.

Anastasia, Bruno, and Giuseppe Tattara. 2003. Come mai il Veneto è diventato così ricco? Tempi, forme e ragioni dello sviluppo di una regione di successo. Università Ca' Foscari, Venice.

Anbinder, Tyler. 2001. *Five points*. New York: Free Press.

Anderson, Jon Lee. 1997. *Che Guevara: A revolutionary life*. New York: Grove Press.

Arana, Ana. 2005. How the street gangs took Central America. *Foreign Affairs* 84 (3): 98–110.

Arlacchi, Pino. 1983. *Mafia, peasants, and great estates: Society in traditional Calabria*. Cambridge: Cambridge University Press.

————. 1993. *Men of dishonor. Inside the Sicilian mafia: An account of Antonino Calderone*. New York: William Morrow and Co.

————. 1996. *Addio Cosa Nostra. I segreti della mafia nella confessione di Tommaso Buscetta*. Milan: Rizzoli.

Arlacchi, Pino, and Roger Lewis. 1990. *Imprenditorialità illecita e droga: Il mercato dell'eroina a Verona*. Bologna: Il Mulino.

Asbury, Herbert. [1928] 1998. *The gangs of New York: An informal history of the underworld*. New York: Thunder's Mouth Press.

————. 1950. *The great illusion: An informal history of Prohibition*. Garden City, NY: Doubleday, Doran and Company, Inc.

Baily, Samuel L. 1983. The adjustment of Italian immigrants in Buenos Aires and New York, 1870–1914. *American Historical Review* 88 (2): 281–305.

————. 1999. *Immigrants in the lands of promise: Italians in Buenos Aires and New York City, 1870–1914*. Ithaca, NY: Cornell University Press.

Baker, Bruce. 2004. Protection from crime: What is on offer for Africans? *Journal of Contemporary African Studies* 22 (2): 165–88.

Bandiera, Oriana. 2003. Private states and the enforcement of property rights: Theory and evidence on the origins of the Sicilian mafia. *Journal of Law, Economics, and Organization* 19 (1): 218–44.

Barak, Gregg. 2001. Crime and crime control in an age of globalization: A theoretical dissection. *Critical Criminology* 10:57–72.

Bauman, Zygmunt. 1998. *Globalization: The human consequences.* Cambridge, UK: Polity.

Beck, Ulrich. 1999. *What is globalization?* Cambridge, UK: Polity.

Becucci, Stefano. 2006. *Criminalità multietnica. I mercati illegali in Italia.* Bari-Rome: Laterza.

Behr, Edward. 1997. *Prohibition: The 13 years that changed America.* London: Penguin Books.

Bell, Daniel. [1953] 1988. Crime as an American way of life: A queer ladder of social mobility. In *The end of ideology: On the exhaustion of political ideas in the fifties,* 127–50. Cambridge, MA: Harvard University Press.

Beyrer, Chris, Myat Htoo Razak, Khomdon Lisam, Jie Chen, Wei Lui, and Xiao-Fang Yu. 2000. Overland heroin trafficking routes and HIV-1 spread in south and south-east Asia. *AIDS* 14 (1): 75–83.

Birindelli, Anna Maria. 2004. Migrazioni. In *Il Veneto,* ed. Gianpiero Dalla Zuanna, Alessandro Rosina, and Fiorenzo Rossi, 227–48. Venice: Marsilio.

Blanco Pazos, Roberto, and Raúl Clemente. 2004. *De La Fuga a La Fuga. El policial en el cine argentine.* Buenos Aires: Corregidor.

Block, Alan A. 1983. *East Side, West Side: Organizing crime in New York, 1930–1950.* London: Transaction Publishers.

Boardman, Paul. 2005. China's building boom. Paper presented at the Sustainable Forestry Initiative Annual Conference, Washington, DC. Available at http://www.forestprod.org/internationaltrade06boardman.pdf.

Bonaguidi, Alberto, ed. 1985. *Migrazioni e demografia regionale in Italia.* Milan: Franco Angeli.

Bonanno, Joseph, with Sergio Lalli. 1983. *A man of honour: The autobiography of Joseph Bonanno.* New York: Simon and Schuster.

Bonura, Francesco. 1929. *Gli Italiani in Tunisia ed il problema della naturalizzazione.* Rome: Luce Edizioni.

Bosworth, Barry, and Susan M. Collins. 2008. Accounting for growth: Comparing China and India. *Journal of Economic Perspectives* 22 (1): 45–66.

Bovenkerk, Frank. 2001. Organized crime and ethnic minorities: Is there a link? In *Combating transnational crime: Concepts, activities, and responses,* ed. Phil Williams and Dimitri Vlassis, 109–26. London: Frank Cass.

Brown, Philip. 1993. *Central authority and local autonomy in the formation of early modern Japan: The case of Kaga domain.* Stanford, CA: Stanford University Press.

Bruck, Connie. 2008. The brass ring. *New Yorker*, June 30, 42–57.

Brugoli, Giuseppe. 1985. Una trasformazione tumultuosa con industriali da "nuova frontiera." In *Associazione degli industriali della Provincia di Verona. 1945–1985: Quaranta anni di presenza attiva nel tessuto socio-economico di Verona*, 9–21. Verona: Associazione degli industriali.

Cacopardo, Maria Cristina, and José L. Moreno. 1985. Características regionales, demográficas y ocupcionales d ela inmigraticón italiana a la Argentina (1880–1930). In *La inmigración italiana en la Argentina*, ed. Fernando Devoto and Gianfausto Rosoli, 63–86. Buenos Aires: Biblos.

Caimari, Lila. 2007. "Suceso de cinematográficos aspectos." Secuestro y espectáculo en el Buenos Aires de los años treinta. Available at http://www.unsam.edu.ar/escuelas/politica/centro_historia_politica/material/ayerza.pdf.

Campana, Paolo. 2010. La Camorra: Struttura e Mercati. Tesi di Dottorato, Università di Torino.

Callucci, Davide, and Giuseppe Caruso. 2009. *A Milano comanda l' `Ndrangheta*. Milan: Salani Editore.

Carrasco, Gabriel. 1886. *Descripción geográfica y estadística de la provincia de Santa Fé*. 4th ed. Buenos Aires: Stiller and Laass.

Carse, Robert. 1961. *Rum row*. London: Jarrolds Publishers.

Caselli, Stefano. 2003a. Bardonecchia, l'unico Comune sciolto per mafia al Nord. *Omicron* 39 (March): 2–4.

———. 2003b. Il senso di Rocco per la neve. Il crimine in Val di Susa. *Narco-mafie* (June) 4: 21–24.

Castells, Manuel. 2000. *End of millennium*. 2nd ed. Oxford: Blackwell Publishers.

Castleman, Deke. 2009. *Whale hunt in the desert: Secrets of a Vegas superhost*. 2nd ed. Las Vegas: Huntington Press.

Cerillo, Augustus. 2000. Gaynor, William Jay. In *American national biography*. New York: Oxford University Press. Available at http://www.anb.org/articles/05/05-00913.html.

Chan, John. 2002. *Workers' protests continue in northeast China*. World Socialist Web Site, May 25. Available at http://www.wsws.org/articles/2002/may2002/chin-m25_prn.shtml.

Chandler, David Leon. 1976. *Criminal brotherhoods*. London: Constable.

Chang, Leslie T. 2008. *Factory girls: From village to city in a changing China*. New York: Spiegel and Grau.

Chao-Tzang, Yawnghwe. 1993. The political economy of the opium trade: Implications for the Shan state. *Journal of Contemporary Asia* 23 (3): 306–26.

Chin, Ko-lin. 1990. *Chinese subculture and criminality: Non-traditional crime groups in America*. New York: Greenwood Press.

———. 2003. *Heijin: Organized crime, business, and politics in Taiwan*. Armonk, NY: M. E. Sharpe.

———. 2009. *The golden triangle: Inside southeast Asia's drug trade*. Ithaca, NY: Cornell University Press.

Chin, Ko-lin, and Roy Godson. 2006. Organized crime and the political-criminal nexus in China. *Trends in Organized Crime* 9 (3): 5–44.

Chong, Gang, and Yu Pu, eds. 1997. *Reports on campaigns against the criminal underworld in contemporary China* [in Chinese]. Beijing: Qunzhong Press.

Chu, Yiu Kong. 2000. *The triads as business*. London: Routledge.

———. 2002. Global triads: Myth or reality? In *Transnational organized crime and international security: Business as usual?* ed. Mats Berdal and Monica Serrano, 183–93. Boulder, CO: Lynne Rienner Publishers.

Ciccarello, Elena. 2009. La carica dei colonnelli. L'ascesa dei nuovi boss a Torino. *Narcomafie*, May, 4–8.

Ciconte, Enzo. 1992. `Ndrangheta dall'Unità a oggi. Bari: Laterza.

———. 1996. *Processo alla `Ndrangheta*. Bari: Laterza.

———. 1998. *Mafia, Camorra e `Ndrangheta in Emilia Romagna*. Rimini: Panozzo Editore.

Cohen, Rich. 1998. *Tough Jews: Fathers, sons, and gangsters*. New York: Simon and Schuster.

Cohen, Stanley. 2006. *The execution of officer Becker: The murder of a gambler, the trail of a cop, and the birth of organized crime*. New York: Carroll and Graf Publishers.

Coleman, James. 1990. *Foundations of social theory*. Cambridge, MA: Harvard University Press.

Collier, Paul. 2008. *The bottom billion: Why the poorest countries are failing and what can be done about it*. Oxford: Oxford University Press.

Cressey, Donald. 1969. *Theft of the nation: The structure and operations of organized crime in America*. New York: Harper and Row.

Critchley, David. 2006. Buster, Maranzano, and the Castellammare War, 1930–1931. *Global Crime* 7 (1): 43–78.

———. 2009. *The origins of organized crime in America: The New York City mafia, 1891–1931*. London: Routledge.

Cruz, José Miguel. 2010. Central American *maras*: From youth street gangs to transnational protection rackets. *Global Crime* 11(4): 379–398.

Csáki, György, and Gábor Karsai. 2001. Evolution of the Hungarian economy, 1848–2000. Vol. 3, *Hungary from transition to integration*. New York: Columbia University Press.

Czitrom, Daniel. 1991. Underworlds and underdogs: Big Tim Sullivan and metropolitan politics in New York, 1889–1913. *Journal of American History* 78 (2): 536–58.

Dash, Mike. 2007. *Satan's circus: Murder, vice, police corruption, and New York's trial of the century*. London: Granta.

———. 2009. *The first family: Terror, extortion, and the birth of the American mafia*. London: Simon and Schuster.

Davis, John H. 1993. *Mafia dynasty: The rise and fall of the Gambino crime family*. New York: Harpertorch.

De Amicis, Edmondo. ([1886]2001). *Cuore. Libro per ragazzi*. Edited by Luciano Tamburini. Turin: Einaudi.

Densley, James. 2009. The signalling mechanisms in gang members recruitment. Paper presented at the Workshop on Recruitment into Extra-Legal Organisations, Department of Sociology and Nuffield College, University of Oxford, December 14.

Deshingkar, Priya. 2006. Internal migration, poverty, and development in Asia. *Asia 2015: Promoting Growth, Ending Poverty* (London), March 6–7. Available at http://www.eldis.org/vfile/upload/1/document/0708/DOC21176.pdf.

Desjardins, Chris. 2005. *Outlaw masters of Japanese film*. London. I. B. Tauris.

Drehle, David von. 2003. *Triangle: The fire that changed America*. New York: Atlantic Monthly Press.

Dickie, John. 2007. *Cosa Nostra: A history of the Sicilian mafia*. London: Hodder.

Dimitrov, Martin K. 2009. *Piracy and the state: The politics of intellectual property rights in China*. Cambridge: Cambridge University Press.

Ding, Xueliang. 2001. The quasi-criminalization of a business sector in China: Deconstructing the construction-sector syndrome. *Crime, Law, and Social Change* 35:177–201.

Dixit, Avinash K. 2004. *Lawlessness and economics: Alternative modes of governance*. Princeton, NJ: Princeton University Press.

Doria, Paolo Mattia. [1709–10] 1973. *Massime del governo spagnolo a Napoli*. Edited by Vittorio Conti. Naples: Guida.

Druijven, Peter C. J. 1993. Trends of urbanization in the Pearl River delta. In *Urban problems and urban development in China*, ed. Wolfgang Taubmann, 143–66. Hamburg: Institut für Asienkunde.

Dunn, Guy. 1997. Major Mafia Gangs in Russia, in *Russian organized crime: the new threat?* Ed. Phil Williams, 63–87. London: Frank Cass.

Dunning, John H. 1993. *Multinational enterprises and the global economy*. Reading, MA: Addison-Wesley.

———. 1998. Location and the multinational enterprise: A neglected factor. *Journal of International Business Studies* 29 (1): 45–66.

Dunning, John H. Regions, globalization, and the knowledge economy: The issues stated. In *Regions, globalization, and the knowledge-based economy*, ed. John H. Dunning, 7–41. Oxford: Oxford University Press.

Eckerson, Helen F. 1966. Immigration and national origins. *Annals of the American Academy of Political and Social Science* 367:4–14.

Facchini, Dino. 1982. Colpire lo spaccio e la grande criminalità, assicurare la convivenza civile e democratica. In *Droga: Nuovo volto del potere. Atti del convegno regionale del PCI. Verona 5–6 Marzo 1982*, ed. Carla Pellegatta and Chiara Benetti, 11–20. Venice: Arsenale Cooperativa Editrice.

Falcone, Giovanni, with Michelle Padovani. 1993. *Cose di Cosa Nostra*. 2nd ed. Milan: Rizzoli.

Farrell, Henry. 2009. *The political economy of trust: Institutions, interests, and inter-firm cooperation in Italy and Germany*. Cambridge: Cambridge University Press.

Farrell, Joseph, ed. 1997. *Understating the mafia*. Manchester: Manchester University Press.

Feng, Shuliang. 2001. Crime and crime control in a changing China. In *Crime and social control in a changing China*, ed. Jianhong Liu, Lening Zhang, and Steven F. Messner, 123–32. London: Greenwood Press.

Finckenauer, James O., and Ko-lin Chin. 2006. Asian transnational organized crime and its impact on the United States: Developing a transnational crime agenda. New York: U.S. National Institute of Justice.

Finckenauer, James O., and Elin J. Waring. 1998. *Russian mafia in America: Immigration, culture, and crime*. Boston: Northeastern University Press.

Fitzgerald, Francis Scott. [1925] 1998. *The Great Gatsby*. Edited by Ruth Prigozy. Oxford: Oxford University Press.

Flynn, William James. 1919. *The barrel mystery*. New York: J. A. McCann Publication.

Fogliata, Rosanna, Sergio Carrarini, and Pietro Mazzoccoli. 1987. Tossicodipendenza e servizio pubblico nell'ULSS 27: indagine conoscitiva-descrittiva. Bovolone-Verona: Regione Veneto, ULSS 27.

Forgione, Francesco. 2009. *Mafia export: Come 'Ndrangheta, Cosa Nostra e Camorra hanno colonizzato il mondo*. Milan: Baldini Castoldi Dalai.

Franchetti, Leopoldo. [1876] 1993. *Condizioni politiche e amministrative della Sicilia*. Rome: Donzelli.

Frid, Carina. 1993. Los inmigrantes y la adquisición de la ciudadanía en argentina (1890–1912). Paper presented at the Fazer a America conference, São Paulo.

Frid de Silberstein, Carina. 1991. Inmigración y selección matrimonial. El caso de los italianos en Rosario (1870–1910). *Estudios Migratorios Latinoamericanos* 18:161–91.

————. 1992. Italianos en Rosario. Un perfil demográfico y ocupacional (1870–1914). *Estudios Interdisciplinarios de America Latina y el Caribe* 3 (1). Available at http://www.tau.ac.il/eial/III_1/silberstein.htm.

————. 1993. Parenti, negozianti e dirigenti: la prima dirigenza italiana di Rosario (1860–1890). In *Identità degli Italiani in Argentina. Reti sociali, famiglia, lavoro*, ed. Gianfausto Rosoli, 129–65. Rome: Studium.

————. 1994. Más allá del crisol: matrimonios, estrategias familiares y redes sociales en dos generaciones de italianos y españoles (Rosario, 1895–1925). *Estudios Migratorios Latinoamericanos* 9 (28): 481–520.

Friedman, Robert I. 2000. *Red mafia: How the Russian mob has invaded America*. Boston: Little, Brown.

Frye, Timothy. 2002. Private protection in Russia and Poland. *American Journal of Political Science* 46(3):572 84.

Gabaccia, Donna R. 1984. *From Sicily to Elizabeth Street: Housing and social change among Italian immigrants, 1880–1930*. Albany: State University of New York Press.

Gaburro, Giuseppe. 1985. Struttura e dinamica dell'industria nello sviluppo dell'economia veronese. In *Associazione degli industriali della Provincia di Verona. 1945–1985: quaranta anni di presenza attiva nel tessuto socio-economico di Verona*, 73–86. Verona: Associazione degli industriali.

Galeotti, Mark. 2000. The Russian mafia: Economic penetration at home and abroad. In *Economic crime in Russia*, ed. Alena V. Ledeneva and Marina Kurkchiyan, 31–42. The Hague: Kluwer Law International.

Gallo, Ezequiel. 1970. Agricultural colonization and society in Argentina: The province of Santa Fe, 1870–1895. PhD diss., University of Oxford.

————. 1976. *Farmers in revolt. The revolutions of 1893 in the province of Santa Fe, Argentina*. London: Athlone Press of the University of London.

————. 1983. *La pampa gringa*. Buenos Aires: Editoral Sudamericana.

Gambetta, Diego. 1988. Mafia: The price of distrust. In *Trust: Making and breaking cooperative relations*, ed. Diego Gambetta, 158–75. Oxford: Blackwell.

————. 1993. *The Sicilian mafia: The business of private protection*. Cambridge, MA: Harvard University Press.

————. 2009. *Codes of the underworld*. Princeton, NJ: Princeton University Press.

Gambetta, Diego, and Peter Reuter. 1995. Conspiracy among the many: The mafia in legitimate industries. In *The economics of organised crime*, ed. Gianluca Fiorentini and Sam Peltzman, 116–36. Cambridge: Cambridge University Press.

Gandolfo, Romolo. 1991. Inmigrantes y política en Argentina: La revolución de 1890 y la campaña en favor de la naturalización automática de residentes extranjeros. *Estudios Migratorios Latinoamericanos* 6 (17): 23–55.

Gentile, Nick. [1963] 1993. *Vita di Capomafia*. Memorie raccolte da Felice Chilenti. Prefazione di Letizia Paoli. Rome: Crescenzi Allendorf.

Gill, Vincent E., Marco Wang, Allen F. Anderson, and Guao Matthew Lin. 1994. Plum blossoms and pheasants: Prostitutes, prostitution, and social control measures in contemporary China. *International Journal of Offender Therapy and Comparative Criminology* 38 (4): 319–37.

Glenny, Misha. 1996. *The fall of Yugoslavia*. 3rd rev. ed. London: Penguin.

———. 2008. *McMafia: Crime without frontiers*. London: Bodley Head.

Glonti, Georgi, and Givi Lobjanidze. 2004. *Vory-v-Zakone: Professionalnaya prestupnost v Gruzii*. Tbilisi: Transnational Crime and Corruption Center.

Godinho, Jorge A. F. 2006. Credit for gaming in Macau. *Gaming Law Review* 10 (4): 363–68.

Goldin, Claudia. 1994. The political economy of immigration restrictions in the United States, 1890 to 1921. In *The regulated economy: A historical approach to political economy*, ed. Claudia Goldin and Gary D. Libecap, 223–57. Chicago: University of Chicago Press.

Goldman, Merle. 2006. The post-Mao reform era. In *China: A new history*, by John King Fairbank, 406–56. 2nd ed. Cambridge, MA: Harvard University Press.

Goris, Esther. 1999. *Agatha Galiffi. La flor de la mafia*. Buenos Aires: Sudamericana.

Gower Chapman, Charlotte 1971. *Milocca, a Sicilian village*. London: George Allen and Unwin Ltd.

Grant, Aleksandr. 1996. *Protsess Yaponchika*. Moscow: AST.

Gratteri, Nicola, and Antonio Nicaso. 2006. *Fratelli di sangue*. 11th ed. Cosenza: Pellegrini Editore.

Gullotti, Enrico. 2003. Lo scioglimento dei consigli comunali per infiltrazioni e condizionamenti di tipo mafioso. *Nuova rassegna di legislazione, dottrina e giurisprudenza* 16:1849–53.

Guy, Donna J. 1991. *Sex and danger in Buenos Aires: Prostitution, family, and nation in Argentina*. Lincoln: University of Nebraska Press.

Hasbrouck, Alfred. 1935. The conquest of the desert. *Hispanic American Historical Review* 15 (2): 195–228.

He, Bingsong. 2002. *Studies on mafias and mafia-related crimes in mainland China* [in Chinese]. Beijing: China Fazhi Press.

———, ed. 2003. *Deciphering mafia related crimes* [in Chinese]. Beijing: China Procuratorial Press.

Hess, Henner. [1973] 1998. *Mafia and mafiosi: Origin, power, and myth*. 2nd ed. Trans. Ewald Osers. London: C. Hurst and Co. Publishers Ltd.

Hershatter, Gail. 1997. *Dangerous pleasures: Prostitution and modernity in twenti-eth-century Shanghai*. Berkeley: University of California Press.

Hill, Peter B. E. 2002. Tokyo: la rete della yakuza. *Lettera Internazionale* 71:53–55.

———. 2003. *The Japanese mafia: Yakuza, law, and the state*. Oxford: Oxford University Press.

———. 2004. The changing face of the Yakuza. *Global Crime* 6 (1): 97–116.

———. 2005. Kabuki-chō gangsters: Ethnic succession in Japanese organized crime? Mimeo.

Hsing, You-tien. 1998. *Making capitalism in China: The Taiwan connection*. New York: Oxford University Press.

Information Office of the State Council. 2005. China: Arms control and disarmament. Available at http://news.xinhuanet.com/employment/2002-11/18/content_633187.htm.

Jacobs, James B., Coleen Friel, and Robert Raddick. 1999. *Gotham unbound: How New York City was liberated from the grip of organized crime*. New York: New York University Press.

Jeffreys, Elaine. 2004. *China, sex, and prostitution*. London: Routledge.

Jian, Xinhua, and Jianwei Zhang. 2005. From "the wave of migrants" to "the shortage of migrants": The institutional analysis of the effective transfer of rural surplus labor [in Chinese]. *Renkou Yanjiu* [*Population Research*] 29 (?): 49–55.

Jiang, Lihua, and Ping Fu. 2006. The role of law and government in protecting the rights of migrant workers [in Chinese]. Available at http://www.sachina.edu.cn/Htmldata/article/2006/04/958.html.

Jiang, Qing-Yun. 2004. Court delay in developing countries with special references to China. *German Working Papers in Law and Economics* 2004, article 36. Available at http://www.bepress.com/gwp/default/vol2004/iss1/art36.

———. 2006. *Court delay and law enforcement in China: Civil process and economic perspective*. Wiesbaden: Deutscher Universitäts-Verlag.

Johns, Michael. 1991. The urbanization of a secondary city: The case of Rosario, Argentina, 1870–1920. *Journal of Latin American Studies* 23 (3): 489–513

———. 1994. The making of an urban elite: The case of Rosario, 1880–1920. *Journal of Urban History* 20 (2): 155–78.

Kalyvas, Stathis N. 2006. *The logic of violence in civil war*. New York: Cambridge University Press.

Kang, Shuhua, and Xinwen Wei. 2001. *Organized crime from an analytical perspective* [in Chinese]. Beijing: Peking University Press.

Kang, Shuhua, ed. 1998. *Organized crime, prevention, and countermeasures* [in Chinese]. Beijing: Fangzheng Press.

Karush, Matthew B. 1999. Workers, citizens and the Argentine nation: Party politics and the working class in Rosario, 1912–3. *Journal of Latin American Studies* 31 (3): 589–616.

Karyshev, Valery. 2001. *Solntsevskaya Bratva. Istoriya Gruppirovski.* Moscow: Izdatel'stvo Eksmo.

Kefavuer, Estes. 1951. *Crime in America.* Garden City, NY: Doubleday.

Kerr, K. Austin. 1985. *Organized for Prohibition: A new history of the Anti-Saloon League.* New Haven, CT: Yale University Press.

King, Gary, Robert Keohane, and Sidney Verba. 1994. *Designing social inquiry.* Princeton, NJ: Princeton University Press.

Klein, Herbert S. 1983. The integration of Italian immigrants into the United States and Argentina: A comparative analysis. *American Historical Review* 88 (2): 306–29.

Kochan, Nick. 2005. *The washing machine: Money, crime, and terrorism in the offshore system.* London: Duckworth.

Kong, Pingping. 2004. History of the underworld in Hong Kong and Macao, and present situation of its infiltration to the mainland [in Chinese]. *Fujian Public Security College Journal* 16 (2): 30–35.

Kornai, János. 1990. *The road to a free economy. Shifting from a socialist system: Hungary's example.* New York: W. W. Norton.

———. 1996. Paying the bill for goulach communism: Hungarian development and macro stabilization in a political economy perspective. *Social Research* 63:943–1040.

Kukhianidze, Alexandre. 2009. Corruption and organized crime in Georgia before and after the "Rose Revolution." *Central Asian Survey* 28 (2): 215–34.

Kupchinsky, Roman. 2009. Gazprom's murky games in Hungary. *Jamestown Foundation-Eurasia Daily Monitor* 6 (86). Available at http://www.jamestown.org/.

Kwist, Dana F. 1991. The Soviet withdrawal from Eastern Europe: A move in crisis. Carlisle Barracks, PA: U.S. Army War College.

Lackó, Mária. 1997. *The hidden economies of Visegrád countries in international comparison: A household electricity approach.* Budapest: Institute of Economics, Hungarian Academy of Sciences.

Lanciotti, Norma S. 2004. Las transformaciones de la demanda inmobiliaria urbana y el acceso a la propiedad familiar, Rosario 1885–1914. *Revista CICLOS en la Historia, la Economía y la Sociedad* 28:208–36.

———. 2009. *De rentistas a empresarios. Inversión immobiliaria y urbanización en la pampa argentina. Rosario, 1880–1914.* Santa Fe: Universidad nacional del Litoral.

Landesco, John. [1929] 1968. *Organized crime in Chicago.* Intro. Mark Haller. Chicago: University of Chicago Press.

———. 1932. Prohibition and crime. Special issue, *Annals of the American Academy of Political and Social Science* 163 (September): 120–29.

Lane, Frederic C. 1958. Economic consequences of organized violence. *Journal of Economic History* 18:401–17.

Lankevich, George J. 2002. *New York City: A short history.* New York: New York University Press.

Lardner, James, and Thomas Reppetto. 2000. *NYPD: A city and its police.* New York: Henry Holt and Company.

Laudi, Maurizio. 2003. Prepariamoci per i Giochi del 2006. *Omicron* 39 (March): 5.

Lee, Ching Kwan. 2007. *Against the law: Labour protests in China's rustbelt and sunbelt.* Berkeley: University of California Press.

Leong, Angela Veng Mei. 2002. The "Bata-Ficha" business and triads in Macau casinos. *Queensland University of Technology Law and Justice Journal* 2 (1): 83–97.

Lerner, Michael L. 2007. *Dry Manhattan: Prohibition in New York City.* Cambridge, MA: Harvard University Press.

Li, Rongshi. 1996. Some considerations on the floating population in contemporary China [in Chinese]. *Population Studies* 20 (1): 12–17.

Li, Wenyan, and Liangdong Ke, eds. 2006. *Prevention of mafia-type crimes and countermeasures* [in Chinese]. Beijing: China People's Public Security University Press.

Lintner, Bertil. 2004. Chinese organised crime. *Global Crime* 6 (1): 84–96.

Liu, Jianqiang. 2004. Real experience with Emperor Hotel [in Chinese]. *Southern China Weekend,* December 23. Available at http://www.jinchuanmei .com/Article_Show2.asp?ArticleID=236.

Liu, Qian. 2004. The blue paper of Shenzhen cancels the temporary residential certificate. *Nanfang Daily.* Available at http://www.southcn.com/news/ dishi/shenzhen/shizheng/200405110199.htm.

Liu, Wei, Donghui Zhao, and Jie Su. 2005. Attention should be paid to the foreign mafia activities in the mainland [in Chinese]. *Globe,* December 29. Available at http://news.xinhuanet.com/globe/2005-12/28/content _3982290.htm.

Lo, Hingshiu. 2005. Casino politics, organized crime, and the post-colonial state in Macau. *Journal of Contemporary China* 14 (43): 17–34.

Loader, Ian, and Neal Walker. 2007. *Civilizing security.* Cambridge: Cambridge University Press.

Lombardo, Robert M. 2004. The Black Hand: A study in moral panic. *Global Crime* 6 (3): 267–84.

Lupo, Salvatore. 1988. "Il tenebroso sodalizio": Un rapporto sulla mafia palermitana di fine Ottocento. *Studi Storici* 29 (2): 463–89.

———. 1996. *Storia della mafia dalle origini ai giorni nostri.* 2nd ed. Rome: Donzelli.

———. 2008. *Quando la mafia trovò l'America. Storia di un intreccio intercontinentale, 1888–2008.* Turin: Einaudi.

Lupsha, Peter. 1986. Organized *crime in the United States.* In *Organized crime: A global perspective,* ed. Robert Kelly, 32–57. Totowa, NJ: Rowman and Littlefield.

Maas, Peter. [1968] 2003. *The Valachi papers.* New York: Perennial.

———. 1997. *Underboss: Sammy the Bull Gravano's story of life in the mafia.* New York: HarperPaperbacks.

Mahoney, James, and Gary Goertz. 2004. The possibility principle: Choosing negative cases in qualitative research. *American Political Science Review* 98 (4): 653–69.

Maksimov, Aleksandr. 1997. *Rossiyskaya Prestupnost'. Kto est' Kto?* Moscow: Izdatel'stvo Eksmo.

Malamud, Carlos. 1997. *Partidos políticos y elecciones en la Argentina: la Liga del Sur (1908–1916).* Madrid: Universidad Nacional de Educacion a la. Distancia.

Mallee, Hein. 1995. China's household registration system under reform. *Development and Change* 26 (1): 1–29.

Mangano, Antonello. 2010. *Gli africani salveranno l'Italia.* Milan: Rizzoli.

Maresco, Manuela, and Luana Serpone. 2005. Democrazia sospesa, per mafia. *Narcomafie* 6:7–9.

Martino, Paolo. 1988. Per la storia della 'ndràngheta. Rome: Dipartimento di studi glotto-antropologici dell'Università di Roma. Available at http://www.lumsa.it/LUMSA/Portals/docenti/Martino/%20Per%20la%20storia.pdf.

Massari, Monica. 1998. *La sacra corona unita. Potere e segreto.* Bari: Laterza.

———. 2001. La criminalità mafiosa nell'Italia centro-settentrinale. In *Mafie nostre, mafie loro,* ed. Stefano Becucci and Monica Massari, 3–38. Turin: Comunità.

Mawby, Robert, and Alan Wright. 2001. Police corruption in transitional states: The case of Hungary—"the best police money can buy"? Manuscript.

Merz, Charles. 1932. *The dry decade.* Garden City, NY: Doubleday, Doran and Company, Inc.

Mete, Vittorio. 2007. La quiete dopo la tempesta. Politica e società civile in un Comune sciolto per mafia. *Meridiana* 57:13–43.

Miguel, Edward. 2004. Tribe or nation? Nation building and public goods in Kenya versus Tanzania. *World Politics* 56 (3): 327–62.

Milhaupt, Curtis J., and Mark D. West. 2000. The dark side of private ordering: An institutional and empirical analysis of organized crime. *University of Chicago Law Review* 67 (1): 41–98.

Milson, Jeremy. 2005. The long hard road out of drugs: The case of Wa. In *Trouble in the triangle: Opium and conflict in Burma,* ed. Martin Jelsma, Tom Kramer, and Pietje Vervest, 74–100. Chiang Mai: Silkworm Books.

Mink Andras. 1997. Crime and corruption after communism: An interview on crime with Geza Katona, former chief of the Investigation Department of the National Police and currently a researcher at the Police Research Institute in Budapest. *East European Constitutional Review* 6 (4): 78–79. Available at http://www1.law.nyu.edu/eecr/vol6num4/feature/interviewoncrime.html.

Minuti, Diego, and Antonio Nicaso. 1994. *'Ndraghete. Le filiali della mafia calabrese.* Vibo Valentia: Monteleone.

Modestov, Nikolay. 1996. *Moskva Bandistskaya.* Moscow: Tsentrloligrag.

Molino, Nico. 1996. *La ferrovia del Frejus.* Sant'Ambrogio: Susa Libri.

Montalto, Saverio. [1940] 1973. *La Famiglia Montalbano.* Chiaravalle Centrale (Cosenza): Frama's

Moray, Alastair. 1929. *The diary of a rum-runner.* London: Philip Allan and Co. Ltd.

Morgan, W. P. 1960. *Triads societies in Hong Kong.* Hong Kong: Government Press

Mori, Cesare. 1933. *The last struggle with the mafia.* Trans. Orlo Williams. London: Putnam.

Mormino, Gary S., and Georges Pozzetta. 1998. *The immigrant world of Ybor City: Italians and their Latin neighbors in Tampa, 1885–1985.* Tampa: University Press of Florida.

Mynz, Rainer. 1995. Where did they all come from? Typology and geography of European mass migration in the twentieth century. Paper presented at the European Population Conference/Congrès Européen de Démographie, United Nations Population Division. Available at http://www.un.org/popin/confcon/milan/plen3/3rdplen.html.

Nagy, László. 2000. Illegal trade of arms and connected crime. Paper presented at the Council on Christian Approaches to Defense and Disarmament conference, Loyola Retreat House, Faulkner, Maryland, September 17–21. Available at http://website.lineone.net/~ccadd/.

Nash, Robert J. 1993. *World encyclopedia of organized crime.* Cambridge, MA: Da Capo Press Inc.

Nelken, David. 2003. Criminology: Crime's changing boundaries. In *Oxford handbook of legal studies,* ed. Peter Cane and Mark Tushnet, 250–71. Oxford: Oxford University Press.

Nelli, Humbert S. 1969. Italians and crime in Chicago: The formative years, 1890–1920. *American Journal of Sociology* 74 (4): 373–91.

———. 1976. *The business of crime: Italians and syndicate crime in the United States.* Chicago: University of Chicago Press.

Ngai, Pun. 2005. *Made in China: Women factory workers in a global perspective.* Durham, NC: Duke University Press.

Nozick, Robert. 1974. *Anarchy, state, and utopia.* New York: Basic Books.

Pagden, Anthony. 1987. The destruction of trust and its economic consequences in the case of eighteenth-century Naples. In *Trust: Making and breaking cooperative relations,* ed. Diego Gambetta, 127–41. Oxford: Blackwell.

Palacio, Juan Manuel. 2004. *La paz del trigo. Cultura legal y agricultura pampeana.* Buenos Aires: Edhasa.

Pan, Philip P. 2008. *Out of Mao's shadow.* New York: Simon and Schuster.

Paoli, Letizia. 1995. The Banco Ambrosiano case: An investigation into the underestimation of the relations between organized and economic crime. *Crime, Law, and Social Change* 23 (4): 345–65.

———. 2003. *Mafia brotherhood: Organized crime, Italian style.* Oxford: Oxford University Press.

Pap, András László. 2001. Street police corruption. Paper presented at the Socrates Kokkalis annual workshop, John F. Kennedy School of Government, Cambridge, Massachusetts, February 9.

Pedrini, Maurizio. 1979. Droga a Verona. *Verona Popolo* 6–7:5.

People's Government of Guangdong. 2006. *About Guangdong* [in Chinese]. Available at http://www.gd.gov.cn/gdgk/.

Pileggi, Nicholas. 1987. *Wise guy: Life in a mafia family.* London: Corgi Books.

———. 1996. *Casino: Love and honor in Las Vegas.* London: Corgi Books.

Pistone, Joseph D., with Charles Brant. 2007. *Donnie Brasco: Unfinished business.* Philadelphia: Running Press.

Pistone, Joseph D., and Richard Woodley. 1997. *Donnie Brasco: My undercover life in the mafia.* New York: Signet.

Pitkin, Thomas M., and Francesco Cordasco. 1977. *The Black Hand: A chapter in ethnic crime.* Totowa, NJ: Littlefield, Adams.

Portes, Alejandro. 1998. Social capital: Its origins and applications in modern sociology. *Annual Review of Sociology* 24:1–24.

Posner, Daniel. 2004. The political salience of cultural difference: Why Chewas and Tumbukas are allies in Zambia and adversaries in Malawi. *American Political Science Review* 98 (4): 529–45.

Putnam, Robert D. 1993. *Making democracy work: Civic traditions in Italy.* Princeton, NJ: Princeton University Press.

———. 2000. *Bowling alone: The collapse and revival of American community.* New York: Simon and Schuster.

Qu, Jing, Sizhen Qin, and Yuzhuo Li. 2005. Trend of border trade in Helongjiang [in Chinese]. *Heilongjiang Daily*, September 9. Available at http://www.hlj.xinhuanet.com/xw/2005-09/09/content_5089393.htm.

Raab, Selwyn. 2005. *Five families: The rise, decline, and resurgence of America's most powerful mafia empires.* New York: St. Martin's Press.

Repetto, Thomas. 2004. *American mafia: A history of its rise to power.* New York: Holt Paperbacks.

Reuter, Peter. 1985. *The organization of illegal markets: An economic analysis.* New York: U.S. National Institute of Justice.

———. 1987. *Racketeering in legitimate industries: A study in the economics of intimidation,* Santa Monica: RAND Corporation.

———. 1995. The decline of the American mafia. *Public Interest* 120:89–99.

Riis, Jacob. [1890] 1970. *How the other half lives: Studies among the tenements of New York.* Edited by Sam Bass Warner Jr. Cambridge: Belknap Press of Harvard University Press.

Rose-Ackerman, Susan. 1998. Bribes and gifts. In *Economics, values, and organization,* ed. Avner Ben Ner and Louis Putterman, 296–328. Cambridge: Cambridge University Press.

———. 2001a. Trust and honesty in post-socialist societies. *Kyklos* 54:415–44.

———. 2001b. Trust, honesty, and corruption: Reflection on the state-building process. *Archives Européennes de Sociologie* 43:526–70.

———. 2007. *From elections to democracy: Building accountable government in Hungary and Poland.* Cambridge: Cambridge University Press.

Rosoli, Gianfausto, ed. 1978. *Un Secolo di emigrazione italiana, 1876–1976.* Rome: Centro studi emigrazione.

Rossi, Adriana. 2003. Il ruolo delle donne nella criminalità organizzata in Argentina. In *Donne e mafie. Il ruolo delle donne nelle organizzazioni criminali,* ed. Giovanni Fiandaca, 146–75. Palermo: Dipartimento di Scienze Penalistiche e Criminologiche.

Rozenblat, Anatoly. 2006. *Hello, America!* Available at http://www.authorhouse
.com/.

Ruggiero, Vincenzo, and Antony A. Vass. 1992. Heroin use and the formal
economy: Illicit drugs and licit economies in Italy. *British Journal of Criminology* 32 (3): 273–91.

Sabetti, Filippo. 1984. *Political authority in a Sicilian village.* New Brunswick,
NJ: Rutgers University Press.

Saccomanno, Francesco. 2005. Operatività, ritualità delle `ndrine ed infiltrazione della `Ndrangheta in Piemonte. Tesi di laurea, Università degli Studi
dell'Aquila.

Sárközy, Tamás. 1993. A legal framework for the Hungarian transition, 1989–
1991. In *Hungary: An Economy in Transition*, ed. Istvan Szekely and David
M. G. Newbery, 239–48. Cambridge: Cambridge University Press.

Saviano, Roberto. 2007. *Gomorrah: Italy's other mafia.* London: Macmillan.

Sawyer, Albert E. 1932. The enforcement of national Prohibition. Special issue,
Annals of the American Academy of Political and Social Science 163 (September): 10–29.

Sciarrone, Rocco. 1998. *Mafie Vecchie, Mafie Nuove.* Rome: Donzelli.

———. 2008. L'organizzazione reticolare della `Ndrangheta. *Questioni di Giustizia* 27 (3): 70–89.

Selvaggi, Giuseppe. 1978. *The rise of the mafia in New York.* Indianapolis: Bobbs-
Merrill.

Sergi, Pantaleone. 1991. *La "Santa" violenta, Storie di `ndrangheta e di ferocia, di
faide, di sequestri, di vittime innocenti.* Cosenza: Edizioni Periferia.

Sharma, Charu. 2003–4. Enforcement mechanisms for endangered species protection in Hong Kong: A legal perspective. *Vermont Journal of Environmental Law* 5 (1): 1–34.

Shelley, Louise. 1999. Identifying, counting, and categorizing transnational
criminal organizations. *Transnational Organized Crime* 5 (1): 1–18.

———. 2006. The globalization of crime and terrorism. *eJournal USA* 11 (1): 42–
45. Available at http://www.america.gov/media/pdf/ejs/ijge0206.pdf#popup.

Shelley, Louise, John Picarelli, and Chris Corpora. 2003. Global Crime Inc. In
Beyond sovereignty: Issues for a global agenda, ed. Mayann Cusimano, 143–
66. Florence, KY: Thomson/Wadsworth.

Shih, Victor. 2004. Dealing with non-performing loans: Power politics and financial policies in China. *China Quarterly* 180:922–44.

Sifakis, Carl. 1999. *The mafia encyclopedia.* 2nd ed. New York: Checkmark Books.

Silber, Laura, and Allan Little. 1996. *The death of Yugoslavia.* Rev. ed. London:
Penguin.

Sinclair, Andrew. 1962. *Prohibition: The era of excess*. Boston: Little, Brown and Company.

Siu, Ricardo C. S., and William R. Eadington. 2009. Table games or slots? Competition, evolution, and game preference in Macao's casino market. *Journal of Gambling Business and Economics* 3 (1): 41–63.

Skolnik, Fred, ed. 2006. *Encyclopaedia Judaica*. Detroit: Macmillan Reference USA in association with the Keter Pub. House.

Smith, Alastair, and Federico Varese. 2001. Payment, protection, and punishment: The role of information and reputation in the mafia. *Rationality and Society* 13 (3): 387–431.

Sonnino, Eugenio. 1995. La popolazione italiana: dall'espansione al contenimento. In *Storia dell'Italia repubblicana*, 2 (1): 532–85. Turin: Einaudi.

Spaventa, Luigi. 1999. Intervento al Convegno "Le nuove mafie in Italia," Milan, Palazzo Marino, March 18–19. Available at http://www.camera.it/_bicamerali/antimafia/forum/19990318/fr.htm.

Sterling, Claire. 1995. *Crime without frontiers: The worldwide expansion of organised crime and the pax mafiosa*. London: Warner Books.

Swanström, Niklas. 2006. Narcotics and China: An old security threat from new sources. *China and Eurasia Forum Quarterly* 4 (1): 113–31.

Thomas, Lately. 1967. Tammany picked an honest man. *American Heritage* 18 (2): 34–39.

———. 1969. *The mayor who mastered New York: The life and opinions of William J. Gaynor*. New York: William Morrow.

Thompson, Ruth. 1984. The limitations of ideology in the early Argentine labour movement: Anarchism in trade unions, 1890–1920. *Journal of Latin American Studies* 16 (1): 81–99.

Tian, Hongjie. 2001. *The reasons for the emergence of gangs in China* [in Chinese]. Available at http://www.bjpopss.gov.cn/bjpopss/cgjj/cgjj200308012.htm.zh.

Tilly, Charles. 1985. War making and state making as organized crime. In *Bringing the State Back In*, ed. Peter B. Evans, Dietrich Rueschemeyer, and Theda Skocpol, 169–90. Cambridge: Cambridge University Press.

Tóth, István János. 1997–98. The importance of hidden economy in Hungary, 1995–96: An estimate based on empirical study of household expenses. *Acta Oeconomica* 49 (1–2): 105–24.

Tuñón, Max. 2006. *Internal labour migration in China: Features and responses*. Beijing: International Labour Organization.

Turner, George Kibbe. 1909. Tammany's control of New York by professional criminals. *McClure's Magazine* 33 (2): 117–34.

Urbán, László. 1997. Privatisation as institutional change in Hungary. In *The political economy of property rights*, ed. David L. Weimer, 239–55. Cambridge: Cambridge University Press.

Varese, Federico. 1994. Is Sicily the future of Russia? Private protection and the emergence of the Russian mafia. *Archives Européenes de Sociologie* 35:224–58.

———. 2001. *The Russian mafia: Private protection in a new market economy*. New York: Oxford University Press.

———. 2003. Mafia. In *Concise Oxford dictionary of politics*, ed. Iain McLean and Alistair McMillan. Oxford: Oxford University Press.

———. 2006a. How mafias migrate: The case of the 'Ndrangheta in northern Italy. *Law and Society Review* 40 (2): 411–44.

———. 2006b. The secret history of Japanese cinema: The Yakuza movies. *Global Crime* 7 (1): 107–26.

———. 2006c. The structure of a criminal network examined: The Russian mafia in Rome. Oxford Legal Studies Research, no. 21.

———. 2009. The Camorra closely observed. *Global Crime* 10 (3): 262–66.

———. 2010. What is organized crime? In *Organized crime: Critical concepts in criminology*, ed. Federico Varese, 1:1–33. London: Routledge.

Veltri, Elio, and Antonio Laudati. 2009. *Mafia pulita*. Milan: Longanesi.

Von Drehle, David. 2003. *Triangle: The fire that changed America*. New York: Atlantic Monthly Press.

Waldinger, Roger. 1995. The "other side" of embeddedness: A case-study of the interplay of economy and ethnicity. *Ethnic and Racial Studies* 18 (3): 555–80.

Wang, Chunguang. 2006. The changing situation of migrant labor. *Social Research* 73 (1): 185–96.

Wang, Wuyi, and William R. Eadington. 2008. The VIP-room contractual system and Macao's traditional casino industry. *China: An International Journal* 6 (2): 237–60.

Weenink, Anton, and Franca van der Laan. 2007. The search for the Russian mafia: Central and Eastern European criminals in the Netherlands, 1989–2005. *Trends in Organized Crime* 10 (4): 57–76.

Weinstein, Liza. 2008. Mumbai's Development Mafias: Globalization, Organized Crime and Land Development. *International Journal of Urban and Regional Research* 32 (1): 22–39.

Williams, Phil. 1995. The international drug trade: An industry analysis. In *Global dimensions of high intensity crime and low intensity conflict*, ed. Graham H. Turbiville Jr., 153–83. Chicago: Office of International Criminal Justice, University of Illinois at Chicago.

———— 2001. Transnational criminal networks. In *Networks and netwars: The future of terror, crime, and militancy*, ed. John Arquilla and David F. Ronfeldt, 61–97. Washington, DC: Rand Corporation.

Wright, Alan. 1997. Organized crime in Hungary: The transition from state to civil society. *Transnational Organized Crime* 3:68–86.

Wu, Xiaogang, and Donald J. Treiman. 2004. The household registration system and social stratification in China: 1955–1996. *Demography* 41:363–84.

Wuorinen, John H. 1932. Finland's Prohibition experiment. Special issue, *Annals of the American Academy of Political and Social Science* 163 (September): 216–26.

Yearwood, Douglas L., and Richard Hayes. 2000. Perceptions of youth crime and youth gangs: A statewide systemic investigation. Raleigh, NC: Governor's Crime Commission.

Yunnan Provincial Department of Commerce. 2005. Report on the border trade in Heilongjiang, Jilin, and Inner Mongolia [in Chinese]. Available at http://yunnan.mofcom.gov.cn/aarticle/sjzhongyaozt/200512/20051201247989.html.

Zaheer, Srilata, and Shalini Manrakhan. 2001. Concentration and dispersion in global industries: Remote electronic access and the location of economic activities. *Journal of International Business Studies* 32 (4). 667–86.

Zedner, Lucia. 2009. *Security*. London: Routlege.

Zhang, Deshou. 2006. *Study on mafia-natured crimes and countermeasures* [in Chinese]. Beijing: China People's Public Security University Press.

Zhang, Sheldon, and Ko-lin Chin. 2003. The declining significance of triads societies in transnational illegal activities. *British Journal of Criminology* 43:469–88.

Zheng, Chao. 2005. *Servicemen reduction over the past two decades* [in Chinese]. Available at http://news.xinhuanet.com/mil/2005-09/02/content_3431290.htm.

Zheng, Cheng, and Fan Xia. 2006. Justice is the guarantee for establishing the authority of the judicial system: Interview with Chief Justice Botao Lu of the Guangdong Provincial Higher People's Court [in Chinese]. *South China* 29 (May 9). Available at http://www.nfyk.com/former/public/article/view.asp?id=1890.

Zheng, Tiantian. 2007. From peasant women to bar hostesses: An ethnography of China's karaoke sex industry. In *Working in China. Ethnographies of labor and workplace transformation*, ed. Ching Kwan Lee, 124–44. London: Routledge.

————. 2009. *Sex lights: The lives of sex workers in postsocialist China*. Minneapolis: University of Minnesota Press.

Zinni, Hector Nicolas. 1975. *La mafia en Argentina*. Rosario: Centro Editorial.

Aberdeen, Camorra in, 18, 192

Abruzzi region (Italy), and migration to Argentina, 128

Act on Business Organizations, 1988 (Hungary), 87–88

Administrative Department for Industry and Commerce (China); and regulations regarding debt collection in China, 159, 160, 231n32

Afghanistan, 172

Agrigento (city, Italy), 130, 134

Agrigento province (Italy), 101, 130, 138; and migration to Argentina, 128; and migration to Rosario, 129; as place of origin of mafiosi in Rosario, 131, 138

Agroprom Bank (Russia), 1

Alcohol, 2, 23, 115, 116, 200, 223n38, 226n81; consumption, 28, 59, 125

Alessandria (Italy), 37

Alessandria della Rocca (Sicily), 101; birthplace of Pendino, 130; migration from, 129

Alien conspiracy theory, 16

Allegra, Melchiorre, 121, 220n10, 220n12

Álvarez, Juan, 132

Alzogaray, Silvio, 139

Amato, Arturo, 138

America, Latin, 181; North, 106, 125, 173; South, 129

American Jewish Joint Distribution Committee, 72

Amsterdam, 55

Anti-Mafia Parliamentary Commission (Italy), 4, 31, 34, 42, 43

Antwerp, 188; as the destination of Russian Jewish refugees, 72

Appalachian meeting, 32; see also Italian-American mafia

Apulia region (Italy), 15

Arbat International, 90

Arena di Verona (newspaper), campaign against drugs, 58

Arena di Verona (Roman amphitheater), 53

Argentina, 5, 101, 104, 131, 132, 134, 152, 227n95; Galifii in, 130, 140, Italian migration to, 126, 128, 132, 219n6; Pendino migration to, 130; trade unions in, 133

Arigon Ltd., 91

Arlacchi, Pino, 53, 55

Arms trafficking, in Hungary, 91; in the former Yugoslavia, 91; in Val Susa, 48

Army, Soviet, 86

Arroyo Seco (Argentina), 129, 138

Artamova, Raisa,* and Yakovlev's crew in Rome, 74, 83; role, 84

Asbury, Herbert, 116

Asesinos (movie), 140

Aspromonte (Calabria, Italy), 32

Association of Concerned Families against Drugs (Verona), 58

Asti (Italy), 37, 51
Australia, 32; `Ndrangheta in, 34
Austria, 2; banks in, 77
Averin, Viktor, 66; in Budapest, 86, 91, 92
Ayerza, Abel, 140

Backer, Charles, 197
Baff, Barnet, murder of, 115
Bajo las garras de la mafia (movie), 140
Bakassi Boys (Nigeria), 200
Ballestreri, Nicolás, 139
Bamboo United crime group (Taiwan), 15, 152; in China, 152, 162; origins of, 230n11; outside Taiwan, 230n11
Banca Popolare dell'Adriatico di Pesaro, and Monya Roizis, 69
Banco Ambrosiano, 20
Banditism, in Argentina, 133; in Sicily, 102
Bangkok, 175
Bangladesh, 55
Bank of New York, 69; scandal, 70, 86
Bardonecchia, 5, 9, 11, 26, 30, 36, 39, 41, 44, 57, 58, 59, 60, 75, 95, 143, 177, 196; city council disbanded, 49; civic engagement in, 52; compared to Rosario, 134–137, 142; construction firms in, 40; construction sector in, 37–39, 45–46, 52, 93, 134, 135, 136, 227n89; elections in, 48–50; geographical position of, 34–35; labor racketeering in, 41, 43, 52; licenses to build new homes in, 39–40; `Ndrangheta in, 46, 125; omertà in, 211n64; police and mafia in, 47; politics in, 48; population, 209n26; protection in, 46, 47; violence in, 41, 46–47, 52
Barreca, Pasquale, 33
Basilicata region (Italy), 212n78; and migration to Argentina, 128; social capital in, 22
Baxter Street (New York City), 106
BBC, 91
Beijing, 154, 158, 163, 176, 180, 195; migration to, 147, 229n4; television, 154

Belfiore crime family (`Ndrangheta), 46
Belfiore, Mimmo, 46
Belgium, `Ndrangheta in, 34
Belgrade, 91
Berlin, 119
Bevacqua, Antonio, 139
Big Eddie, 116
Bivona (Agrigento, Italy), 129
Black Hand (extortion), 112, 114; in Rosario, 139
Boemi, Salvatore, 33
Bogdanovich, Oleg,* and protection activities in Rome, 81; and resource acquisition in Rome, 80; and Yakovlev's crew in Rome, 74
Bonanno crime family (New York City), 19, 105, 225n64; name, 123
Bonanno, Joseph, 104, 120; and Maranzano, 119, 120; as boss, 121, 123; on extortion and protection, 204n12; on Masseria, 119; on Mussolini, 105
Bongiovanni construction company (Rosario), 134, 135
Borgata, 119, 120, 121, 123; see also cosca
Borgia, Cesare, 68
Boros, Tamás, 91
Boston Globe (newspaper), on the mafia in Hungary, 90
Bourbon dynasty, 102
Bowling Alone (book), 22
Brenno, Riccardo,* and investments in the Italian economy, 79; and Yakovlev's crew in Rome, 75; trip to Moscow, 77
Brescia (Italy), 55
Brezhnev, Leonid, 71
Brigada, 67, 189, 192; see also Russian mafia
Brighton Beach (New York), 72
Bronx, 119
Brooklyn, 17, 104, 119, 120
Brussels, as the destination of Russian Jewish refugees, 72
Buccinasco (Milan, Italy), `Ndrangheta in, 37
Budapest, 9, 70, 95; Solnstevskaya in, 15, 69, 86, 91–93; trust in, 30
Buè, Santiago, 130

Buenos Aires, 131, 132, 139; Agata Galiffi in, 141; Italian migration to, 126, 129; Juan Galiffi in, 130; kidnapping for ransom in, 139; murder of Marrone in, 131; prostitution in, 228fn99
Buenos Aires province, 133
Burgio (Agrigento, Italy), 129
Burma (Myanmar), 172, 173, 175, 176, 178, 228n1
Buscetta, Tommaso, 105, 221n12; and the Castellammare War, 225n65; on the Italian-American mafia, 123, 224n60; on the 'Ndrangheta, 31
Byrnes, Thomas, 112

Caccia, Bruno, 46
Cacciatore, Carlo, 130
Calabria region (Italy), 7, 22, 41, 42, 44, 45, 46, 51, 52, 58, 59, 61; migration from, 54
Calderone, Antonio "Tonino," on mafia transplantation, 14, 105; on extortion/protection, 204fn14
California, 190, 191
Calò, Giuseppe "Pippo," in Rome, 20, 192, 206n33
Caltanissetta (Italy), and migration to Argentina, 128
Calvi, Roberto, 1; murder of, 20
Cambodia, 15
Camera, Antonio, in Verona, 57
Camera, Felice, in Verona, 57
Camorra, 24; expansion to Apulia, 15; in Aberdeen, 18, 192; pentiti in, 33
Campana, Paolo, 96
Campania region (Italy), 22, 212n78; and migration to Argentina, 128; migration from, 54
Campieri (field armed guards), 193
Canada, 32; 'Ndrangheta in, 34
Canavese Valley (Piedmont), 40, 45, 51
Capo crimine, defined, 32
Capone, Alphonse Gabriel "Al," 121
Case selection, 29–30
Casino (film), 20
Casino Royale (book), 164
Castellammare del Golfo (Sicily), 104, 120

Castellammare War (Italian American Mafia), 119, 121, 222n33, 225n65; and its effect on recruitment into the Italian-American mafia, 123
Castells, Manuel, 3
Catania (Italy), 13, 14, 105, 139; migration to Argentina from, 128, 130
Catholic Church, 102; against drug trafficking in Verona, 58
Caucete (Argentina), 141
Celestial Alliance crime group (Taiwan), 152; formation of, 151; in China, 152, 153
Centeno, Carlos, 138
Central America, 191
Ceretto, Mario, 44
Chandler, David, 105
Chang, Anlo (White Wolf), 152
Chang'an town (Dongguan, Guangdong province, China), 162, 168, 169
Changping town (Dongguan, Guangdong province, China), 157
Chechen crime groups (Moscow), 66
Chechnya, 74, 189
Chen, Bosheng (Big Jie), 167, 168
Chen, Kai, prostitution ring led by, 172
Chen, Nuoquan, 152
Chen, Zhixiong (Four-Eyed Xiong), 167, 168
Chernomyrdin, Viktor Stepanovich, 77
Chiavari (Liguria), 225n73
Chicago, 6, 20, 27, 121, 175, 192, 226n75; Black Hand in, 22n36
Chicago outfit (mafia group), and Las Vegas, 20, 27, 192
Chin, Kolin, on Taiwanese triads in China, 17, 162, 168
China, 5, 11, 29, 146, 149, 153, 154, 156, 167, 177, 180, 181, 228n1; and democracy, 196; courts in, 155–156, 230n21, 231n22; debt collection in, 159–163, 178, 232n44; drug trafficking in, 172–177; gambling in, 163, 164, 165, 166, 178, 233n51; Hong Kong triads in, 150; informal economy in, 10, 156; internal migration, 147, 149, 229n4; labor disputes in, 230n18; mafia/

China (*continued*)
mafiosi in, 14, 153; prostitution in, 169–172, 178; protective umbrellas in, 125, 158, 171, 172, 177, 178, 180; special economic zones in, 147; Taiwanese triads in, 17, 125, 151–152, 162–163; trust in, 30
China Central Television, 163
China Daily (newspaper), 172
Chinese Communist Party, 170, 171
Chisinau (Kishinev), birthplace of Monya Elson, 68
Christian Democratic Party (Italy), 41
Chu, Yiukong, 13
Churchill, Winston, 109
Cianciana (Agrigento, Italy), 129
Cinema, as a form of advertisement for mafias, 26
Cirio, 24
Citizen Kane (film), 197
Civic Community Index, 36, 53
Civic culture, 22
Civic engagement, 8, 23, 29; in Bardonecchia, 52, 61; in Verona, 58, 61
Civil Service Board (New York City), 107
"Clean Sweep" police operation (Taiwan), 151
Cleveland, 121
Clodo, Dietmar, 92
Code of Silence/*omertà*, in Bardonecchia, 49–50
Cold War, 71
Coleman, James, 21
Collective action, 21; in Bardonecchia, 47, 50, 211n64
Colombo crime family (New York City), 121, 123
Columbian drugs cartels, 3, 25
Communist Party of Burma, 173
Condizioni politiche ed amministrative della Sicilia (book), 102
Connecticut, 117
Construction firms, in Bardonecchia, 40; in Rosario, 134–136
Construction sector, 5, 9, 23–24, 25, 26, 61; boom in, 8, 28, 134, 137; cartels in, 8, 9, 23; in Bardonecchia, 37–40, 42,

45–46, 52; in Margherita Laziale, 75; in Rome, 75; in Rosario and Bardonecchia compared, 136–137, 142; in Rosario, 134–137
Construction Workers Trade Union, 47
Container Security Initiative (USA), 176–177, 178
Content analysis, 75; of phone wiretaps, 96–97
Conventillos, 134; see construction sector
Córdoba province (Argentina), 131
Corino, Mario, 41, 43, 47; and elections in Bardonecchia, 48; death, 50
Corruption, 9; in Hungary, 88; in New York City, 107–111, 125; in Verona, 58
Corsaro, Antonio, in Verona, 57
Corsaro, Francesco, in Verona, 57
Corsaro, Vincenzo, in Verona, 57
Cosa Nostra, 5; see also Sicilian mafia
Cosca (mafia family), 103, 119
Costello, Frank, 116
Cotai Strip (Macau), 163
Cottian Alps, 35
Counterfeiting, in New York City, 112, 114, 125, 222n33; in Rosario, 131, 140, 141, 142
Crane, Stephen, 197
Crime without Frontiers (book), 3
Criminal Code (Argentina), 140
Critchley, David, 119
Croatia, 91
Csáki, György, 87, 88
Cuffaro, Giuseppe, 226n75
Cuffaro, José, 129; gang led by, 139, 228n97
Cuneo (Italy), 37, 51
Cuorgnè, 45; violence in, 46
Curabà, Esteban, 129, 137
Curb Exchanges, for the sale of alcohol in New York City, 117–118
Curti construction company (Rosario), 135; and Pendino, 134
Cutolo, Raffaele, 15

Dalian (Liaoning province, China), 171
D'Aquila crime family (New York City), 118, 120, 121; See also Gambino crime family

D'Aquila, Salvatore, 118, 120; murder of, 121
Dash, Mike, 107
Debt collection, in China, 154–156, 159–162, 163, 178, 180, 231n31, 231n32, 231n35; in gambling, 163, 166–169; in Hungary, 89; in Macau, 232n44
Democracy, and mafias, 5, 12, 142
Democracy in America (book), 102, 191
Deng, Xiaoping, 147
Deodati, Antonio, 17, 105; murder of, 112
Department of Justice (Guangdong province, China), 167
Department of Justice (USA), 173
Detroit, 121
Ding, Xueliang, 180
Don Chicho (play), 140
Dongguan (Guangdong province, China), 147, 154, 157, 178; "concubine villages" in, 150; industrial area in, 157; Taiwanese triads in, 152
Diagna, Jack, 115
Drugs, consumption in Verona, 55; in Burma, 172–173; in China, 172–177; in New York City, 198; in Val Susa, 48; market, 29, 64; trade, 11, 61; trafficking, 10, 55, 84
Du, Xiangu, 15
Duisburg (Germany), 33

Economic power, 3
Eighteenth Amendment (US Constitution), 115
18th gang (US and Salvador), 191
El Salvador, 190, 191, 234n2
Elections, and registration of voters, 48; European, 63; in Bardonecchia, 48, 49, 50, 63
Elizabeth (city, NJ, USA), 175
Elizabeth Street (New York City), 101, 106
Elson, Monya, and Vyacheslav Kirillovich Ivan'kov, 69; and Yossiff Roizis, 69; arrest in Fano, 70; birth, 68; in Fano, 69, 78; in New York City, 68, 69
Emilia Romagna region (Italy), 22, 78

Employment, illegal, 10, 63
Enterprises, illegal, 13
Erdélyi, Nándor, 92
Esquilino (Rome), and the Russians, 72
Ethnicity, 4
Eural Trans Gas, 91
European Union, 198, 199
Export-oriented economy, 8, 10, 24, 25; of Verona, 63
Extortion, 6, 203n9; and protection, 204n12; defined, 204n10; in Calabria, 208n13; in China, 161, 231n31; in New York City, 112, 114, 118, 125; in Rosario, 131; in Verona, 57–58
Extra-legal governance, mafias as forms of, 6

Facchini, Dino, 55
Facchini, Giorgio,* 82; and resource acquisition in Rome, 80; and Yakovlev's crew in Rome, 75
Famiglia Montalbano (book), 31
Fano, 78; Russian mafiosi in, 68; structure of the economy, 68
Fascism, 15, 17; mafia repression during, 105, 131
Federal Bureau of Investigation (FBI), 66, 92; and Semën Yudkovich Mogilevich, 86; and Monya Elson, 70
Ferrari, Marco,* 81–82; threatens Yakovlev, 81–82; wife of, 82
Ferraris, Maria, 138
Fiat (car manufacturer), 40
Financial crimes, 95
First World War, 104, 126, 135; and economic situation in Rosario, 133–134
Five Families (Italian-American mafia), 5, 121, 123, 126; see also Bonanno, Colombo, Gambino, Genovese, Lucchese crime families
Five Points (New York City), 106, 107
Flaccomio, Antonio, murder of, 112
Florida, 31
Flying Eagle crime group (China), 152
Forced resettlement (soggiorno obbligato), 6, 7, 11, 16, 50, 61; Gasparre Mutolo on, 17; to Emilia-Romagna, 37; to

Forced resettlement (*continued*)
  Lombardy, 37; to Piedmont, 37; to
  Turin province, 209fn30; to Tuscany,
  37; to Verona, 54
Ford, Gerald Rudolph Jr., 71
Foshan (Guangdong province, China), 166
Four Seas crime group (Taiwan), in China,
  152, 167
14K crime group (Hong Kong and Macau),
  167, 230n13; and gambling, 168; in
  China, 152, 167
France, 2, 35, 39, 131; `Ndrangheta in,
  34; Sicilian mafia in, 105
Franchetti, Leopoldo, 102
Frejus tunnel, 36, 39
Frid, Carina, 129, 225n73, 225n74
Fujian province (China), 152, 172; and
  Taiwan, 152, 177; as a special economic
  zone, 147; crime groups in, 167; migra-
  tion to, 147; Taiwan triads in, 152
Furforo, Nicodemo, 138
Fuzhou (Fujian province, China), Taiwanese
  triads in, 152, 153; prostitution in, 172

Gagliano, Tommaso, 115
Galicia (Spain), 3
Galiffi, Agata "Gatta," 140–141
Galiffi, Juan, and connections to political
  elite, 138–139; background, 130–131;
  criminal activities, 131, 138, 140; in
  Italy, 140, 141; known as "Al Capone
  Argentino," 130
Gálvez (Argentina), 131, 138
Gambetta, Diego, 4, 8, 13, 14, 25, 26
Gambino crime family (New York City),
  in Bardonecchia, 51–52
Gambling, 10; in China, 163; in Macau,
  163–169; in New York City, 107, 125;
  police protection of, 108
Gangs of New York (book), 116
Garbage collection, 9
Garment industry, 9; mafia protection in,
  115
Garton Ash, Timothy, 180
Gaynor, William Jay, 196, 197; reforming
  the New York City police, 109–111,
  114, 120

Gazprom, 91
Genoa (Italy), 36
Genovese crime family (New York City),
  123
Genovese, Vito, 119
Gentile, Nick "Zu Cola," 101, 120; back-
  ground, 219n1; dual membership of
  Sicilian and American mafias, 121
Germany, 3, 99; `Ndrangheta in, 33, 34;
  Russian mafia in, 192
Gioiosa Ionica (Calabria, Italy), 41, 45,
  51, 57
Global Trading, 2, 3
Globalization, 8, 21, 26, 79, 84; and orga-
  nized crime, 3, 4, 192; as a factor affect-
  ing mafia transplantation, 10–12, 192
Gorbachev, Mikhail Sergeyevich, 1
Great Ring Gang crime group (Macau), 167
Greenwood Cemetery (New York City),
  105
Guangdong province (China), as a
  special economic zone, 147; Courts
  in, 155; crime groups in, 166; drugs
  trafficking in, 173, 175; gambling in,
  163, 165, 232n38; GDP in, 147; Hong
  Kong triads in, 150–151, 167, 177;
  migration to, 147, 229n4; recorded
  crime in, 229n4; Taiwan triads in, 151,
  152
Guangzhou (Guangdong province, China),
  147, 154, 232n44; debt-recovery in,
  168; Macau triads in, 167–8; prostitution in, 171; recorded crime in, 229n4;
  Taiwan triads in, 152
Guatemala, 190, 191
Guevara, Ernesto "Che," 225n73

Haikou (Hainan province, China), Taiwan-
  ese gangsters in, 152
Hainan province (China), as a special eco-
  nomic zone, 147; Taiwan triads in, 152
He, Bingsong, 150, 151
Hearst, William Randolph, 197
Henan province (China), gambling in,
  233n51
Herald (newspaper), 197
Hill, Henry, 24

Hill, Peter H., 13, 14, 15
Historical Index of Civic Traditions, 36
Ho, Stanley Hungsun, 164, 165
Holland, Camorra in, 18; `Ndrangheta
    in, 34
Hong Kong, 5, 10, 33, 146, , 149, 150,
    153, 164, 165, 167, 169, 234n67; and
    drugs trafficking, 173, 175, 176, 178;
    anti-triads crackdowns in, 150, 151;
    investments into China, 147
Hoover, Herbert Clark, 115
Horse theft, in New York City, 112, 125
Hubei province (China), 156
Hungary, 9; Civil Law in, 89; Commercial
    Code in, 87; confidence in the legal
    system in, 88; courts in, 88; dispute
    settlement in, 89; economic criminal-
    ity in, 88; gross domestic product, 87;
    migration to, 97, 99; real estate registra-
    tion system in, 89; Red Army defectors
    in, 149; Russian gangs in, 86, 95; Soln-
    tsevskaya in, 86–93; tax avoidance in, 88

Ierinò, Cosimo, arrest, 59; in Calabria, 59;
    in Verona, 57
Il Libro Cuore (book), 225n73
Inagawa-kai crime group, 13; see also
    yakuza
Incaprettare (mafia-style murder), 57
India, 12
International organized crime, 3, see also
    transnational organized crime
Investments, and resource acquisitions, 83;
    as discussed in phone intercepts, 75–79,
    83; by the Russian mafia in Italy, 76–79,
    83; defined, 19, 75; in the economy by
    the mafia, 11, 61, 75
Inzerillo, Salvatore, 52
Ishii Susumu crime group, 13; see also
    yakuza, Inagawa-kai
Israel, 72
Italian-American mafia, 6, 16, 19, 25, 26,
    101, 112, 143, 197, 206n23, 207n8;
    admission into, 120–121, 123, 126;
    admission ritual, 112; and Prohibi-
    tion, 116–120; and relationship to the
    Sicilian mafia, 121, 123, 126; birth of,

114–120, 125, 196; Commission, 121;
    New York families, 121, 123; see also
    Five Families
Italy, 2, 30, 34, 78, 79, 84, 125, 129,
    134, 140, 141; Central, 15, 78, 126,
    133; fascism in, 105, 131; medieval,
    206n35; migration from, 137; money
    laundering in, 95; Northern, 11, 15,
    22, 30, 61, 78, 126, 128, 133, 137,
    141, 205n17, 209n28; Southern, 16,
    61, 126, 128, 137, 181, 198, 205n17,
    209n28, 210n48; unification of, 193
Ivan'kov, Vyacheslav Kirillovich, 188; and
    Monya Elson, 69; investments in Hun-
    gary, 91; in the United States, 17
Izmailovo crime group (Russia), 78

Jackson, Henry Martin, 71
Jackson-Vanik Amendment, 71
Japan, 12; and the transition to the market
    economy, 194, 195; foreign criminals
    in, 15, 151, 230n11; origins of the
    yakuza in, 194
Japanese Mafia, The (book), 13
Jerome, William Travers, 109
Jiang, Jinxin, 167
Jiang, Qingyun, 156
Jiangmen (Guangdong province, China),
    167
Jiangsu province (China), 147
Jiaotou, 151, 205n11; see triads, Taiwanese
Jinan Daily (newspaper), 156
Johns, Michael, 132, 134
Judiciary, in Bardonecchia, 63; in Verona,
    63

Kamenskaya, Alina,* 75; and maintain-
    ing internal order in Rome, 82; and
    resource acquisition in Rome, 80
Kandov, Abner, 92
Kanonieri kurdebi, see vory-v-zakone
Kansas City, 20, 101
Karsai, Gábor, 87, 88
Katona, Géza, on the mafia in Hungary,
    88–89
Kelly, Paul (Paolo Vaccarelli), and Five
    Points gang, 114

Kezich, Tullio, 26
KGB (Komitet gosudarstvennoy bezopasnosti), 71, 86
Khabarovsk (Russia), Chinese organized crime in, 15
Kidnapping, and Masseria, 118; in Rosario, 129, 131, 139–140, 142; in Verona 57
Korea, 77, 82
Kostina, Sonya,* role in the Russian mafia group in Rome, 83
Krysha ("roof" protection arrangement, Russia), 67, 158
Kurgan crime group (Russia), 78

La Boca (Buenos Aires), 126
La Crítica (newspaper), 131, 139
La Maffia (play), 140
La Rioja province (Argentina), 131
La Stampa (newspaper), 50
La Torre, Pio, 42
La Veronese (type of heroin), 56
Labor market, 3, 9
Labor racketeering, in Bardonecchia, 41, 43, 52
Ladispoli (Italy), 72; camp for Soviet refugees in, 72
Landesco, John, 6
Lao Da (Big Brother), 15
Las Vegas, 20, 21, 27, 163, 164, 192
Latin Kings gang (US and Guatemala), 191
Lavagna (Liguria), 225n73
Law enforcement, in Bardonecchia, 63; in Verona, 63
Lazio region (Italy), 74
Lei, Hanshan, 160
Lemlich, Clara, 109
Lewis, Roger, 53, 55
Lexow Committee (New York State Senate Inquiry, 1894–1895), 108, 109
Li, Deliang, 168
Lianping county (Guangdong province, China), 163
Liga del Sur (political party, Argentina), 138
Liguria region (Italy), and migration to Argentina, 128, 129, 132, 134, 225n73

Liquor Dealers' Association (New York City), 109
Little Italy, 118
Liwan district (Guangzhou, Guangdong province, China), 168
Lo Presti, Rocco, 51, 57; and politics, 48, 63; control of construction sector in Bardonecchia, 44, 49; convictions, 44; death, 45, 50; move to Bardonecchia, 44–46, 50; salary of, 64
Locale, defined, 32
Lombardy region (Italy), 78; and migration to Argentina, 128, 129, 134; forced resettlement of mafiosi to, 16, 37; social capital in, 28
London, 70; arrests rates in, 108; as the destination of Russian Jewish refugees, 72; murder of Roberto Calvi in, 20
Long Island, 116, 117
Lu, Botao, 155
Lubavitch Movement, 72
Lucchese crime family (New York City), 115; in lathing and plastering industry, 115
Luciano crime family (New York City), 123; see also Genovese crime family
Luciano, "Charlie Lucky" (Salvatore Lucania), 114, 206n22; and Prohibition, 116; Boss, 121
Lupara (sawed-off shotgun), 44
Lupo, Ignazio, 104, as a counterfeiter, 112
Lvov University, 86

Macau, as a Special Administrative Region of the People's Republic of China, 163; gambling in, 163–166; loan sharking in, 163–164; Triads, 164, 167, 178; VIP rooms in, 164–166
Machiavelli, Niccolò, 68, 81
Mafia limpia (Rosario), 137
Mafias, 4, 6, 23, 41, 143; ability to collect information by, 14, 25, 26; advertisement by, 26; agency problems in, 14, 25, 26, 27; as a form of extralegal governance, 6; emergence of, 5, 12; liquid, 4, 143, 190; localized, 13, 191; recruitment into, 19

Mafiosi, 8, 156; communication among, 14; fake, 25; migration of, 27, 93, 104–6, 129–131, 150–153, 177, 190, 192 ; supply of, 9, 11, 61, 86

Magazzolo Valley (Agrigento, Italy), 129

Mai, Guoqing, 168

Maintaining internal order, in mafia groups, 76, 96; in the Russian mafia group in Rome, 81–83

Manhattan, 106, 107, 114, 116, 118, 121

Mano Negra, 139, 142, 227n95; see also Black Hand

Mara Salvatrucha gang (US and Salvador), 191

Maranzano, Salvatore, and Castellammare War, 121, 123; and Prohibition, 119, 224n57; as boss, 121; background, 119, 221n13; death, 121, 123; in Sicily, 220n10; in the Schiro crime family, 120

Marche region (Italy), 78; and migration to Argentina, 128, 134, 137; economy of, 68; Russian mafiosi in, 68

Margherita Laziale* (Italy), 73, 75

Maritati, Fabio, murder of, 58

Market economy, transition to, 12, 29, 87 90, 194–195

Markets, emergence of new, 8, 28, 64, 87, 93; illegal, 8, 24, 75; legal, 154–163

Marrone, Francisco "Don Chico," 130; criminal activities in Rosario, 137; death, 131, 140; migration to Argentina, 131

Martiré, Jose, 139

Maspoli construction company (Rosario), 135

Masseria, Giuseppe "Joe the Boss," 104, 117; and Castellammare War, 121, 123; and Prohibition, 118–119; arrival in the USA, 220n7; Boss, 118, 121; death, 123

Maxi Trial of the Sicilian mafia, 104

Mazzaferro crime group (Italy), 9, 29; in Bardonecchia, 36, 51, 63; in Verona, 29

Mazzaferro, Francesco "Ciccio," 44; charges, 45; control of excavation business in Bardonecchia, 45; convic-

tions, 45; in Bardonecchia, 50; move to Bardonecchia, 45

Mazzaferro, Giuseppe, 57

Mazzaferro, Vincenzo, 57

McAdoo, William, 108

McClellan Committee (US Senate), 123

McClure Magazine, 106

McCoy, Bill, 116

Meiji period (Japan), and the transition to the market economy in Japan, 194

Messina (Italy), 112

Micheletti construction company (Rosario), 135

Middle East, 55

Middle Kingdom, 10, 146, 158; see also China

Migration, 3, 6, 7, 10; as a factor conducive to mafia transplantation, 16, 36–37, 53–54, 61, 71–72, 86, 104, 126, 128, 147, 149, 191; from South to North of Italy, 37; of Hong Kong and Taiwan triad members to China, 150–153; of Italians to Argentina, 126–128, 141–142; of Italians to Rosario, 129; of mafiosi, 27, 93, 104–6, 129–131, 150 153; of organized crime, 3; of population, 5, 16, 27, 104, 126–129, 141–142, 147, 149; of Russians to Hungary, 86, 97, 98; of Russians to Rome, 71, 73; of Soviet Jews to the USA, 71–72; to New York City, 104; to Verona, 54; within China, 147, 149

Mikhailov, Sergei, biography, 65–66; in Budapest, 86, 91

Milan, 3, 140; migration from South of Italy to, 37, 54, 61

Milwaukee, 20

Ministry of Public Security (China), 153, 159, 229n4, 231n32

Mochin, Andrey, 92

Modane (France), 36

Mogilevich, Semen Yudkovich, 86, 92; in the oil business, 91; money laundering in Hungary, 90

Moises, Naim, 3

Moldova, 68

Money laundering, in Bardonecchia, 48, 51, 64; in Hungary, 90; in Italy, 76
Mong Kok (Hong Kong), 146
Montevideo, 140
Moray, Alastair, 116
Morello, Giuseppe, 104; arrest, 120, 222n33; as a counterfeiter, 112, 120; *borgata*, 121; death, 222n33
Morello, Tony, 112
Morello, Vincent, 112
Mori, Cesare, 105
Morozov, Akim,* 189
Morozov, Nikita,* 188
Morozova, Ekaterina,* 189
Moscow, 1, 3, 65, 71, 73, 74, 77, 82; Georgian *vory-v-zakone* in, 17; protection activities of the Russian mafia in, 81
Motivations to open a mafia outpost, 4, 6, 18–21, 75–81; acquisition of arms as, 12
Movimento Sociale Italiano (Political Party, Italy), in Verona, 58
Mulberry Street (New York City), 106, 117
Munich, 55
Mussolini, Benito, 105
Mutolo, Gasparre, on forced resettlement, 17

Nanjing (Jiangsu province, China), 155, 159
Nanshan district (Shenzhen, Guangdong province, China), 152
Naples, 24
Nassau county (New York), 116
National Security Authority (Hungary), on organized crime, 92
`Ndrangheta, 5, 9, 13, 125, 199; expansion of, 33; in Bardonecchia 41–53, 63; in the drug market, 64; in Verona, 53–61, 64; origin of the word, 31; role of kin, 33–4
`Ndrina, defined, 31
Népszava (newspaper), 92
Netherlands, 3
Network analysis, 97
New Jersey, 116, 117, 118, 175

New York City, 5, 12, 17, 70, 111, 133, 136, 142, 146, 196–197; Black Hand crimes in, 139, 142, 222n36; consolidation of, 196, 235n10; docks in, 198; economic structure, 106, 224n57; immigrant population residential patterns in, 106, 223n47; Italian migration to, 101, 104, 106, 125, 126, 142; police corruption in, 143; Sicilian mafiosi in, 18, 105, 111–114, 129
New York Morning Journal (newspaper), 197
New York Police Department, 109, 197
New York State, 119, 125
New York Times (newspaper), 108, 197; on curb exchanges, 117; on horse stealing in New York City, 112
New York World (newspaper), 197
Newark (NJ, USA), 175
Newell, Claudio, 138
Nixon, Richard, 71
North Korea, 78
Northern League (political party, Italy), 16, 50
Nuclei Armati Rivoluzionari (terrorist group, Italy), in Verona, 54
Nuovo Banco Ambrosiamo (Bank), 1
Nuvoletta crime group (Italy), 24

Obshchak (common fund), of Solntsevskaya crime group in Moscow, 68
Oil sector, in Hungary, 89, 91, 93
Olivetti, 77
Omertà, see Code of Silence
Operation Thunderbolt (Taiwan), 151
Orekhovskaya crime group, 66; see also Russian Mafia
Organization for Economic Cooperation and Development, 198
Organized crime, 4, 22, 190, 199, 200; and democracy, 195, 196; and EU subsidies, 198; and globalization, 3, 4, 192; groups in China, 181–187; in Hungary, 86, 89, 92; in New York City, 120; in Taiwan, 151–152, 205n11; official Chinese definition of, 153; see also *jiaotou*
Outsourcing, 12

Padroni system, 137
Pakistan, 55
Palermo, 103
Parkhurst, Charles H., 196
Parmalat, 24
Partido Comunista de la Argentina, 133
Partido Radical (Argentina), 133, 138, 139, 142; see also Unión Cívica Radical
Partito Comunista Italiano (Italy), 55, 58, 59, 63, 74, 75
Partito Democratico della Sinistra (Italy), 49
Partito Social Democratico Italiano (Italy), and ' Ndrangheta's attempt to penetrate it in Verona, 58–59
Paz del Trigo, 133
Pearl River (China), 147, 152
Pendino, Gaetano, 101, 130, 139; and the construction sector in Rosario, 134–135, 227n87; criminal activities, 137, 138, 227n91; mafia boss in Rosario, 130, 138
Pennochio, Tommy, 118
Pennsylvania, 119
Pentitoli (state witnesses), 19, 33, 34, 46, 209fn21
People's Republic of China, 146, 163, 180; see also China
Pepe, Giovanni,* and investments in the Italian economy, 79; and Yakovlev's crew in Rome, 75
Pesaro (Italy), 68
Philadelphia, 120
Philippines, Taiwanese gangsters in, 151, 152, 230n11; yakuza members in, 17
Phnom Penh, 15
Piazza dei Signori (Verona), drugs trading and consumption in, 55
Piazza Delle Erbe (Verona), 53, 59; drugs trading and consumption in, 55
Piedmont region (Italy), 5, 9, 10, 11, 22, 30, 45, 53, 61, 78, 196; forced resettlement of mafiosi to, 16; migration to Argentina, 129, 132
Pine Union crime group (Taiwan), in China, 152
Pisa (Italy), 72

Pittsburgh, 120
Poland, 99
Police, 28, 177, 191, 196, 200; and protection of prostitution in China, 171–172; corruption in China, 161, 171; corruption in New York City, 107–111, 114, 143, 197, 221n23; in Bardonecchia, 63; in China, 150, 151, 159, 163, 168, 175, 178, 180; in Hong Kong, 150, 153; in Hungary, 88; in Rosario, 131, 133, 137, 138, 139, 140, 141, 142; in Taiwan, 151, 153; in Verona, 63; investigation into the Russian mafia in Rome, 83, 85, 95–96, 188, 189; Italian, 70, 76, 83; reform in New York City, 109–11, 197, 222n27; religious, 200
Polifroni, Cesare, 32
Politics, in Bardonecchia, 48, 52, 63; in Verona, 63; penetration by the mafia, 25, 48, 63
Porta Nuova crime family (Palermo), 20, 192
Porto Empedocle (Sicily), 120
Possibility principle, 29
Poultry production, 9
Prague, protection activities of the Russian mafia in, 81
Prioni construction company (Rosario), 134, 135
Prisoners' dilemma, cartel agreements as a solution to, 6
Privatization, in Hungary, 87
Profaci crime family, 121, see also Colombo crime family
Progressive Movement, 114, 115, 125, 197
Prohibition (USA), 9, 28, 61, 115–120, 142, 143, 197; and Finland, 223n38; and the emergence of the Italian-American mafia, 125, 126; and the New York crime families, 121, 197; end of, 224n56
Promstroybank, 1
Property rights, 8, 12; state's ability to define and protect, 28, 93, 95; theory of mafia emergence, 12, 193–195
Prostitution, 10, 23, 84, 177, 178; Chinese legislation on, 171; fight against, 180; in Budapest, 91; in China, 150,

Prostitution (*continued*)
153, 161, 162, 170–172, 233n56; in
Dalian, 171–172; in Fuzhou, 172; in
Macau, 169–170; in New York City, 9,
107–108, 125, 126, 197; in Rosario, 228n99; in Zhuhai, 167; police
protection of, 108, 171, 178; protective
umbrellas and, 172, 178
Protection, 5, 6, 8, 9, 24, 42; and transplantation, 8–9, 143; as a market, 16;
by the Italian mafia in New York City,
114–120; by the Russian mafia in
Rome, 81; criminal, 10, 11, 22, 23, 28,
89, 93; defined, 75–76; demand for
criminal, 7–8, 11, 21, 23, 25, 63, 89,
93, 133, 134, 143; in Hungary,
89, 91–93; in Russia, 93, 158; state,
10, 63
Protectionism, 23
Protective umbrellas, in China, 10, 125,
158, 171, 172, 177, 178, 180; in New
York City, 106–111, 196
Protector/s, local, 63; see also mafia,
mafiosi
Pulitzer, Joseph, 197
Putin, Vladimir Vladimirovich, 1
Putnam, Robert D., 11, 22, 23, 27, 36, 53

Qinhuai district (Nanjing, Jiangsu province, China), 155
Quatertaro, Carlo, 112

Raffadali (Agrigento, Italy), 129, 130, 138,
226n75
Randisi, Francisco, 137
Rapporto Sangiorgi (police report), 103
Ravanusa (Agrigento, Italy), 130
Red Badge of Courage, The (book), 197
Reggio Calabria (Italy), 32, 33, 53
Reina crime family (New York City), 115,
121; see also Lucchese crime family
Reina, Gaetano "Tom," 115
Reputation, 4; for violence of mafia
groups, 4, 14, 25, 26
Resource acquisition, 4; and investments
in the economy, 83; as a motivation to
open a mafia outpost, 4, 11, 18–19, 61;

as discussed in phone intercepts, 79–80,
83; defined, 75; ficticious marriages as a
form of, 80
Reuter, Peter, 4, 8, 13, 14, 25, 26
Riina, Salvatore "Totò," in Bardonecchia, 52
Río de la Plata, 126
Rise of the Network Society, The (book), 3
Rizzi construction company (Rosario),
134, 135
Roizis, Yossiff, 68; and cooperation with
authorities, 70; and Monya Elson, 69;
bank transactions, 69; drug dealing, 69;
in Budapest, 69; in Fano, 69, 78
Romania, 99
Rome, 1, 2, 3, 5, 10, 11, 21, 30, 70,
71, 74, 75, 86, 90, 93, 96, 125, 177;
and Russians, 72, 73, 97; migration
from South of Italy to, 37, 54, 61;
money laundering in, 76; population of,
216fn15; Solntsevskaya in, 5, 15, 83,
84, 85, 97, 188, 189, 190, 192
Romeo and Juliet (play), 53
Ronco (Verona), 57
Roof protection system, see *krysha*
Rosa dei Venti (terrorist group), in Verona, 54
Rosario, 5, 29, 102, 225n73; as the
Chicago Argentina, 226n75; capital
of Argentina, 132; construction sector
in, 24, 134–137, 142, 143, 227n88,
227n89; criminality in, 137–142; economic conditions, 10, 131–133; Italian
migration to, 104, 129, 225n74; mafia
in, 5, 29, 126–131, 137–142; police
repression of trade unions in, 133, 142;
prostitution in, 228n99; Sicilian mafiosi
in, 18, 101, 129–131
Rosarno (Italy), 199
Rosas, Juan Manuel de, 132, 133
Rose Revolution (Georgia), 17
Rose-Ackerman, Susan, 22
Rostovtsev, Konstantin,* and Yakovlev's
crew in Moscow, 74
Rothstein, Arnold, 116–117
Rum Row, 116, 119, 125; see also Prohibition
Russia, 2, 17, 33, 71, 75, 76, 77, 78, 79,
85, 86, 158, 189, 190, 195, 205n1; de-

fault on international loans in 1998, 83; migration from, 93; post-Soviet, 12, 194
Russian mafia, 3, 9, 13; in Hungary, 86–93; in Rome, 68–86; origins, 194; see also Izmailovo crime group; Kurgan crime group; Orekhovskaya crime group; Solntsevskaya crime group
Russian Orthodox Church, 65

Sabella, Salvatore, 118
Sacra Corona Unita, 15
Saint Louis, 20
Saint Petersburg, 1, 71
Salta province (Argentina), 131
San Juan province (Argentina), 141
San Lorenzo (Argentina), 131
San Luca (Calabria, Italy), 32, 33
Sanctuary of Our Lady of Polsi, 32
Santa Fe (city, Argentina), 131
Santa Fe province (Argentina), 131, 138; criminality in, 139; Italian migration to, 176; land tenancy in, 132; political elite in, 139
Santo Stefano Quisiquina (Agrigento, Italy), 129
Santos, Diamantino, 164
Saracco, Cayetano, 138
Satan's Circle (New York City), 106, 196, 197; vice in, 106–107
Schiro crime family (New York City), 119, 120, 121, 221n13
Schiro, Nicolò "Cola," 120
Sciarrone, Rocco, on mafia transplantation, 15
Second World War, 20,53, 68, 87
Serbia, 91, 99
Seres, Zoltán, 91
Sergeev, Boris,* 1, 2, 188; and resource acquisition in Rome, 80; background, 74, 188; cities where he resided, 2, 188; crimes committed by, 2; murder, 3, 83, 189–190
Sergeev, Sasha,* 2
Sergeeva, Nadia,* 2; role in the Russian mafia group in Rome, 83
Serondino (Argentina), 129
Shakespeare, William, 53

Shan State (Burma), 172
Shanghai, debt-recovery in, 168; migration to, 147, 229n4; port of, 176; Taiwan triads in, 152
Sharpe, Ali Ben Amar de, see Francisco Marrone
Shelley, Louise, 3
Shenzhen (Guangdong province, China), 146, 149, 154, 157, 180, 229n8; concubine villages in, 150; crime in, 229n4; drugs trafficking in, 173, 175, 176, 178; economic situation in, 228n3; history of, 147; Hong Kong triads in, 150, 151, 152, 153; migration to, 229n4; Taiwanese triads in, 152, 153
Shenzhen river, 146
Sichuan province (China), 176
Sicilian mafia, 3, 102–104; and Fascism, 17; branches outside Sicily, 15; in Rome, 20, 84; in Tunis, 15, 18, 105; origins, 102–3, 193–194; pentiti in, 33
Sicilian Mafia, The (book), 13
Sicily, 7, 12, 17, 22, 33, 45, 105, 111, 114, 115, 119, 120, 125, 129, 136, 220n8, 220n12, 226n78; banditism in, 133; mafia in, 102–104; migration from, 54, 128, 134, 142, 221n12; transition to the market economy in, 195; western, 103, 132
Siciliana (Sicily), 101
Sidelnikov, Fedya,* 73; and Yakovlev's crew in Rome, 74; tasks, 79, 82
Siderno (Calabria), 32
Sidorov, Vladimir,* 98; tasks, 82
Silvestrokie (followers of Timofeev), 73; see also Solntsevskaya crime group
Size of territory, as a factor affecting transplantation, 63
Smith, Harald, 36
Smith, Trigwe, 36
Social capital, 11, 22, 23; and transplantation, 64; in Bardonecchia, 51; in Piedmont, 36; measured, 51
Sociedad Cosmopolita de Obreros Albañiles (Rosario), 134, 135
Società dei Mulini (Sicily), 102

Society of Tammany (New York City), 107, 115

Soggiorno obbligato, See forced resettlement

Solnstevo district (Moscow), location of, 65; meaning of the word, 65

Solntsevskaya crime group, 3, 5, 9, 74, 77, 82, 95; as a form of extralegal governance, 6; control of businesses, 68; fictitious marriages of members in Rome, 80; in Budapest, 5, 15; in Italy, 68; in Moscow, 29; in Rome, 5, 15, 17, 84, 97; in the United States, 17; internal division of labor in Rome, 79, 80, 81, 84; *obshchak* (common fund), 68, 84; origins, 65–66; protection activities in Rome, 81; rituals, 85; role of women in Rome, 82; ruling council, 68; size of, 67; study of, 95–97; see also Russian mafia

Sotto-`ndrina, defined, 31

Soviet Union, 1, 3, 17, 65, 72, 81, 97, 158, 181

Spain, Georgian *vory-v-zakone* in, 17

Spatola crime family (Sicilian mafia), in Bardonecchia, 52

Special Economic Zones (China), 147, 173

Spilotro, Anthony, in Las Vegas, 20, 26, 192

State witness/es, see *pentito/i*

Steigura, Leonid Goldstein, 92

Sterling, Claire, 3

Suffolk county, 116

Suifong (Water Room) crime group (Macau), 166, 167

Suizhou (Hubei province, China), 156

Sullivan, Timothy Daniel "Big Tim," and Democratic political 'machine' in New York City, 107–8

Sun Yee On crime group (Hong Kong), in China, 150–151, 152

Switzerland, 78

Taiwan, 10, 33, 146, 147, 150, 157, 169; ban on visiting China lifted, 147; campaigns against organized crime in, 17, 151–153; investments to China, 147

Taiwan Strait, 152

Taiwanese language (Hokkien), 152, 177

Tenderloin, see Satan's Circle

Terranova, Ciro, 112

Thailand, "speed" epidemic in, 173; Taiwanese gangsters in 25, 151, 152

The Criminal Brotherhood (book), 105

The Prince (book), 68

Times, The (London newspaper), 105

Timofeev, Sergei, nicknamed Sil'vestr, and Yakovlev, 73; founder of the Orekhovskaya crime group, 66

Tocqueville, Alexis de, 102, 191

Torre, Lisandro de la, 138

Trade unions, 9; in Bardonecchia, 42, 47; in New York City, 114, 196; in Rosario, 133

Transnational organized crime, 3, 7; consensus, 4; see also International organized crime

Transplantation of mafia groups, 4, 5, 12, 15, 23, 24, 25, 61, 142–143; and presence of local protectors, 25; and relationship with mafia of origin, 7, 51, 64, 92; and size of the new territory, 25, 28, 143; as an un-intended consequence, 21; defined 6–7; factors conducive to, 16–21, 27, 61; failed, 11, 86; in order to conquer new markets, 20; investments in the legal economy as a factor conducive to, 19, 192–193; long-term, 11; to escape mafia wars, 7, 17, 27, 73, 93, 105, 125, 142–143; to escape state prosecution, 7, 8, 17, 18, 105–106, 125, 131, 151–153, 177, 198; to Hungary, 93, 95; to Piedmont, 37; to Rome, 93, 95; to Rosario, 129–131, 137–142; to Verona, 60; what is not, 7

Trapani (Italy), 102

Triads, 3; as a form of extralegal governance, 6; Hong Kong, 6, 10, 13; in China, 125, 150–153; Taiwanese, 5, 6, 10, 25

Trust, 21, 22, 61, 190, 192, 206n35; and mafia transplantation, 64, 143; generalized, 11, 21; high level of, 11, 143, 195; in Bardonecchia, 52; in China, 156; in Piedmont, 36; in Sicily, 219n3; interpersonal, 29, 36, 47, 61, 156; lack

of, 8, 219n3; low level of, 28; social, 11;
within criminal groups, 193
Tucumán (Argentina), 139, 141
Tunis, Sicilian mafia in, 15, 18, 105
Turin (city, Italy), 5, 35, 36, 37, 46, 50,
52; 'Ndrangheta in, 51; migration to,
54, 61; unemployment in, 40, 60
Turin (province, Italy), 48, 212fn79; elec-
tions in, 51; murders in, 46; *soggiorno
obbligato* in, 37, 209fn30; the judiciary
in, 63; the police in, 63
Turkmenistan, 91
Tuscany, 77, 78
Tverskaya hotel murder, 3–4, 189–190;
See also Sergeev, Boris

Ukraine, 91, 99
Unemployment, 12
Unión Cívica Radical (Argentina), 138
Unión Cívica Radical Antipersonalista
(Argentina), 138
United Nations, 188
United States, 5, 9, 16, 17, 19, 25, 33,
60, 61, 68, 115, 121, 147, 149, 177,
190, 197; as the destination of Russian
Jewish refugees, 71–72, 215n8, 215n10;
drugs route into, 175, 176, 178, 198;
Italian migration to, 101, 104, 105,
106, 120, 126, 219n5, 221n12; Italian-
American mafia in, 114–126, 224n60;
Latino gangs in, 191; 'Ndrangheta in,
34; Solntsevskaya in, 90, 188, 205n22
United States Coast Guard, 119
Urbán, László, 87
Urbino (Italy), 68
Ursini-Scali crime family (Italy), 51
Ursino, Giuseppe, 51

Val Susa (Piedmont), 34, 35, 36, 51, 52,
212fn64, 212fn70; arms trafficking in, 48
Valachi, Joe, 123; testimony of, 123, 126
Variation on the dependent variable, 29–30
Vario, Paul, 24
Vasin, Evgenii Petrovich, 15
Vendetta crime, 137, 138
Veneto region (Italy), 5, 22, 29, 30, 53,
61, 70

Venezuela, 77
Venice, 78
Verbanio-Cusio-Ossola (Piedmont), 51
Verona, 10, 11, 29, 30, 75, 143;
'Ndrangheta in, 54, 57–59, 125; drug
consumption in, 53, 55; drug traffick-
ing in, 55, 56, 59; economic structure
of, 53; extortion, 57; forced resettle-
ment to, 54; kidnappings in, 57; migra-
tion to, 54, 61, 213n102; neofascists
in, 54; population of, 53; violence in,
56–58
Via Aurelia (Strada Statale number 1,
Italy), 72, 73
Victory crime group (Hong Kong), 150,
230n8
Vienna, 2, 70, 72, 74, 188
Vietnam, 25
Villa Constitución (Argentina), 141
Villa Gobernador Gálvez (Argentina), 129
Violence, as a resource for mafias, 14;
in Bardonecchia, 41, 46–47, 52; in
Hungary, 89, 90; in Rome, 82–84; in
Rosario, 131; in Verona, 56–58; indus-
try, 89; supply of people trained in, 12
Vladivostok, Chinese organized crime in, 15
Vlasilo,* and Yakovlev's crew in Moscow, 75;
cheating on Yakovlev, 82; murder, 82
Volstead Act (USA), 115
Vory-v-zakone (thieves with a code of
honor), 81; in Georgia, 17

Wa area (Burma), and drugs production
and trafficking, 172–173, 176, 178,
233n63
Wa Army, 173
Waldo, Rhinelander, 109
Washington Post (newspaper), on the mafia
in Hungary, 90
Water Room crime group (China), 166
Welles, Orson, 197
White Fence crime group (US and Guate-
mala), 191
Williams, Phil, 3
Wiseguy (book), 24
Wo Shing Tong crime group (Taiwan), in
China, 152

Wo Shing Yee crime group (Macau), in China, 167
Women, in the Russian mafia in Rome, 82, 85
World Trade Center (USA), 176
World War Two, see Second World War
Wu, Tungtang, 152, 153; see also Celestial Alliance

Xiamen (Fujian province, China), 152

Yakovlev, Ivan,* ally of Timofeev, 73; and maintaining internal order, 82, 85; and resource acquisition in Rome, 80; and Sergeev, 188, 189; and the Moscow criminal underworld, 74; arrest, 85; companies, 188; escaping from Moscow to Rome, 17, 73, 83, 125, 192; in Margherita Laziale, 75; in Miami, 73; Italian police investigation into, 70–71;

* indicates that the name is a pseudonym.

member of the ruling council of the Solntsevskaya crime group, 70, 73; money laundering in Italy, 76, 77, 78, 79, 192; use of violence, 216n39
Yakovleva, Marina,* and maintaining internal order in Rome, 82
Yakuza, 13; as form of extra-legal governance, 6; members in the Philippines, 17; origins, 194
Yuan, Jiuhong, 160
Yugoslavia, 15, 55
Yunnan province (China), 173, 175

Zedda, Aldo, 40
Zedda, Iginio, 40
Zeng, Jijun, 167
Zhai, Yunfeng, 155
Zhejiang province (China), 147
Zhuhai (Guangdong province, China), 167, 228n3
Zunyi (Guizhou province, China), 161
Zurich, 3